Praise for
Do Unto Earth

"A must-read book for everyone who cares about the future of humanity and our planet."
—**Dr. Ervin Laszlo**, bestselling author of Science and two-time Nobel Peace Prize nominee, recipient of the Goi Peace Prize and International Mandir of Peace Prize, bestselling author of Science and the Akashic Field, founder of the Laszlo Institute of New Paradigm Research and The Club of Budapest, fellow of the World Academy of Art and Science and the International Academy of Philosophy of Science

"A 911 call from Planet Earth herself, *Do Unto Earth* is a potent manifesto for living life today and forward. This book should be required reading in schools. We must act now!"
—**Mary Madeiras**, three-time Emmy-Winning director, screenwriter, Akashic Records practitioner, activist, and author

"*Do Unto Earth* is full of empowering messages and mind-bending assertions that you won't find in science or history textbooks. Given the urgent need for new solutions on this endangered planet, the ideas are worthy of further investigation."
—**Mark Gober**, author of *An End to Upside Down Thinking*, board of directors of the Institute of Noetic Sciences (IONS) and the School of Wholeness and Enlightenment (SoWE)

"From page one, I was hooked! *Do Unto Earth* merges spirituality with our environmental crisis and does it in a way that is as gripping as a blockbuster movie. Brava to Hayes, Borgens…and Pax."
—**Temple Hayes**, author, spiritual leader, animal activist, and founder of illli.org

Do Unto Earth

Do Unto Earth

It's Not Too Late

PENELOPE JEAN HAYES
WITH
CAROLE SERENE BORGENS

Waterside Productions

Waterside Productions
2055 Oxford Ave
Cardiff, CA 92007
www.waterside.com

For you—
so you know for certain that you are the
change and you have the power

Acknowledgements

Where to start with acknowledgements on a project such as this? Firstly, we are grateful to be in a moment where we can express our gratitude to those individuals who make up what has now become an A-list publishing team (We've come a long way, Baby!), and even more than that—a mission-driven and provident team.

To the best literary agent in spiritual non-fiction, Bill Gladstone, who has now also become our co-publisher: Bill, you are imbued with many remarkable gifts, including the most extraordinary ability to heat-seek the next big phenomenon in new consciousness Self-Help. You are a dream to work with and we are honored to have your leadership and guidance.

Gayle Gladstone, our co-publisher from Waterside Productions and an intuitive businessperson with a keen eye for beauty in all its iterations: you are magnetic and creative and elegant and peace personified. What a woman!

To our editor, Ainsley Schoppel: You are so good at what you do. You are more than a trusted editor, you are one of those very essential members of the Tetris of what has become a tower of creation. Thank you for Fairy Godmothering the punctuation and sentence style while also questioning where our readers might benefit from clarification.

Andrew Green, our cover and interior illustrator: Andrew, you have given life and story to *Do Unto Earth*. You are a visionary artist and your depth of passion and purity of intention flows through your consciousness, down to your hand and fingers, and onto the drawing board. Your talent is a wonder.

To our publicist, Dea Shandera-Hunter: With you, it was love at first meeting and we are much stronger with you on the team. You are a true soul-sister and your media expertise is second-to-none. Namaste, dear one.

Erika Zapecza, our top gun digital marketer: From day dot, you just got our brand and clearly and beautifully share with the world the Pax Wisdom message of peace, love, and unity. We sleep well at night with you covering our six in the digital channels.

To our readers: This is for you and about you. While we hover over keyboards, all of this is a long love letter from the Divine Source directly to you.

And, to the Spirit Energy who has brought us together on these projects—Pax: Thank you for your patience when we've chipped away at a curiosity and pressed you for more. Thank you for your humor at times, your steering-on-the-journey at other times, and your unabridged truth always. Thank you for using us for your messages—we want to be used for good. Thank you for your divine protection as we march forward in what has been an exciting ride, and sometimes one that has required bravery beyond our earthly personalities.

Contents

Introduction

"We are running out of time and it is now incumbent upon all of us—all of you, activists, young and old—to please get involved, because the environment and the fight for the world's poor are inherently linked. The planet can no longer wait; the underprivileged can no longer be ignored. This is truly our moment for action. Please take action."
Leonardo DiCaprio
Academy Award-winning actor
and environmental activist

" *I*t's time to wake up. It's time to wake up. *It's time to wake up*," your inner-knowing whispers with ever-increasing urgency to unslumber.

"Dear Beloved, please wake up," Mother Earth pleads as she bares the marks of blatant abuse and indifference.

And still, so many sleep.

We have become anesthetized to our true nature and we are living as though our environment and all creatures and creation are outside of ourselves, and yet, the reality is that what we do unto Earth and each other and all creatures and creation, we do unto ourselves.

This moment—this writing—is a call-to-action, a warning, a challenge, a prayer, and a message of healing to the world. You are about to read something unlike anything you've read before. This book brings us to the threshold of a life-changing decision, and we are asked to be the change.

Do Unto Earth is an extraordinary conversation intended to quantum leap us forward in our spiritual evolution and journey to enlightenment. Within these pages is the blueprint for environmental repair and peace and unity on Earth. However, this is not a directive delivered from a thousand feet up; this is a very personal message from and dialogue with the Divine Wisdom Source directly to you and for you.

Please accept this gift with eyes clear and wide. Be inspired and be an inspiration. Arrive like a child again. Look at this world in wonder and awe again. Be gentle and respectful and kind. Do what Love would do. Utilize your voice and stick out your neck as Love would. Choose love every time and every day and in every action.

Yes—you can.

As you begin this journey, you might like to know how this collaboration of writing began.

It is indeed my great joy and honor to communicate with the Spirit Messenger, Pax, channeled by Carole Serene Borgens. From a young age, Carole, a former nurse, diligently studied all things metaphysical. This Spirit Messenger first visited her in the early 1990s when she was new to channeling by automatic writing. When her pen wrote the opening introduction and request for her to be a channel, she recognized the profound responsibility attached and jumped up from her office chair to pace the floor—not easy with three sleeping Irish Wolfhounds covering the carpet. Carole's initial response was to ask if she could think about it and take some time to respond, which she was given. Asking, "Why me?" Spirit responded to her: "You are new to this, you have no bad habits, and you will change none of my words." In time, Carole came to be comfortable with this blessing and so began her journey.

I, too, have been a seeker and spiritualist since my years as a teenaged runaway, and so it is a useful tool at times for me to reach out to a reputable intuitive for deeper guidance. Beginning on the fourth of February 2019, I had several long-distance Spirit channeling sessions with Carole—she was in British Columbia and I was in Florida. I had copious questions for Spirit as I sought further direction for my second title, *Do Unto Earth* (which, incidentally, is also the name of my business), while building upon the message of my first title, *The Magic of Viral Energy*. I was expanding and broadening the message of "viral energy" from personal and interpersonal goals to global concerns facing humanity and Planet Earth. I was also simultaneously establishing the Viral Energy Institute, a learning and research platform for the study of Viralenology.

Through our talks, this Spirit Messenger and I were getting to know each other and Spirit felt my passion for the plight of abused animals and species extinction, as well as my intention to bring awareness to our environmental crisis and to share the impacts of "viral energy masses"—large energetic fields created by both light and heavy intentions and action by communities, populations, industries, governments, and cultural beliefs—on Planet Earth. These disruptive energy masses create massive vibrational pockets of particular energies including love, hate, peace, discord, gratitude, violence, forgiveness, indifference, and compassion.

The Spirit Messenger seemed very interested in this direction and before long, Carole contacted me to say that Spirit wished to offer wisdom to be used by and shared through the Viral Energy Institute regarding this mission of planetary healing.

The writing began on the second of October 2019 when I sent questions to Carole who then channeled Spirit's responses by automatic writing (today, she does this via typing). It was *during* the writing that it became clear to all that this conversation would take book form and adopt the title *Do Unto Earth*.

As the answers were returned from Spirit, Carole and I both had many moments of excitement and more than a few gasps followed by, "Ooooh crikey, this is going to change everything!" The first of such revelations came in Chapter One when I asked the Spirit Messenger who they are…

Volume 1

Do Unto Earth
Pax and Our Starseeded Origins

"You cannot get through a single day without having an impact on the world around you. What you do makes a difference and you have to decide what kind of a difference you want to make."
Jane Goodall
English primatologist and anthropologist, world's foremost expert on chimpanzees, and UN Messenger of Peace

Chapter One
Divine Wisdom

*I*t would seem that many people do not live in harmony with nature and with respect and love for the
Earth. Why do we matter to God when we are so destructive
to ourselves, others, and our planetary home?

Well now, this is indeed an interesting question for it is well
known that your God considers everything worth mattering.
Penelope, it is the overall love that defines Planet Earth's people
as those to whom God matters, so it is their understanding they
also matter to God. We suggest each organized religion has their
own name for who they follow, and this question relates to the
love each deity has for followers. Love is unconditional; this is
why you matter.

I suspect that there's a reason why you've said, "*your*
God", and certainly, this piques my interest. I am aware that
I'm speaking to a great Spirit Messenger and Spirit Energy
from the Spirit World, however, I'd like to know more about
you.

Were you once from Earth; from a former and far more evolved people? Please help me to understand the source of your wisdom so that Earth's people will listen.

We do not incarnate as solid and we do not "reside" in one place—this is our gift. "My" origins do not include your planet, no, but having watched the development of society and where you are today, it is clear that a guiding hand is needed.

It is the case that my/our interest in communicating with Earth's people today is to share wisdom. Is this not the way to growth and evolution, to share with others what one has learned? Our speak, our words, our wisdoms are generated for the purpose of sharing guidance and the path to wellness for your planet. We have no linear time and refer only to soon time and far time. We in the Spirit World have duty and obligation to assist those in need and where requested, to offer wisdom to assist others. I care as we should all care, as should Earth's people care about your future.

Okay, so you were never a physical being or from Planet Earth; you are and have always been Spirit. Would it be accurate to think of you as the Guardian Angel for Earth?

Ah, no, that is not our role. *Conscience* in each of you, when activated, is collectively a guardian angel for Mother Earth.

There needs to be continued action and awareness to this end. Without being aware, your people have placed your planet in jeopardy and are moving forward with life as usual. There are some who wrap their lives around the correction of damage done and the prevention of future evils in this regard. They are the saints and saviors of your world but are not enough by themselves.

Consciousness needs raising in a maximum way to allow your people to have the meeting of minds which will create the global power necessary to effect change. Together you are a force. Come together in your thinking—the rest will follow.

Has a cosmic course been plotted for this message at this time and why did you choose me?

We knew, we waited, and when the time was right to write (cosmic smile here), we met, and it is good.

Penelope, in many past lifetimes, you have been a champion of causes, and a common thread running through them was your love and concern for the wild animals of the Earth. Your transferring of that to and inclusion of domestic animals has you on a long-established course of action for yourself. You have lived as an aboriginal and First Nations person. You have seen the ways wounded by those who would move in and take over the land, destroying all that came before. You have experienced the hostility and shame of being hunted and removed from your known life in place and time. You can feel these feelings and know that the vibration of Mother Earth now reflects these feelings. You have watched Earth being done unto in a very bad way in past lifetimes, and you bring with you the depth of feeling to expose what is, today.

Your greatest gift is the ability to raise the consciousness of a population and bring the message of healing to your world. You have the purity, the energy, the ability, and the resources. We think that is a good basis for trust in action for now and into our future works together.

Penelope, you have many questions; there will be no end to these questions, and they are all dedicated to the cause you feel and work you wish to continue on behalf of your planet.

Is this a heavy load? Not for Penelope who, after considering all of this information for a time, will understand and accept your challenge. You are the one. We support your journey and are pleased to be a part, with Carole Serene. Trust in this and go in peace and love.

Gosh, that *is* a commission. (And, I do have a lot of questions.)

You have a confidence and directness that is very compelling. I'll go ahead and ask outright: who are you, exactly?

We are one with the Universe, not the Universe alone. We are the Divine Universe, yes, and the God being and the greater wisdom, that which knows and supports all and is healing, non-judgmental and tolerant, all-seeing, all-knowing, and Peace.

(Gulp!)

Who-You-Are makes our discussion extraordinary: "*We are the Divine Universe, not the Universe alone, the God being and the greater wisdom.*" I'm humbled and honored to be having this dialog with you.

So then, you *are* who we would call God?

This question does not regard that there are other religions and groups who do not define themselves as related to "God". You are to know that organized religion on your Earth plane relates to other deities and those who study the Bible, Quran, and many other holy texts, and consider themselves related to their own varieties of your God. Think of Shiva or Allah and remember—variations on the theme are reality.

We are wisdom and history and benevolence. We are not a deity. We are who we report to be and have always reported to be. We are forever, we are infinity, and we are always and will be always—this is infinity, and this is us.

Oh, I see, "God being" and "God" have different connotations, and "Divine" and "deity" are not synonymous. This is a revelation.

Perception, it is, that defines us in the hearts and minds of your people. Our Universe is not of the proportion of what you might expect and *our range also greater in both future and past and all-being.*

We wish to engage in action as opposed to brackets and confines of description. To define further is folly as it is the finite amount of fear your people have around deities and religions as organized and what may and may not be permitted within those confines. It is our functioning outside of these discussions that is preferred. Your earthly religions hold value and offer solace to the many. For those who function outside of those realms, our energy is defined and available.

We support and offer love—unconditional love—for this is how our Universe functions.

I'm understanding that the issue of a name is about ensuring inclusivity to all people including those following any one of the many world religions and the name that each calls their deity or Divine Being, as well as those who follow no religion at all. Today, these names cause division. Am I getting your point correctly?

We are here to say the rose smells as sweet without our name of Rose.

That's a simple yet effective analogy. Still, I'd like to know how I should address you. May you provide an approved

moniker for the purpose of these volumes; one that crosses borders and religions and can connect all to the message?

> *Pax.*
>
> Pax reflects our goodwill and wish for peace. Yes, this is us—Pax. Relate to this as Spirit Messenger of Truth, Peace, and Goodwill. It is our mission, and yours.
>
> We are blessed to be with you and it has become your mission to ensure our words reach those in need, our direction is heard, and a potential global disaster averted if people can be activated and energized and empowered to begin to have their voices heard and the movement toward planetary repair enlarged.

Thank you, *Pax*. Your chosen name has a nice ring to it! It feels right and there's something about it that deeply resonates within me; almost like a memory that I can't quite place. It feels paternal and maternal and grandparental at the same time: warm and wise.

I just took a moment to search the word online. "Pax" is Latin for peace, but of course you knew that. Additionally, the acronym PAX stands for Private Automatic Exchange, which is an accurate description of the Spirit channeling process. (No coincidence, I'm sure.)

At this time, I would like to address that some people will not trust this information because it wasn't written thousands of years ago and it doesn't appear in the Bible or another holy text. How can people know that this conversation is provident and good work?

> It is to be known that our wisdom of the ages comes to the people of Mother Earth with love and respect and the intention to pass along what is seen in the big picture.

What I'm really trying to get at is to address that some people—*even some of my own family members*—might say or worry that to have a conversation with an unknown-to-them Spirit Messenger is the devil misleading me. I need a little help here because some will not hear this message due to close-mindedness and fear, and they too need to hear this message.

It is the case that fear of the unknown is a large part of life for many. We are not here to revolutionize their thinking. We are here to speak our messages and ensure that those who can hear do, those who need to but are unsure, will, and those who are fearful and unbelieving remain in the loop and have access to the teachings. Their fear comes from the depths and we are not here to preach against their beliefs.

Suffice it to say that if these family members believe in you, Penelope, they will be open, and if they don't believe in you enough to at least hear and consider our messages, then perhaps their opinions are to be not considered so highly going forward. We touch who is ready, and those who are not have the messages and can take time considering the material and determining their own willingness to explore it further. It is not ours to reverse thinking of those set against anything not in the Bible. Narrow vision is its own reward.

I appreciate your help with this thoughtful response.

And, just a bit of "housekeeping" as we say: Those who read this book will want to know how to correctly address or speak of you. Would we say, "he" or "they"? Are you male or female energy? Are you to be referred to in the plural, "we"?

We are collected consciousness, and for these purposes you may refer to us as Carole Serene does—"he" is how she calls us. Despite our self-reference as "us", we are both, don't you see?

9

Pax, now that we have a name to call you, I'd like to go a step further and ask you what you look like, but I suppose that you might tell me that you don't have a "look" because you're Spirit. But, *if* you had a look, what would it be?

We are a puff of cloud, a breath of wind, a library filled with knowledge, a raging river, and a vast ocean. We are the circumference of your globe and the weight of it. We are the sound of the jungle and the quiet of the snow, while all the while being the figure like Atlas, holding the weight of your world on his shoulder while attempting to support humankind. This is our *who* and our *why* and *our reason for being with you as a constant.*

You are beautiful.

I'd like to summarize what you have said regarding who you are:

You are the Spirit World; you can be in all places and all times at once and you are; you have no linear time; you are infinity, always was and will be always; you are the Divine Universe, yet not the Universe alone; you are the God being and the greater wisdom, yet you are not a "deity"; your message is for all. For these conversations you choose to call yourself, "Pax".

I must say, you're rather modest, Pax, because *in my book*, you're a pretty big deal!

Yours are the ideas and we are the support, resource, and cheer-leading section, too. We see this as a beginning, and all good beginnings contribute to growth and emergence of what is meant to come, to take shape, and form. It is a collaborative effort, we say, and it is our belief that this is a good team we three, and it is our enjoyment to be a part of assisting your world today in healing.

Chapter Two
Who We Are

Some people believe that we are aliens to this planet because we live and behave out of balance with the natural rhythm and laws of Earth—are we humans "aliens" to Earth and do we actually originate from elsewhere?

You do originate from light years away and this will be controversial.

Was there a "big bang" and you appeared out of the dust? Not so, but you were formed elsewhere and delivered to your present round sphere in the space and time continuum.

Are you evolving? Yes, and you are also devolving in your lack of care and consideration for your planetary host.

We suggest walking carefully forward now as this is the now when there is no turning back. Forward now into care of your resources, or forward into planning for alternative lifestyle and place—the choice is yours. Yes, colonizing other planets will be reality—it may not seem so in your today, but there are people making these plans and they will be considered by the mainstream in a short period of Earth time. Stranger things have happened.

Okay, that was a jaw-dropper. Although I asked the question, I was not expecting *that* answer—not at all. There's a lot to talk about here.

Why did we leave the planet from which we came? Is there a planetary collapse story that relates in some ways to our current situation on Earth?

Well it was the case, Penelope, that exploration was timely and the visit to your Planet Earth led to putting down roots, depositing settlers as it were. There was no need to leave but there was a want to resettle and attempt to bring forward evolution to another place. That is what is done in advanced civilizations.

The few who came brought what would seed the new place, then went on their way. Historical notations of those visits are to be found in ancient art and stories.

It was advanced civilizations that monitored Earth from time to time who determined that growth of knowledge would benefit development, so contributed what they did from time to time. They did not deposit a large number of people to populate this new land; that is not the way of it. These seed people are known in history and represented in early art and oral histories.

Did these advanced peoples bring any plant or animal species when they came?

Of those who settled there were those who brought growing seeds and options to local food to your planet, yes, but animals, no. The planet had animals and growth, just not more highly evolved people and ideas—this was deposited.

Interesting: no animals were brought here, though plants were. Which plant species were Starseeded to Earth?

There were those that would become food plants and the forerunners of what was needed to fertilize soil to receive and enable germination and growth. It is not rocket science that in order to reap there must be sensible sowing. To harvest and utilize for man and animal is the way.

Those organisms contributing to the transition from seed to produce were the ones. Much more will be learned of what was, when your people begin to move off-planet for survival, and what will be.

We're moving off-planet?

Yes, but first it is intended that your people will become more aware of their responsibility in saving your planet, not just leaving it fallow while all move off to another globe in the sky. This will not be. Responsibility must be accepted for what has been done to your Earth and what is now needed to rectify your actions.

That's fair.
Our ancestors who remained on their planet of origination, did they evolve differently than we did?

Evolution of Earth peoples is not compatible yet with the host planet's peoples. It is of a different sort and that is the way of it.

Our anthropologists have certainly made a seemingly clear case through fossil remains for our evolution from apes to modern man, all having happened on this Planet Earth. Is this not accurate?

Your people's introduction to this Earth planet was, as we indicated, a delivery from an advanced society to "seed" your place with those who could provide guidance and direction. There was a coming together of growth and evolution with some areas of the planet growing in knowledge and skills at a faster rate than others, naturally, as these are the areas with the guidance and examples to follow provided by the "star seeds".

What are "star seeds"?

This term is used in reference to those hosts from the home planet and those they sent to your people as teachers, leaders, and helpers. They seeded your world with star wisdom. The visitations referred to were thousands of years ago in origin and continued forward for the purpose of depositing information and technology. They carried advanced wisdom and came and went, visited for a time, returned to their home base and again visited at a later date—it was done in cycles to ensure lessons learned and advancement and progression. This was not a settling forever or even a long period of time. This was a bringing and teaching and sharing and mentoring only—a new beginning for growth in knowledge on your planet. They came to observe and contribute where they felt it was needed. It was not for these advanced visitors to relocate and assimilate, no, they came and went throughout time, and still do to see how the current civilization is faring.

You were right: this will be controversial, especially as it will throw a wrench in our evolution-from-apes theory.

So then, if not from our lineage, who are the fossils that we've found of extinct primate species such as Homo neanderthalensis, Homo heidelbergensis, Homo erectus, Homo naledi, and so on—those beings from which we currently believe we descend, including the chimpanzee and even earlier species of monkeys and lemurs?

Some walked on four legs and some on two legs and their evolution continued in those directions with different results. There is no mystery here, but it would seem so to many. The primates remained and the star seeds took another form.

To understand that origin is not one place and one species is important: that Planet Earth was "seeded" and had advanced species assistance brought evolution to a new place; twinning as it were, although the end result isn't identical at all.

That some primates became upright is what your science says. That others *began that way* is not known. It was a different time and life progressed in stages and speeds as designed by location.

To distinguish our uses in this text of the word "primates", you said that no animals were brought to Earth but rather all animals on Earth were already here, and so we will confirm that the star seeded primates are completely different from the primates that are indigenous to Earth such as chimpanzees, gorillas, monkeys, and so on. Correct?

Yes.

The star seeded primates that you've been talking about are those ones that we have always thought of as early primitive mankind; the ones that we call "cavemen", and all of the species on two or four legs for which we've found fossil remains. *These* primates were brought from other far-away planets, and more than one planet's primates seeded Earth. Is this correct?

The thought of a ship filled with "monkeys" is amusing, yes? And yet, like Noah's Ark, there were some being transported for reasons not to do with just seeding. These were advanced in training and programming and, yes, thinking and acting as helpers. It is true that they took little space and contributed much to the projects.

It was the case—yes—that these advanced helpers were transported and relied upon for their given tasks. While they were not primates as you think of primates today, they also were not the more highly evolved leaders of these civilizations. They were to be included in these journeys for their reliability and expertise. Did some stay behind, yes, and did some return with the crew to home base, yes also.

Seeding was accomplished in increments as time and place varied with it.

Were *any* of our human race peoples *ever* apes that then evolved into humans?

Your beginnings as Earth people were originated elsewhere and you were planted, like seeds, in your current place.

That you evolved from seeds of humans to where you currently are and in what form is not a mystery. The blueprint was there for your form and function.

That your science can trace a likely evolution from primitive forms to upright walking forms is their contribution.

Ours is that your peoples were formed in their DNA from another place. Can the two co-exist? As many are found to co-exist on Planet Earth in the way of plants and animals, so do humanoids. In addition, those visitors among you from interstellar sources do so as well.

Do any of these star seeded primates for which we have found fossil remains still exist on Earth or were they all extinct?

Evolution of species to suit environment was responsible for change, and in some areas, extinction, yes. It is known that those who moved and grew and changed their ways of living became a different looking species. Some survived and some not; bones are found and distinctions drawn between early and later primates and their ways of life. Some morphed into uprights while others, in completely different areas and lifestyles, remained as earlier seen—nothing could be the same in all as they spread throughout your geography and were changed by it.

I suppose what I'm getting at is—is there such a thing as "Bigfoot" as many people claim to have seen?

As your species continues to evolve, it is the case that anomalies exist. Given enough time in nature, particularly isolated nature, interbreeding becomes reality. Do some ask of human interbreeding with animals? There are genetic modifications and genetic quirks and recessive genes that come to the fore in all species. Is this one? We say there is evidence as stated by some and refuted by others—it shall remain a mystery.

Well, that is a cliffhanger! Must it remain a mystery? Can you tell us a bit more...pretty please?

We see that the way for us to speak to the many is for us to be the line between our knowledge and the curiosity of the many.

We speak again of genetic modifications and "throw-backs" and know that it is the case in your world that these exist in all species, and this is no different. It is simply a hidden mystery to all but a few, and they know the existence of this mammal is real.

Wow. I didn't see that coming. This will make a lot of Sasquatch sleuths very happy. (By the way, Pax, you should never play cards; *you gave this up pretty quickly.*)

As for mankind's roots, I want to be sure that we understand this correctly; the following will be a pivotal point. At what stage in our development did humans arrive to Earth? Were they already fully developed as our current species called Homo sapiens upon arrival on Earth?

They were, as you say, fully developed, although looking somewhat different than earlier man who was in place and walking upright.

As we have stated, star seeds arrived from other galaxies, as they still do, and they were the advanced ones in technology and thinking and became the wise ones leading the development of your Earth peoples. The visitations and people touched were variable. Evolution was underway during the visits.

Ah, so an even *earlier* species of man—*also star seeded*—was already in place and walking upright, and then—at a later time—arrived the ones we call Homo sapiens: us. I do recall that you said, "To understand that origin is not one place and one species is important." This is beyond fascinating and it will interest the world's population to learn that the human race is alien to Earth.

That is being understood now in your science, although not well documented for fear of, what?

For fear that by disproving our evolution theory it would set back advanced scientific thinking to the dark ages; that disproving the theory of evolution from ape to mankind would result in our collective thinking defaulting to the only other current theory option: the biblical theory of creation that rests on a singular first man and woman giving life to

all of humanity. In this story, women are seen as tempt-
resses because Eve bit the forbidden apple; you see, much
old thinking comes with the religious creationism theory,
and yes, forward-thinkers would be fearful of reverting back
to these close-minded ideas. However, what you are sharing
is quite clearly not an Adam and Eve scenario, but a new
knowing of our beginnings.

To go over it one more time—if I correctly understand
all of this, some of our peoples were delivered to Earth as
the species they are now—humanoids. While other beings
were upright walking primate-type helpers (also Starseeded)
which then evolved to some extent (although not from the
animal primates, such as chimpanzees/apes, native to Earth)
before those species became extinct (with the exception of a
possible few lingering anomalies). Is this correct?

As we have said, it is so. It is and was the way of it.

I guess this starseeding is why we've never found "the
missing link" in our evolution theory.

It would be good to work on a new timetable and chart
of our lineage. How long have we been on Earth?

Ah yes, this is the question. Earth people have been Earth
people for as long as science currently estimates, however star
people were visiting Earth that long and longer to determine
habitability. As it was a habitable space, and also a hospitable
space, it became so. Linear time is not always a descriptor
of history in the truest form, although it is relied upon by
scholars.

And, star people still visit Earth?

As long as there is time, there are visitations and entrance into thoughts of colonizing other planets—this is the way of explorers whether on your Earth plane or from other galaxies.

"As long as there is time." Was there ever a "time" before time?

As long as there is time refers to the hope that your planet has not self-destructed before this process completes.

Time before time—your philosophers enjoy this discussion. All time is.

Thanks for the clarification. (We'd better get on with it then.)

From time to time, and that is not your Earth time, there have been star people buzzing by and sometimes stopping and staying—it is throughout the history of life on your planet. And you should know it continues that they watch and hope you find peace in your world.

I think that I'm starting to see the big picture: several/many advanced civilizations from different planets came to Earth and colonized various regions with their peoples. If that is the correct big picture, then does this mean that the human race currently on Earth today is really not of *one* race? Many of our cultural races look distinctly different from each other; are we actually many distinct peoples descending from *different planets* in the Universe, rather than one human race that simply evolved somewhat differently in various geographic places and climates on Earth?

Bingo! You have it, yes, the differences are many and it is fair to say that your varying cultures were seeded and succeeded, or not, with some help from their source. Some did fail while others grew and prospered and do still. It was a time of growth and experimentation and the visitors determined to bring what they could to strengthen the resolve of the new peoples to survive and grow and find their way. It was not always successful, and some did not prevail over adversity of nature.

Oh my goodness, Pax—this is another monumental disclosure.

Earlier, you mentioned the Big Bang and I can't let the news of the inception of the universe slip by. Was the Big Bang the beginning event of our universe?

The Bang wasn't so big as your people may believe.

You had me at hello; do tell. Our cosmologists and the general population must then have a rather sizeable (pun intended) misconception of the "Big Bang". How big was the bang and what was it *really* if not a big bang?

Bigger bangs have occurred elsewhere and not resulted in such fanfare as this apparently initiates.

Do we understand the notion of eternal, forever, always was, or the sense of wonder at what appears that was not previously there, or was it and we simply missed it? The mists of time cover what was to be and allow those mists to lift when what is to be, now, is coming together with its now.

It was always there, eternally present, and like help from a loved one, becomes reality when needed and the time is right. Until then, it rests.

"The mists of time cover what was to be and allow those mists to lift when what is to be, now, is coming together with its now." I'm gushing over these words, the way they romance and dance, and yet I still want to know: what do they mean?

While the wisdoms and technology all exist, they may be accessed only when your civilization is truly ready for the knowledge and will use it for peaceful and positive outcomes. The mist lifts and what has always been can be seen and accessed for your technological—or other—growth, as in it "is coming together with its now"—it's time. It is a protection, of sorts, for your people and their advancement in this time. All things are there, all wisdom and knowledge, the cosmic library exists and those who are evolved may access it. To everything there is a season.

You're good, Pax, you're good!

While you confirm that bigger bangs have occurred, is the particular "Big Bang" to which we refer the birthplace of our Universe or do we have this wrong?

It is not wrong, but it was not the only birth of your universe. Your universe began in earnest when visitors dropped in and deposited their wisdom.

You see, you say these subtle sentences that could very easily slip by unnoticed; nearly encrypted codes. Then, I read and re-read them and a lightning bolt goes off in my head. Your last sentence makes me think of the quantum physics revelation that particles are just waves of energy vibration until they are observed, and only then do they become a thing (matter).

Pax, are you saying that the Universe is created not at all by physical manifestations of matter such as the so-called Big Bang(s), but rather that the Universe is created in physical form as consciousness is starseeded across the Universe? (No wonder the highly enlightened civilizations have a mission to starseed; they're creating a whole Universe here!)

It's payback time, yes, these civilizations continue to grow and develop throughout your time.

There is also the selective question of whether you consider the Universe to be one Planet Earth, or all you know?

Is this a reflection of mankind believing that everything in the Universe revolves around us (so to speak)?

It is the nature of your reality that you consider Earth the center of your universe, and we refer to the majority of your people. There are those who understand the big picture and that your Earth revolves around *others* and revolves *while others surround it*. If the melding of these realities can include lessons from both, then good will come of it.

Maybe we could call this new theory of our inception, "Starseeded Origins".

It is not to say your evolution theory isn't correct, but it was augmented by the arrival of the star seeds to lead your civilization toward technology and development they would have not managed otherwise. They were few but they shared widely their methods of travel and creation of building and exploration. They were light beings who assimilated for a time and then departed; leaving behind the knowledge they shared. They were seeding

Planet Earth with people and knowledge far advanced from what existed. To think all became on your Planet Earth at the same time, is to not think it through. There are pockets of people and growth around this Earth plane that were planted like crops and flourished, or not, over time.

Call it what you may, it was a turning point, and there were many throughout time. The entire globe was not visited in its entirety each time.

As visitors came to early civilizations, they assessed and left what was determined to be of most use, whether knowledge of agriculture or building, or higher learning ideas to leave a path to further curiosity and growth. Civilization existed as it was evolving on Earth, the visitors watched and waited and came from time to time to further grow the abilities of Earth people and leave their mark in written, painted, and oral histories.

From which planets did the various humanoid races originate?

Oh, you do have the curiosity, yes? Those visitors of early times were planting their people seeds, as it were, and encouraging growth like a garden. They came and went and delivered what assistance they could to early inhabitants, some failed and some grew just like crops, nothing is guaranteed.

While you look at the multitudes of races today on Planet Earth, it is clear their differences are remarkable, while they have similarities also. One is that they all wish to thrive and survive and will do so given the tools. This is what the visitors offered, tools for survival. It was their gift to early civilizations that advanced technologies were shared, used to support growth and building as well as to entice the people to explore their own ways of exploration and development of tools and methods. It is the case that the records of this, both written and drawn in pictures, were representative of those plans and some were recorded for posterity while others were spoken so that the idea would not be forgotten. There wasn't paper on which to write, so walls and rocks and pieces of hide, anything that would take a mark was used. This applied to many civilizations if not all.

After seeding, we say the visitors "buzzed by" to see how the local people were faring—this they did often along their journeys. To identify the galaxies they came from is not to be as not everything has a name, as your people seem to believe, and that they came from afar is about the closest descriptor. It matters not in the big picture. There will be more on this in time.

The races were different, yes, the appearances physically were different, and these were the appearances of the visitors who seeded these areas. It is an interesting study and we share that there was a reason why these visuals were created by varying colors and shapes and sizes, and it was to be the lesson in acceptance and integration and inclusivity.

You have led me to a ginormous epiphany: while we're not the center of the Universe, we Earthlings are special because our being-ness and identity as Earthlings was uniquely created to grow and spread unconditional love, equality, and unity!

We see it still is not resolved on your Earth plane.
Your people should ask how long they will discriminate.

Maybe, just maybe, discrimination will stop once the people learn through this conversation that each race is quite deliberate and perfect in their differences, and that all races share a history as intrepid explorers of the Universe with a binding mission to bring us together in acceptance, integration, inclusivity, and peace. Maybe this knowledge

will begin to enlighten humankind to the truth that each race is to be respected as the beloved starseeded descendants of the Enlightened Ones.

This would be the desired outcome, yes, and do we think this one set of words alone will enable this change? We do not, but we are pleased to contribute our wishes that your Earth people begin to be enlightened about this seeding and begin to understand differences for what they are—strengths.

Each seeding on your Earth plane brought skills and strengths and likelihoods of growth and success of a culture. As your Earth turned and your time continued, peoples came and went, struggled and succeeded, were overcome by Mother Nature or learned to work *with her* for survival and even successes above this, and others quietly succumbed to their challenges and did not prevail. There are lessons in each. There is no failure to be found but rather a need to regroup and try again in another format—this was done. Each of your people-groups have contributions to make in your world of today; each has beliefs and strengths and also challenges, and all contribute, when shared, to a strengthened society. This is the lesson.

The wide variety of languages that we have on Earth must also then have origins tied to the various starseeded peoples. Do our languages today still somewhat resemble the languages of the peoples from our starseed planets of origination?

Well this is a no-brainer to some while being a great conundrum to others. Do these divisions in looks and language bear resemblance to origins? We say they do, and they are remnants of the beginnings of diversity on your planet. We see it is not yet accepted in many of your locations, countries, and we ask how long does it take to assimilate those who contribute and happen to appear different? We say it is the source of so much upheaval in your civilization as a whole, with no need for it in this time and place. We wonder at it.

So, our variety of human races, or "people-groups" as you say, came from different peoples from various galaxies. However, were they all from galaxies within our Universe, or also from other Universes?

Ah yes, there were visitors from afar (other Universes) as well as from your galaxy. They do buzz about and visit and leave traces sometimes and none at others. When it is considered a possibility to spread good and knowledge of advanced ways, they have done so. It was not always the desired outcome, however, when less than hospitable inhabitants were encountered. Those were left untouched and sometimes approached at a later time with successful outcomes for all.

This whole "Planet Earth Project" depends on a certain place and presence, which we too often take for granted, and yet, she is the hostess and platform.
For our people to feel a true kinship and connection to Earth we'll need to know why Earth should be considered *our* "Mother Earth" when she is not the planet from which we originated?

To adopt a homeland and call it so is the way of your people. One need not originate from a place to feel at home there. Knowing your Mother Earth supports your life and happiness is the basis for a relationship. At this time in your evolution there is no alternative. There will be, but this is not the question.

Pax, my dear, we are going to rock the boat—in a very good way, I think—on this intriguing topic of our evolution and its replacement with the truth of who we are.

I wonder, did our major religions and deities originate from the different planets from which we were starseeded? Or, did the peoples once here on Earth then form their own beliefs and deities?

Oh yes, the question of religious origin. Populations on Earth determined their own paths to follow in worship based upon experiences and beliefs of what or who protected them.

Some believed in nature, some in animals, and some in living people. As time went on and generations came and went, those beliefs grew and deepened and what began as a transfer of power—from a people to another for their belief that they were protected—grew to legend.

That these people were responsible for knowing the way and protecting themselves had been forgotten, and that power given over to another for worship. It is common amongst your people today, yes?

Yes.

While we have developed many differences in our religious beliefs, there are some references and experiences that many can relate to, I hope.

If you consider the ways of your aboriginal first peoples, this is how your Planet Earth does best. Everything has a soul, is their belief, whether plant or animal or rock or river or tree, everything has soul, and to treat each being in this way is to practice love and compassion for all. This is how to educate your people to protect Earth and her environment. For the people of your time to continue to flourish on Planet Earth, wisdom and guidance from advanced civilizations would be helpful, however, wisdom and guidance from your aboriginal peoples will be even more valuable to preserve what you have and repair Mother Earth where needed. You must look to the past to see the future ways.

Speaking of first peoples, of the many Starseeded Peoples from many other planets in this galaxy and beyond, which people were the very first to arrive to Earth?

The First Peoples of your planet are here now and show themselves as aboriginals, and their people, and their people, are descended from the off-planet visitors who came and went and seeded populations around the globe.

There is common DNA to be found among people with no way of physical contact in those earliest days when travel was impossible beyond local inhabitant's areas.

Are the First Nations people of North America related from the same home planet of Starseed Origin to, say, the indigenous people of the Asian sub-continent of India, or are the African nations peoples related through Starseed Origin to the aboriginal Australian people; that kind of thing?

Oh yes this is the way of it. These continents split apart over time, eliminating ways of journeying from place to place other than by water. There have been treks far and wide and peoples were starseeded, planted as it were, and DNA can be and is noted today in its similarities among people spread far and wide. Gives new meaning to the term, distant cousin, yes?

It is the case that these "earlys" were seeded far and wide and cultures developed differently as a result of topography and climate. This was a given and these things still rule development in many geographical areas of your globe.

Yes, it was a common goal to develop Planet Earth as best it could be done to find another center of life and intelligence to add to those out there in the galaxy and further. Like you now send up to a space station as an artificial planet and place, people live there for extended periods as a test, so too was Earth used for this experiment.

That it has survived is surprising to some who watch and wait for the demise due to present massive growth of pollution and poisoning in all ways.

Who watches? Who are "those visitors among you from inter-stellar sources"? You used this sentence earlier and it sounds like a present-time happening. Are these interstellar visitors among us *now*?

Always, in one form or another, not always solid. We have stated they buzz by to monitor progress. Some will watch longer than others before departure.

When you say, "not always solid", does this indicate that interstellar visitors can be present among us in a form that is not seen or detected?

Well yes, they have this means of travel and being that is in thought form as well as solid. They may monitor progress on your Earth without being seen and they may also take form and participate at times.

Another way is akin to remote viewing and another is via thought-form communication and watching. There is choice. Each is designed to be not worrisome to your people and this is considerate, yes?

I'd say so.

There is no intention to be intrusive and yet there is intention to be watchful as they consider how to proceed with contact or not.

At present your Earth politicians, government, industry, and ordinary citizens are not sufficiently informed about extraterrestrials and their intentions to manage this contact without fear and aggression. Your watchers do not intend harm, nor do they intend anything other than communication. This would not be understood at this time, so they watch and wait—this is their reasoning behind the actions.

Do our ancient relatives who Starseeded us here care about us or are we just a disappointing experiment?

Now, it is not your ancient relatives caring at this time, but rather those continuing to buzz by to view progress. It is they who marvel at what once was pristine now being smoke and haze covered with air not breathable in many areas. It is they who are saddened.

Where have our ancient relatives gone? Why don't they check on us and on this "experiment" of putting many races together on one planet?

Well now, consider that ancient and still present are not always compatible. That they may have "gone on" is to be considered, and that those who still watch have taken up that mantle, is the case. Not all is forever in the Universe.

As those who seeded your Earth planet had and have great interest in the present and future of your Earth civilization, they also have interests elsewhere and sometimes tire of watching your people's non-authentic, in their view, progress or lack thereof. And so, where do they go, you ask? Away to refresh themselves and place emphasis elsewhere where there could be positive outcomes and joy produced from the lessons they teach. It is not that they no longer believe in the future of Earth people to overcome their self-destructive tendencies, but rather that they tire of waiting.

So, your watchers have changed shift, as it were, and some go on to place their emphasis and talents elsewhere and replacements come to you in hopes of seeing a corner turned toward higher consciousness attainment leading to higher-consciousness living. Some come and some go; it is the way of it.

Your civilization has grown and flourished, then self-destructed and shrunk, and then the cycle repeats. Yours is not the first to begin down a path of corruption and self-interest, but it is doing so now. While many voices are now raised toward a resurgence of what came before in the way of aversion to these destructive lifestyles, they are in themselves not sufficient to the cause.

Who *can* help the cause?

Your current civilization has benefited for a long while now from the arrival of those star seeds, more recently the arrival of highly advanced thinkers, with conscience to match, are with you to lead the way on environmental and humanitarian improvements.

You see them, you hear them, and you wonder at the intensity of their leadership to change your planet for the better. They walk among you and will be responsible for positive change on a global basis. They speak to inform and change outdated thinking and inaction. They accept nothing less than action to make change to save Planet Earth, beginning now. You see and hear them, and they do not go away. It is their purpose in life, so we say listen and learn and act accordingly.

Were these "highly advanced thinkers" born in the here and now by human parents, reincarnated highly evolved souls? Or, are they true *aliens* to Earth?

Oh yes, these are the old souls, the wise ones who have determined that to reincarnate and return to your current world is their purpose now. They are born to human parents, entering the next stage of their evolution to return to Earth to teach; to show the way to wellness.

They bring integrity and knowledge of the ways forward to regain purity of heart for your people and purity of air and water, soil, and methods of resource management.

They are to be considered the wise-ones of your time.

The time of commercialism and disrespect is leaving, not quietly, but it cannot continue and expect the new leaders to emerge in those conditions.

Nowadays, there are many people who speak on the environmental crisis in depth and with passion—and many of them are children or young adults who are so incredibly well educated and well spoken.

They make their thoughts and voices heard, their circles of influence broaden, and the impact is felt. They are the forerunners of the next big change and pave the way by removing from power the corrupt. They do this by being vocal in their concerns and speaking of the inconsistencies, of mankind's inhumanity to mankind, high-level corruption, and the collusion that currently runs rampant in the management of companies and countries. The facts will be heard—the proponents exposed, and the startling outcomes witnessed. People formerly with heads positioned firmly in the sand emerge, horrified, and pledge to make the necessary changes in their own spheres of influence.

The ripple effect is felt, and the positive energy created by the many supports in their decision to follow and create their own changes.

They bring intention and knowledge and attitude and will not be unheard on issues of colossal import to your Planet Earth. You see them and hear them and wonder at their level of knowledge, passion, and expertise.

It is their determination that the leaders of today do not have the understanding of the "big picture" and see the resulting demise of the health of your planet. You will see them being leaders from an early age, yes, and seemingly knowing how to make a difference in your world, whether it be climate change or politics or humanitarian issues. It is they who bring solutions and more, showing the way to a future of peace and wellness for all.

We've taken in a lot of new information and perhaps it's time for a pause of reflection. To recap, you've confirmed that we did not originate from Planet Earth, Bigfoot is real, and there are advanced thinkers among our people who will lead in global wellness.

This is all *very* exciting!

You also said, "Yours is not the first to begin down a path of corruption and self-interest, but it is doing so now." It's compelling to hear that our civilization is not the first to begin down a path of corruption and self-interest. In terms of the peoples of those other planets that went down the path of destruction, was monetary gain the driving force for these ways of self-interest?

Indeed, our reference here is to *early civilizations on Planet Earth.*

There have been many powerful and advanced civilizations. From the Roman Empire to Aztec, there were numerous that rose, prospered, and then fell. It is now awaited that your consciousness-raising trends will flow in the direction of higher evolution and this time your civilization will continue to evolve and thrive in peace and harmony.

A world of no warring and corruption in future, no greed and territorial attitude of control and power grab—how long does it take for this to become the way of your world? Generations will pass on the journey to this higher functioning.

Is it now known that this is to be the goal? We say it is and as alternatives present, they will be considered, but overall wellness comes. As your people view the opposite of this, they see the darkness of the energy created and sustained and want no part of it going forward. This darkness resides within your political powers. It is not new in your world history but is to be removed from the reality of your world.

Has there ever been a planet destroyed by its human occupants, whereby the whole planet was lost? Or, is Earth the only planet being harmed (or that has been destroyed) by its people?

No other planets destroyed by its people, not so, but destroyed by natural phenomena in their solar system, it happens.

Now it is the case that this has become reality on Planet Earth.

On the faraway planets from which all varieties of people *originated***, how did** *those* **people develop? Was it an evolution of life from single-cell organisms all the way up to primates and so on? Or, is there some other magical creation way that you can tell us about?**

Magic indeed, and this is the way of it.

Do not think that all things began with single-cell organisms for they did not necessarily and our ability to describe the journey from there to today is limited to what you need to understand, and that is that awareness and creation come together to plant what is needed, where needed, and suited for that specific purpose. Rather like a custom build or a purpose-specific build—we leave that thought.

Pax, that's a pretty big announcement to just mention in passing. May you please tell us a bit more about how life creation works?

It has been the way through your time that as there is a need, so is there a solution. This accounts for developments and surprise findings in all ways of your civilization as your technology advances exponentially. It brings your people forward in thinking and growing intellectually and becoming curious and acting upon their questions to find answers, noting problems and finding solutions.

As intellect grows, so does civilization.

If traced right back to the beginning of the beginning, did all peoples (from all planets, in all galaxies; everywhere) come from one original planet and peoples?

And where is that beginning it is asked? Was it in one place and time or did beginnings become on many levels and in many locations simultaneously?

Obviously, the latter. I know now how you nicely wrap the answer in a question and ask us to come to it on our own.

It is a thought that scholars wrestle with and bring interesting theories to the fore. We suggest the lingering result of a sparking of interest in *being*: was it an idea and an episode of adventure amongst those creating, those who could create, that which was creation in waiting?

Galaxies had their identities and wisdoms and the source managed to be the wisdom and the identity; the creator.

Who are "those creating, those who could create"?

The source of all, the God-energy, the *being*, and beings who did and do still and will continue—there is that energy overall—encompassing and enveloping and wise.

Does each galaxy have a creator?

It is not the case that there are lines of creators responsible for their portions of the Universe. This remains mystical and thought-provoking for some, but *above all* (no pun intended) is the strength of wisdom and Spirit.

Very cute, Pax, very cute.
"*Above all*, the God-energy,"—however, creators of any kind are not deities, right?

Not deities and no need to be considered such. It is the way of creation, then and now, it is what it is.

Chapter Three
Earth Mysteries Revealed

*I*t's a rare opportunity to be having a dialog with the God being. I'd like to take the opportunity to talk about some of our legends and folklore.

We referred to our self as God being, yes, and it was intended to describe how Earth people may think of our type of energy, our type of essence if you will.

There are many references that do not use the word God. You would not use the term Allah or Krishna for the same reason that using "God" for us causes disruption in the Christian psyche. We suggest not using this term now and in place of it use Divine Source, Divine Wisdom, Divine Guidance or the like.

Yes, we spoke about the importance of inclusivity. Thank you for the reminder.

Let's now start with the mysterious events that have occurred—*especially historically more so than today*—within the area called the Bermuda Triangle located in the western part of the North Atlantic Ocean, such as the disappearance of ships and aircraft.

Ah yes, this is a not-charmed area of your world that has seen its share of disaster. Why is this, you ask? Well, we are here to say it is a place of deep, underground caverns, which harbor the minerals that interfere with navigation now and far back into your history. These elements are not of the area; they were brought for a purpose.

Brought by whom?

These underground caverns have been home to underwater UFO bases and now not occupied, although will be again. With what was there, and remains in place, the magnetics are too powerful to override by commercial navigation of the time. These elements which cause magnetic interference are responsible for far more than interruption to navigation.

Like what? What else are these underground caverns responsible for?

Responsible for the good and useful means of recharging the craft that use the base—it is the overarching reason for the creation of the base. What serves as good for the visitors has created havoc to marine and air travelers, and with combined resources may be amended to reduce the potential of risk for Earth people. We can speak more to this in time.

So, these minerals are not natural to the Earth?

Not natural to the Earth planet. These aspects of the underwater base were included in materials relied upon for their specific purpose and transported with ETs as necessary materials.

What are these minerals that cause magnetic interference for our navigation systems yet are useful to recharge extraterrestrial spacecraft?

As margins of error go, these products of the future will not be named here as references will be negated. Suffice it to say that what was and will be again is not known to your science. When the day comes for awareness; all is revealed.

How long ago did ETs occupy these caverns?

Used as underwater bases for travel and visitation *throughout Earth history*, from time to time recharging was initiated there of flight craft. You will understand the base was a purpose-built creation and all aspects of it were brought to the site from off-planet. It was set up for a specific purpose and operated for the specified time required, after which left in place for future use.

How fascinating. I guess this base goes way back to the initial starseeding of Earth. Given this, these extraterrestrials must certainly feel that they have both a purpose and a right, *perhaps even an obligation*, to occupy such a base at will.

Protection of this area has been foremost in the minds of those watching over it and this will not change.

To be clear, who "watches over" the Bermuda Triangle? (Don't mind me while I shake my head to ring-in this news.)

Those who created the base to suit their needs of travel and visitation watch to ensure it remains untouched. Nothing is of monetary value to Earth people; simply a need to maintain viability of the area for future use. While there is a need for this base, it is to be as it was left and as it is intended—this is the protection.

Can anything be done to make this area safe for ships and planes in present time?

We must say that this present situation of restricted access will continue, and it is best to avoid the area if possible. Otherwise, there are precautions to take which can make a difference.

What kind of precautions?

We say that respecting Mother Earth and her depths is a beginning, and asking for her protection, as mariners do, when passing through challenging weather and locations, is the way. While it is the off-planet creators of these bases who watch, it is heard, by them, that safe-passage is requested through air and water.

There are times when it appears peaceful, this area, and other times when watchfulness steps up to a high level and resulting mysteries occur. They are not mysteries to us, and to your people we say have respect when passing through, ask for permission to do so, much like you should respect the traditional territories of your First Nations peoples. This is a novel idea for your people, but one that is ancient and works. When you respect another's territory and ask permission to pass through, that permission is historically granted when peaceful intentions exist. That no people live in that area does not negate the need for respect of the associated elements, those who create and those who visit.

You've said that the ETs have left, for now, so from whom do we need to ask for permission?

Mother Earth, as explained above in precautions.

And, this ET base will again be occupied?

It will, and until that time there will be relative peace there regarding those ships and planes traversing the waters and skies.

Remain peaceful in intent, speak it and place the blessings on your people and craft—this explains the intention and is a good idea at any time, yes?

Yes, I suppose it is.

This is not the only Earth location of such a base, although has resulted in notoriety of the area through no intention of the visitors. In other locations the coming and going is less of an attention-getter and no disruptions caused in nature or Earth travel.

Really? In what other places on Earth were there similar ET bases?

Oh well now, this is an interesting story as there were and are similar bases. At present, in your time, there are on the North American west coast and near Venezuela as well as in the Northern areas of your globe. There are more but less frequented and harbor nothing that interrupts travel on your planet at this time.

It is purely for the protection of the bases that quiet is kept about their locations, although those residing close do know of their presence as the ships come and go and are noticed. It is a neighborly thing to do, this allowing each to live their lives without interference—like across a fence you know others are there in the process of living lives differently, but friendly allowances for others prevails. This is the attitude of the visitors and of those who see and feel and know their presence and remain quiet and supportive. Live and let live, yes?

Indeed, and let me just go over that: there are, still at this time, *occupied* ET bases on Earth?

Occupied for brief periods of time as the visitors come, monitor and leave—this is their way.

More than you know, it is their wish for peace and harmony around your globe and their visitations show them it is not the way for you, and they depart once again. The day will come when there is change and that is into your future, meanwhile they bring harmony and good intentions only. Allow it.

Pax, what is a wormhole in space?

For the storage of worms?

Ha! You're quite the character sometimes. But, for real, what's a wormhole in space?

In all of the galaxy there are many anomalies and one is the ability to move from place to place in time without effort and without intention, always. It is a time and place and a movement toward another experience that defies logic and brings awe to those attempting to dissect it to understand the step-by-step action of it. Release this and allow it to become for you when the time is right.

Got it: a wormhole is a space-travel highway of sorts, kind of like an intergalactic high-speed train. Now, to why I asked about wormholes...

Some of our current-day pilots, even military pilots, have reported a wormhole-like vortex in the airspace within the area called the Bermuda Triangle. Here's an example: I recently watched a documentary featuring a couple of pilots who said that they had been pulled into a tunnel vortex, yet with great effort they managed to travel through it before it closed behind them. They safely landed at their destination, although ahead of schedule and had used less fuel than the flight should have consumed.

Is there such a "wormhole" in the airspace of the Bermuda Triangle?

Your pilots have experienced this, and we say it is. We clarify that this vortex is a place where entry into another time is possible, and that they, in this example given, landed safely at their chosen destination is example of intention. It was their choice to touch down where they planned, and so it was.

Did ETs create this time-vortex? Is it somehow involved in the protection of the ET base that you spoke of? And, are there other time-vortexes in our Earth atmosphere?

Throughout your time and space there are portals to other dimensions—always have been—and they account for the disappearance of ships at sea and airplanes above. It is the way of the Universe that these cracks in spacetime exist and travelers find themselves other than where they anticipated being. These are dis-associated with the magnetics previously mentioned and not a result of closeness to undersea ET bases. Time warps are and always have been, and a mystery to you they remain.

Ah, so they're a natural phenomenon.

You've given us much to think about. Before we leave this topic, I'd like to ask about the disappearance of the female aviator Amelia Earhart. She disappeared in the central Pacific Ocean, perhaps in the vicinity of the Bermuda Triangle, while in flight on the second of July 1937. There has been much speculation on her disappearance. People want to know if she simply crashed and died (if so, why?) or did she survive for a time.

So, what really happened to Amelia Earhart, her flight navigator Fred Noonan, and her shiny Lockheed Model 10-E Electra craft? What happened that day? What went wrong? Was her aircraft affected by the magnetic minerals of which you spoke? Did she crash yet survive on an island somewhere? Did her aircraft travel through a portal of sorts and end up elsewhere?

Indeed, she flew into a vortex that took her safely into another dimension. It is a continuation of the mystique that surrounds her and her flight and that her aircraft has never been found is a part of this. She was an adventuress and did not dispute what she experienced when it began—she allowed the playing out of the steps that took her into and through the tunnel and deposited her into another place in time.

As she was prepared in her heart for all adventures that came her way, she was not fearful of what she began to experience in this portion of her journey. She was an explorer and allowed this experience to become her next reality. She was chosen. She accepted the challenge and the rest, as they say, is history.

Amelia Earhart, her aircraft, and companion went through a time-vortex to another time dimension! This—all of this—is the makings of a great movie. And, here, another showstopper.

She felt the calling to higher adventure, spiritually, and while she was flying high and, in her mind, touching the face of God, she became exhilarated by the feeling of closeness to the Universe when she came near to the vortex.

In some way she knew there was opportunity to further explore the unknown, and when presented with it she continued on into it.

The Universe provides what the soul craves.

What time-era did they come out into? Was it earlier or later in our history to 1937?

The era, the wrinkle in time, the landing place, the folding into a new reality for this aircraft and passengers is and will remain a mystery for your people. That there always is a defining time and place for all things is not the case.

As this unfolds it will be shown that a space-time adventure continues as this adventuress continues her explorations in another dimension where all flight is possible and continues as desired. There is no beginning or end and there is no definitive flight plan—it is a time-free zone she encounters and enjoys.

Fly free and dream on, the wish of many is hers.

What a beautiful thought for us to hold.

Now, I'd like to ask you about the sunken continents of Atlantis and Lemuria—these lost civilizations greatly interest me. What do you know of them?

Much like Sodom and Gomorrah, there are times when what has gone wrong has gone so wrong that the end result is annihilation, and this was a case of self-destruction. These civilizations had much in common and much to offer. They also had the choice between good and evil. It was the case that the planet, at those times, also underwent a great change from within and it resulted in a climate change type cataclysmic event not fully understood, but suffice it to say, it was a result of the energy emanating from each.

Were there other continents on Earth that are now sunken?

Looking beneath the sea for signs of life will show numerous cities now submerged due to the rising of sea levels, not uncommon. Lost continents are another story.

There are not what you think of as continents imbedded on the sea floor. There have been cataclysmic earth shakings that resulted in the breaking away of pieces of coastal areas and those are hard to identify. It is the case that perusing the ocean's floor turns up much but not this.

Your civilizations of past are most often to be found beneath the sand and soil of your planet. The passage of time has resulted in a diminishing of civilization and abandonment of those civilization's homelands and residences. As growth comes again to these areas it has been common to resurrect what can be and build over what cannot to the extent that antiquities grow, one upon the other in some places, and to go straight down is the way to find history. Not so under water.

In time the cities of North America will suffer the same fate if your world does not adopt cleaner living policies.

You are not immune from the wrath of Mother Nature.

Let's briefly touch back on Sodom and Gomorrah because you bring it up. You've used the example as a parallel to the self-destruction of the two continents—Lemuria and Atlantis—in the sense of energetic impacts resulting from wrongs of dark intentions and actions such as hatred, warring, disrespect to nature, and more. However, let's talk about it further because our people can so easily get things wrong. (It's one of our bad habits.)

Sodom and Gomorrah were cities of antiquity that were mentioned in the Christian Bible, the Hebrew Bible, and the Islamic Quran. The general lesson was that the peoples there had committed great sins—some versions of the story point to acts of homosexuality—and therefore the cities were destroyed by the wrath of the deity that corresponds to each religious tradition. (*I pause here to take a deep breath at what seems so archaic and backwards thinking.*) Let's please clarify the example of the Sodom and Gomorrah story as it relates to the fate of the sunken continents of Lemuria and Atlantis.

If you refer to the demise of these two civilizations, yes, they contributed to their implosion: turmoil and hate and greed and darkness of energy settling, the soil under them gave way to opening and the rest is history.

Do you know your world is looking in that direction now? Although, we see change coming to you to offset the same fate.

May we clear up some ideas about homosexuality? Painfully, it still seems to be a topic of division and debate for some people. We've already mentioned it so we might as well get some insight from the Spirit World on this.

What is it you wish to ask? If it is about equality and acceptance and mutual respect, then of course there should be all this and more shown from one individual to another despite differences. This is not new, but it is still treated as sub-species and shameful.

The shame is in not accepting each individual for who they are.

A part of healing all on your planet is finding total acceptance for life on Earth in all forms. To accept those with differences in makeup is to grow and evolve, and to not do so is to become stuck in a judgmental place where no amount of speaking of the need to will result in people accepting others with differences.

As an extension of this, that judgmental nature makes for a smaller world for individuals so afflicted and they continue to cycle down into a smaller self instead of growing and accepting and spreading this sense of love to all.

Very good insights. Profound. Now I feel we can return to our conversation about Earth's lost continents. The peoples from the advanced civilization of Lemuria: are any still around today, perhaps hidden around or inside Mount Shasta, California, as our legends say?

An interesting theory, this is, but what resides within Mount Shasta is rock and more rock. It is a sacred space to the indigenous peoples of the area and—as part of their traditional territory—it is blessed with some protection. Legends are self-perpetuating, yes?

I've read that highly evolved civilizations keep knowledge of Earth's true history on some sort of crystal discs—is this true?

Crystal discs are mythology for humankind, but one not too far from truth of the interstellar visitors' way of recording history, rather like a logbook of centuries.

Within there will be entries reflecting travel and visits and results, and much like Akashic records, will not be accessed by the many.

Thanks to our Internet, I found this on Wikipedia: "The Akashic records are a compendium of all human events, thoughts, words, emotions, and intent ever to have occurred in the past, present, or future. They are believed by theosophists to be encoded in a non-physical plane of existence known as the etheric plane."

In further researching Akashic records, I've learned that these are also referred to as "white noise extraction systems" and are described as the standing energy waves in spacetime containing all history and all events in all times that ever existed to date.

The Universe must have a reason for such a perfectly designed record system, and someone *must* be able to access these. How can we access the Akashic records?

Ah yes, these records can be accessed by anyone with high spiritual interest and training and powers. It is through the work of Spirit that the door swings open to this hall of records and access is given. You are to consult your Higher Self and whether in meditation or other practices, consider this as a desire. Attaching the intention to use this information for the highest and best good of all, you may move forward.

I will practice this for the highest and best good of all.

Are there any historical and tangible records left specifically from the people of Lemuria?

That would be unlikely, but we can say the search continues and more is to be known when exploration is further enabled.

And what about Atlantis: does any evidence of this continent still exist, if we knew where to look?

There are those who know where to look and believe they are finding ruins they attribute to Atlantis. Is it, is it not? Time will tell as more and deeper examination of remnants is enabled.

Dedication to this cause continues and in your soon time will be interpretation of the findings with what some deem is proof of the existence and demise of Atlantean civilization.

Are there subterranean cities on this planet?

If you ask about living cities, then it is not the case. If you ask about remains of previous civilizations, then yes, very much, as over time the seas have risen, and coastal inhabitants and villages have been taken by the tides. It is a repeating event now on your planet as the seas again rise and those nearby are and will be impacted by loss of land and lifestyle. History repeats itself in climate change, ice ages come and go, warming and cooling cycles, and life goes on. It can be moderated, as your people now think can be done, and time will show it can if attention is paid to the cleaning of your natural resources and protection from future polluting.

Oh, here's another fascinating (to us) question. What happened to the Mayans? The archeological and anthropological evidence shows a people who were there one minute, so to speak, and gone the next. Their cities were abandoned, and no sign of their peoples turns up elsewhere or again. It is said that they disappeared. Did they just "rapture-out" to another world or another dimension like some of us wonder? And, what's the significance of the much-discussed Mayan Calendar and their ties to the stars?

We are here to report that the teleportation of the Mayan peoples took place when their calendar year ended—abruptly but planned evacuation as it were.

Why did they do this, you ask? Theirs had been a civilization of great worship and god-practices and preparation for their ascension in many ways. They had a plan to rise to the epitome of their abilities, do their finest work in growing their civilization to its highest performance level, and then moving on to another home base. They were advanced in their ways and determined to not languish in that one place when it was felt their work there was done.

And so it was that they departed as they had arrived, quietly and with intention.

Well, blow me over with a feather.

Pax, what was the purpose of the Mayan calendar going all the way to the twenty-first of December of the year 2012 when the Mayans successfully teleported off-planet so very many years earlier?

Well this is an interesting philosophical question of your time, yes.

The end of that calendar, dated as it was, indicated a belief at the time that the Universe would be in turmoil and the Planet Earth would catapult out and away from the galaxy. It was the astronomers of the time who set up this belief based on their study of the skies, movements they saw, and intentions of theirs to be at the forefront of exploration of space, from the safety of their cities, while informing the masses through their calendar that plans would be made to evacuate what they thought of as a doomed planet.

Did they think life could be sustained while Earth was hurtling through space in an uncontrolled manner? No, they did not, and therefore quietly prepared to teach the population of the intent to remove themselves from harm. Stated in that way it seemed a natural extension of their civilization to relocate for safety and take their wisdoms, customs, and advanced technology with them to begin again elsewhere. This was accomplished at a time of their choice, the end of calendar date being so far in future their departure could come when they were prepared and well within the calendar deadline.

What was the significance of that precise date of the twenty-first of December of the year 2012?

It was a mathematical equation used to arrive at the numbers as they added in their calendar to a total representing success and higher functioning of the endeavor to relocate. Mathematics was the basis, as it was for much in this civilization.

It is reported that about forty percent of Guatemala's fourteen million people are of Mayan decent. Is this correct; did a portion of the Mayans stay behind?

There are always dissenters to any rule and sure enough, there were those who chose the terra firma they knew over that they did not, so branched out to nearby places to await the departure of their countrymen. They stayed and that is the choice that proved a good one for many. They took their culture with them and contributed to their adopted homeland. What you have today is a melding of cultures and history and if you check DNA you will find interesting mix of mysteries.

Yes, mysteries, and this will show a mix of *other* peoples—we say no more at this time.

DNA and genealogy are easily tested nowadays. Once news of a mystery waiting to be uncovered is out, I'm sure

we'll soon begin to find out about the mix of other peoples. To be continued!

As we're all very interested, what are the Mayans doing these days (those Mayans who teleported out, that is)?

They went far and fast and happily established themselves well onto a hospitable homeland and began their worship and continuation of their excelling in all things. They brought science and astronomy and astrology and healing, of course, and created a hierarchy as they grew into the formidable and highly functioning society they demand. They are outside of your range now but will make themselves known again in time.

We will look forward to the reunion.

This is going to be a wild and fun conversation for many people, and many others will have a very hard time believing in extraterrestrial beings and peoples who travel from planet to planet. What should be considered, however, is the impressive number of astronauts who believe in ETs and who have reported UFOs and other happenings that, to them, can only be explained by the existence of intelligent life outside of our world.

American astronaut, Buzz Aldrin, said this about the moon of Mars: "There's a monolith there. When people find out about that they're going to say, 'Who put that there? Who put that there?'"

Pax, is there a monolith (a large piece of placed rock or structure built as a monument or building) on the moon of Mars? And, who put it there?

To not doubt the word of one who has seen is best, and yes, it is to appear not as a naturally made creation.

How does this appear in a place not seemingly visited in past? Who is to say it was not visited in the past? The past, as you think of it, is quite recent as opposed to the past in terms of galaxies and moons and history of those from outer-ports of advanced life. So, let us inform that some carvings appear to have been planted, *and were*, and it is their anomaly that garners attention.

It is there for wonder and it is there for a statement, somewhat like planting a flag for people of your time. We say the "who" is not as important as the "why" in this case. Suffice it to say the visitors to that place determined it to be a meeting place and not a staying in place. This marker indicated so to those who followed.

Fascinating, to say the least. Dr. Aldrin might be gratified to be validated after all of these years.

And, is there anything extraterrestrial in creation about Ayers Rock in Australia? Called Uluru by indigenous aboriginal Australians, this sandstone monolith dramatically sticks out in an otherwise flat landscape and is sacred to the aboriginals. Is there something interesting to know about it?

Sacred it is and sacred it has always been as a piece of inner earth thrust upward to arrive in that position of no return to below. As that continent flexed and shook and fractured in spots, that which was beneath the surface and wanting to decrease pressure was allowed to escape the darkness and appear to the native inhabitants but there were none present at that time. This came later and the history is recorded to include this as a draw, a pilgrimage for those who, in wonder, came to look and touch and climb to the top. Drawings and carvings appeared to record these events and the belief that Mother Earth had provided a Goddess rock for worship began.

The sacred site gave and gives hope and belief to the indigenous peoples that something greater than themselves exists in their place and time. It is now reverting to sacred trust and being held away from the ravages of unlimited and unwise visitors who damage and deface this wonder of nature.

Talking about "earth thrust" makes me think of the Earth's *crust*: is it thinning as some scientists say? If so, why?

It is the case that Earth's crust thins and recovers through time with warming and cooling and ice ages and heat waves—it remains flexible. Now it is in a period of constriction once again. Nothing in nature is rigid. Periods of growth and periods of decline in areas of your Earth peoples have been the way through history. It is and it will be and is not to be feared as the end of anything—it is a cycle.

What do periods of growth and decline in areas of our Earth peoples have to do with the thinning of the Earth's crust? Are we somehow controlling the Earth's geological cycles?

Well yes, and it is the case that "areas" refers to geographical areas where, over time, natural as well as unnatural events have occurred. It is these warming and cooling periods that make the change, and these are largely created by Earth population. Some are and some are not, and this is the way of it.

As cycles go on your Earth plane and in your history, climate has changed to warm and again to cool, cataclysmic events in nature have occurred and nothing has been constant, nor will it be going forward. Every action has a reaction and here it is in view.

Just know that your people are active, and Earth is largely passive, and you affect your future on Planet Earth.

Let's talk about our population and the bearing limit of our planet. Do advanced civilizations limit their population somehow? What advice do you have for us on this sensitive topic?

Ah yes, sensitive it is, for controlling population growth is not always wise. While some civilizations, countries now on your planet have done so; it was released as a law after a period of time. The people won't stand for it and other means must be found.

Wars and pestilence were means of reducing populations in past; neither of which are wanted in your current time, but the warring continues on parts of the globe and pestilence can be a current-day threat as is pollution and drugs, all of which reduce populations. There are self-governing means of population control such as birth control, widely used in some places and not in others.

We say the overall means of controlling population—as on other planets and in other civilizations—has been wisdom. Those cultures function at a higher vibratory level and understand the ways of peace and love. They do not war and they do not function in hate or anything negative. Their way of going is to find peace and share peace and small communities of intellectual souls prevail. It is not a rule of law, but rather a self-imposed wish to focus on self-awareness and evolution, on furthering their goal of enlightenment, which requires inner focus. Are they self-centered; we say yes in the best possible way. The path to enlightenment is theirs.

Pax, I have so many questions about life, Earth, space. For instance—what is a black hole in space? And what is its purpose?

A black hole is a repository for what comes by and is destined for other places and other uses.

It is the case that a balance is created here, and there is no end-place for the space debris now, but black holes could be a vacuum for what your people have left and describe as "space junk". You aren't really there yet and debris is your legacy already—why do we think your colonization of another planet is a good thing for your Earth? It is to become yet another litter location for your people if minds and hearts do not change on this topic. Why is it you find it necessary to discard and forget about it? Why is lack of planning for resources no longer needed, and still reality? Do you not grow with your forward motion in life? We say it is to be the downfall of your intentions to relocate and revive civilization.

We are here to advise that the mysteries of space are to remain so for as long as needed to entice your people to learn and explore and consider themselves in a very good place, so good, in fact, that mindsets change and cleanup in earnest of Planet Earth accelerates.

I suppose that our space travel does include the steady leaving-behind of space litter such as discarded satellites and rocket stages.

There are others above who watch and are not pleased. As they buzz by to observe, they also must carefully plan their route so as to avoid banging up against your litter—for shame people, clean up your own place before thinking of how to leave your footprint elsewhere.

Infinity is where it ends and there is no end to infinity, yes?

I'm inferring that black holes are part of that infinity: everything that comes by is accumulated and stored for a while, and eventually whatever is collected in that vacuum goes—where?

Do your scientists understand that what goes in will come out elsewhere?

Where? Where does all the matter go that is sucked in?

This is for future consideration, yes, and for now it is to be understood that the Black Hole is the repository for what will appear elsewhere, in time. Where it goes is where it will go and that is to be.

What we can share is that it will burst, yes, for it will fill and like a volcano, spew contents up and out and through and around and down. It would be best to be elsewhere when this occurs, except that the contents will end up "elsewhere", but it will come as a welcome event. No more shall we share at this time, other than to divulge that what is in and comes out form building blocks for future civilizations on future colonies. All good, it is said.

With this— "What is in and comes out form building blocks for future civilizations on future colonies"—you just handed Steven Spielberg his next movie plot!

While our space junk is likely useless to interstellar colonies (after all, space junk is just garbage), perhaps black holes can be a delivery portal. Perhaps we could send a message through a black-hole-delivery-system. Could this be possible? Let's say that we filled a space-tight capsule with messages, pictures, and drawings—could it potentially reach those inhabitants of a space colony?

Well this is an interesting consideration. Not the intended purpose or highest use for the black hole as we know it, but as things go in, they will come out. Although, to aim for a specific end spot would be an exercise in futility. We used the term "spew", and that doesn't come with specific aiming capability. Perhaps the use in this manner can be attained with fine-tuning, and why not consider that a next stage development. All is possible in time and change is to be considered good and constructive and exciting, too.

So, a black hole is a holding place and one day it erupts like a volcano. To be clear, the stuff that is sucked in comes out elsewhere, like through a tunnel?

It has been stated that what goes in comes out elsewhere, and it could and would be random: that elsewhere. So, don't be between one place and the other when it happens. This is a dramatization but not completely as there will be space debris in motion.

Is there plot and plan for this action? We say not, and is there an ideal outcome of this action? Possibly. And what is to be the end result of this action? Now it is to be questioned and conjured and considered and not experienced or clarified for many turns of your Earth planet in another spacetime orbit. For now, it is a vast idea of infinite possibility.

When you spoke about our Starseeded Origins and the starseeded primates, you mentioned "a ship full of monkeys"—perhaps a reference to Noah's Ark. Was there really a guy named Noah, who, as the biblical story goes, built a huge ark and filled it with two of each species to save them from a great flood that destroyed the world as they knew it at that time?

It's a good story, yes? It is the case that writings from early times, as they have been edited and added to and translated into many languages, have become warped and exaggerated and diminished and generally changed to suit the translator or religions involved in the writings. We say to take all lessons with thought and filters and adopt those that feel right on a personal basis. Was there a giant boat—yes. And were there two of each species on the Earth planet—not likely, but there were many, and perhaps the two of everything refers to two of all that were known at the time. Some stories become embellished over time and the basis for this is sound but the story as it appears today includes the growth of the animal numbers to proportions not based on reality. But never mind, we say the lesson is there and the intention was good. Not all is non-fiction.

Pax, I've been meaning to ask you: who designed and built the Great Pyramids of Egypt? Even today, our best architects, physicists, and mathematicians can't figure out the mysteries of the building of these structures and their mindboggling design. Were the pyramids designed by the locals (the people of that area and of that time) or are they the works of extraterrestrial visitors from advanced civilizations? And, who did the building labor—was it slave labor? How did the monstrous size stones get moved through the desert? What technology made that possible?

This is quite the conversation on your Earth plane, and the reality is those extraterrestrial visitors we speak of, those who buzz by from other galaxies to follow-up on Earth peoples' progress, were the advanced knowledge responsible.

It is the case that those who seeded civilization continued to monitor, and in their advanced technological development, it was a simplistic way of building they shared. Physics was well understood, obviously, as they built interstellar capable ships for travel, and they contributed their knowledge to those who accepted.

The movement of building materials was aided by some movement of thought: the intention of moving, teleportation if you will, is the way. As travel from place to place by teleportation is, so is the way to manage large-scale movement of stone. It is a dissolution of plasma in one place and reassembly in another. As your Earth saying goes, it's not rocket science. This is no different than dissolving clouds or creating any number of realities using the mind-power.

Is this how the stones of the Stonehenge circle in England were moved? Our physicists are still stuck on this one, too. It is said by our anthropologists that Stonehenge was built in six stages during the transition from the Neolithic Period (the New Stone Age) to the Bronze Age. It would seem to me that if the stones were moved by highly evolved and enlightened interstellar visitors using thought power, then well, they could have moved them much quicker than that! May you please help us to correct history here and enlighten us to when and why Stonehenge was built?

Gathering for worship has been the incentive for creation of structures such as this monument, and the peoples of the various times came with differing reasons and levels of intention for such a build. While the helpers from afar had capabilities surpassing those of the local inhabitants, they offered what was wanted and needed at the time. If the people wanted a box, they were not given a skyscraper as they would not have known what to do with one.

The evolution of this monument, as with others from early Earth times, came as awareness grew and knowledge grew to match it and the desired end-result was shown. One step at a time.

What is the structure beneath Stonehenge?

What is beneath is more of the same. Although, it will not be excavated, on that space, if so, it would show another but smaller circle. There have been circles in place for centuries and the numbers of those yet undiscovered is large. The worship and giving thanks for their gifts and abundance is the key for the build and the use of such places. To observe lunar cycles and star movements to be aware of the sun and moon, and to time their activities with these rotations was also key. The people of that time and place worshipped and gave thanks for what they had, planned and hoped for additional abundance of crops and lifestyles, and made it a point to show this gratitude daily. When gathering at monuments such as this for special occasions in the lunar calendar, there was heightened awareness of the power of the stars and planets, of the sun and moon, and humility and gratitude were the overriding feelings of the time. This is something that could be emulated in some aspects of your today society.

A daily practice of gratitude is a solid recommendation and is advised by just about every best-life coach and inspirational speaker of today. What is it about gratitude that is so important and powerful?

It is attraction of more to be grateful for.

You know that the laws of life say that what you think about you attract, well, when you are positive and grateful and thankful for the abundance in your lives, you live in a state of grace that is emphasized each time you share your gratitudes with the Universe. You become charmed and a target and magnet for continued abundance and it is a never-ending circle of joy.

To think the bliss and live the bliss and attract the bliss—a natural cycle in life—it is within you to create for yourself.

Charmed is a good way to think of this: lucky or happy as though protected by magic. I also like the description of "a never-ending circle of joy". Gratitude is a generator of more to be grateful for.

Switching gears, another item of speculation is polar axis swap. In the Earth's history, has there ever been a swapping of the poles and the axis of rotation of the Earth?

Not in the way you would think of it, no, and it is the case that the shifts in energy around the globe have been many and varied. Moving forward you will see the continued growth and change, as this is the way throughout your history. There is no need to fear this as your planet always recovers and recharges and restores herself to rightness.

Are you saying that there will never be a future cataclysmic Earth pole shift?

No need to consider this as possibility. What you do need to consider is protection of all of your nature as it roots your planet in the security of future wellness.

What triggered the last ice age?

Ice ages have come and gone throughout history and are often thought of as cataclysmic when in reality they are Earth's way of regrouping and beginning fresh with flora and fauna and purity of air and water. Rapid cooling of the atmosphere due to seasonal change, and by this is meant seasons comprised of thousands of years. It is a flow of air, atmospheric pressures, and change that originate far from your Earth.

The causation of our ice ages is "atmospheric pressures and change that originate far from your Earth"—wow.

This includes wholesale change on many stars and planets and comes from unknown-to-you source. It continues through time and space and is just the way of it.

This is fascinating: the Universe is holistic!
And, are *we* affecting Earth's poles and our magnetosphere?

All you do on and to your Planet Earth affects some aspect of it. Withdraw from injuring the underground with explosions to enable fossil fuel extraction and withdraw from injuring the atmosphere with gasses and pollution and nuclear testing.

Is the danger of nuclear fallout or meltdown just too risky to pursue nuclear power? (*We must scare the pants off of our interstellar visitors!*)

This has its uses and positive features in the right hands of science, but you have world leaders who are demented and consider the use of this power as their own to threaten others into submission. It is a danger to your population to have this as a reality and a tool of warring people.

"World leaders who are demented." (Kinda funny, but not funny.)

Do not think that what you do is isolated—like ripples on the water these actions spread their negativity far and wide. Your people have concerns but feel disempowered to make change on a large scale.

We shall talk of this further—empowerment is a right for all.

I look forward to that discussion.

Scientists today are identifying a drift in the Earth's spin axis; therefore, magnetic north has moved. It has shifted so much so that they had to do an emergency update to the World Magnetic Model and GPS, yet no one can entirely explain the cause of the shift. Why is Earth's axis shifting?

A shift of this magnitude is not abnormal, and the existence and movement of stars and planets tends to be fluid rather than fixed forever. There is spin and change—Earth events that bring massive change to parts of your globe and affect the health of your planet—and the likelihood of future change and the intellectual community fears this. It is to be known that change is natural and does not mean there need be fear.

It is the Mother Earth shifting in her chair and taking a different view of her surroundings.

That's a lovely way of describing it.

You've said that you wish to distribute a message to humanity about our environmental situation. We will continue this conversation in depth, yet first: why are we having this conversation about healing Planet Earth *now*?

You are a young civilization on that planet, and whether you survive to be an older and wiser peoples depends now on the speed at which repair to Earth's resources is undertaken and affected. Damage is severe now to your environment, and that combined with greed and diminished integrity of corporate entities and world governments doesn't bode well for healing before a Failsafe point is reached.

If we weren't to change anything and continued on this current destruction trajectory, is the Failsafe point rather soon—in my lifetime? Some say that the Earth only has eight or maybe twelve years left before we've reached the tipping point of "too late"—that Failsafe point, as you say. Would eight to twelve years be considered about right? I know that you don't speak in linear time, yet please pin this down to an estimated timeline as this will help when communicating this message.

Yes, it is the case that in the very soon time is the Failsafe point we referred to. It is here that a line is drawn in the sand and if minds and hearts aren't changed to the extent that actions are changed, your Planet Earth will continue down the path to the point of no return. This is serious and non-reversible. It is to be respected.

Volume 2

Do Unto Earth
Pax and the Critical Return
to Wisdom

As I walk, as I walk,
The Universe is walking with me.
In beauty it walks before me.
In beauty it walks behind me.
In beauty it walks below me.
In beauty it walks above me.
Beauty is on every side.
As I walk, I walk with Beauty.

Traditional Navajo Prayer

Chapter Four
The Ways

*I*f we had to pick just one anthropogenic issue to fun-
nel our attention, what is the largest threat to our environment and the survival of our planet and life on Earth?

There are numerous current threats to survival of your civilization as it currently exists, but the one overarching situation is
the pollution of your environment, poisoning of your water, air,
and soil to the extent that even growing healthy food is impossible in some areas. That you have genetically modified crops to
suit the wishes of commerce, grow it faster and bigger—what
were you thinking? How could you consider there would be
no negative reaction, no fallout as a result? How did you think
speeding growth of crops and animals in order to sell more and
sell faster would be a good thing? We watch your, what you
consider good intentions, unravel and destroy, slowly and steadily,
your farms, your farm economy, and your planet. Did you think
the spraying of crops with damaging pesticides would spray the
crops only? Had you not considered the leaching into the soil
and the rivers and streams of this poison? Did you not realize
all streams, well almost, lead to the ocean, and the fish resource

affected along the way is yet another calamity and catastrophe of environmental destruction? It is a deafening silence we hear from those corners of commerce where money is all-important and the talk of healthy maintenance and care for the soil and water and air is non-existent. For shame people, this is the path to destruction.

Many people, including our scientific community, say that climate change is the biggest and most pressing issue threatening our planet. In 2020, our scientists released a report pertaining to the rising sea level from melting glaciers and polar icecaps. The report stated that one hundred and fifty million people in their current locations would live below the permanent high tide line by the year 2050. May you please compare the urgency regarding the rate of planetary destruction due to pollution versus climate change?

There is no separation between pollution and climate change as the former is a causative factor of the latter. One aggravates the other, therefore, to reduce pollution contributes to reduction in rate of climate change—balance is needed. Your Earth is out of balance.

I suppose we need only look at the example of the extreme air and water pollution in Delhi, India to know that pollution is the quickest murderer of our planet and life here. Air pollution alone kills one and a half million people each year in India.

When you speak of pollution, we consider that of all resources both above ground and below: the soil and water and the air. What is done underground by the oil and gas industry is a contributor to instability also. Mother Earth shudders at the intrusion.

Yes, we tend to forget about what's happening underground, especially as there is so much pollution visible above ground and in the oceans.
As for climate change, is there a way to reverse it? Or, is there a way for us to invent technology to artificially re-cool the Earth?

Not more technology needed and no "reversing" of climate change. Lowering your ceiling and elevating your temperature—a nasty combination.

This was called "global warming". Now this term is not widely used.

Yes, because for many people, Global Warming sounded too scary, so the term was marketed-up and re-scripted to Climate Change.

What is required is to stop climate change and global warming by changing the ways of your industrial nations. Look at the air and water pollution—what are you thinking, people, that you continue to pour waste and off-products into air and water? We look at this in wonder. As you are a throw-away society this takes it too far as you are leading to the need to throw away your planet. Where does it end? Who begins the fight to overcome corporate greed? Why is there no adoption of cleaner methods of heating and propulsion of vehicles in a large scale? Is it because these methods are not widely enough available? And if so, is this protection of big industry and its profits?

This is a sadness and you should—those of you who can—speak loudly for change. If you choose to not do so then you should be ashamed as you contribute as surely as if you made the rules.

When people unite in a cause, change happens, and you know this. Is it time to cease your silence and speak your truth? Mother Earth weeps.

It is time to become a megaphone for Earth and her animals and plants.

Data can vary by source; however, I'll try to pull together an overview of known environmental statistics. In order of greatest threat, the countries with the most CO_2 emissions today are: China, USA, India, Russia, and Japan. These countries' astronomical CO_2 outputs can be tied to automobile output, methane produced by cattle livestock, and large populations that either consume or manufacture products.

On another list that includes a number of pollution sources, the following nations are among those that have been cited as the highest polluters as it relates to the sum total of CO_2 emissions, non-recycled waste, chemical and garbage dumping into the oceans, and air toxins from dirty manufacturing: Mongolia, Afghanistan, Bangladesh, India, Pakistan, Kuwait, Nepal, Myanmar, Ghana, Lebanon. These nations have varied realities: some are over-populated, others are war-torn, and a few are under-developed countries where it could be that people are most concerned with daily survival over environmental degradation.

Now that we have a little context, I'd like to address the argument by some that the environment should not be considered above things like the need to stabilize geo-politics and growth in the job market and the economy. No matter how much we preach about the environment and how much

Mother Earth weeps, there are many people in the world who are just trying to get by month-to-month or day-to-day. The environmental crisis might not be the issue that people vote on for their political leaders, and it might not be top-of-mind if they don't have adequate food to eat or if they can't pay their rent.

May you please speak to how we survive these daily needs and at the same time change our ways and methods while looking for alternative fuel and food sources?

Inclusivity is the way. To not assume that people in need of support in food and shelter, jobs, and inexpensive goods do not care about the fact that pollution is making them ill—that clean food and water may not be available to them and their children—is the beginning. All people care about their own and their family needs. Teaching the ways to reuse and recycle, for example, teaching the ways of sourcing locally, teaching how growing their own foods, if possible, are more easily done than believed; all these incentives make people feel they are a part of the solution and not part of the problem. It is empowering to people who may be in need, to know they have tools to circumvent their previous ways of living to become more healthy for themselves and their planet. There is a certain amount of pride in learning new ways of preserving Earth wellness and being able to teach their children the ways—it is empowering. This is how to include and expand the soldiers for healthy living and healthy planet. It is to respect all people for having integrity and concern for their Mother Earth's future wellness.

While we know the world must change slowly, one brick at a time is how we build, and one idea at a time is how we change. Throughout this process there are leaders who speak of the necessity of change, but do they describe the route or lead the way? That is needed.

Now we ask for those in the know to participate and contribute to this change. Those who move forward in their thinking are responsible for educating those who do not.

Pax, earlier, when I asked how we can heal our planet, you pointed to our First Nations people and said, "The ways of your aboriginal peoples, this is how your Planet Earth does best," and so let's get right into this and more.

You should know that repair is possible when your world leaders lead and listen to your environmental scholars who are prepared to lead in their way. This must be a combined effort to teach and inspire and act responsibly with wisdom and intention. Speak to the First Nations peoples on the planet—they got it right the first time and kept it well until interference from those determined to take away their lands and culture. When you look closely at history, you see the decline in environmental wellness began when First Nations peoples were removed from their lands, their cultures were stolen, their language was outlawed, and they were considered savages and not worthy of integration into white society. Those guilty of these atrocities now need apologize and ask for leadership to repair the resultant decimation of Earth's resources.

We are here to speak of the times when mankind felt it necessary to begin projects one at a time and do a good job. Why is it now that mankind feels that all work must be accomplished in record time and quality suffers? Materials are poor and workmanship generally is below quality also. It is our belief that the times of old were when items were made with care and concern in the knowledge that they would last generations and that was the intention.

You have become a throwaway society, and this is wasteful and foolish and harms Mother Earth with landfill excesses.

Would it not be prudent to return to the old ways of using high-quality materials and taking pride in workmanship?

Yes, it would.

It is our belief that by returning to the ways of old where community was self-sustaining, you will receive the best you can. To support an artisan in your area, your neighborhood or village, supports the whole village or city and keeps economy buoyant. Not to order from foreign countries where the workers are poorly paid and with no benefits or concern for their welfare other than that they can produce. This is not the way of the future.

As consumers, we need to remember that each and every purchase is a vote for something that we support. We have much more power in the solutions than we own up to.

Again, we say look to the past for the way of the future. Locally made, locally grown, locally raised—this is how you support your future and find the best for your family in terms of food, clothing and more. This also requires little fuel for transport. Know that the Earth's situation is bad enough now without continuing to demand apples to a country where they are not in season.

Do as was done in past times: eat seasonally available produce. How simple. Or preserve the produce so it is available off-season. Generations past preserved all they could, and it got them through. Teach your children and your coworkers and your family members that this is the thing to do.

You need a shift in thinking now. And, it has come to the time that we request you focus on what it will take to move you from such a wasteful society to one which takes care in all areas of sustaining itself.

Looking within we say you will find the wisdom to know that this is the case and begin to work towards re-educating yourself and your families to learn the ways of your forefathers and grandmothers. It will be the best thing you do.

Mother Earth thanks you for taking the next step. You each can do your part for the world.

And, we thank Mother Earth for her patience.

It will be raised by some people that there was warring between many indigenous tribes and histories of great conflict and brutality.

It is the case that in generations ago time, in First Nations peoples' society, there was warring and protection of land, and there was upset and genocide at the hands of white invaders, but when left to their own worlds, these first peoples lived idyllic lives. Culture based on respect for all life, respect for Mother Earth, respect for Elders, respect for traditions; these are the cornerstones of peaceful life.

Yes, First Nations peoples' history was "genocide at the hands of white invaders". This is true and no one could successfully challenge this statement. Yet, I do want to touch on "white" as the descriptor of the invaders throughout history. Was it always the case that "white" people decimated the indigenous peoples? I feel like we might get some push back on using the term "white" people to represent many nations of people over many years. But, I'm not into sugarcoating so if that's the best way to phrase this, then we're good.

The term, which is currently acceptable, is "settlers". It was white settlers in North America and others in different locations. Ultimately, their actions toward indigenous people were similar and the end result was not assimilation, but annihilation; or at least intolerance, persecution, and non-acceptance.

Shameful.

As we seek to emulate the wisdom of First Nations people, are you referring also to the way that they procured medicine from plants, or their spiritual rituals, or the way in which they related to the land as guardians rather than owners of it?

We say to research these ways of the elders and their peoples, touch on the practices that surrounded their community, their society, agricultural and ceremonial practices, and see a time and place where responsible stewardship of resources was the way. Managing resources was a part of their nature—there was no over-fishing or stripping away of topsoil or clear-cutting of forests or wholesale slaughter of animals. Everything taken from Mother Earth was done with respect, prayer, and thanks.

The First Nations people have been the best stewards of your planetary resources, and always will be. They should be consulted, listened to, and included in decisions of world import.

Earth's First Nations peoples live by the belief that they belong to the land and are not owners of the land. If we all lived this way, our environment would be healthy and resources would be available with a healthy balance in place. This perspective shift makes a great difference in all other practices and ways to respect Earth, however, is it likely that we could return to this way of life and release ownership rights?

The First Nations indigenous peoples knew they belonged to the land, yes, but their extended belief was that they were caretakers of the land only; it did not belong to them. They acted in ways to ensure continuation of resources, ensuring they planted and harvested only what they needed, left the soils to fallow and restore nutrients for a later planting. They took only the meat and fish needed to clothe and feed themselves for the season, and respected the spirits of those they took. There was reverence for the land, and this translated into all they did. Under their stewardship the land was healthy and prospered, therefore so did the people who relied upon the land and resources for their wellness. Plant medicine was a part of the cultures and knowing and growing those specimens needed for healing was a large part of their lives. To know that their soils were pure, as was their water, enabled them to live well and long. They also knew that to walk softly and leave no footprints was how to respect Mother Earth.

You know, Pax, First Nations peoples can be wary of outsiders; they are protective, especially of their Elders, and guard them against people unknown to them.

We can learn from the many already published books and writings by First Nations leaders of the past and today, however I wonder: is your message that we should seek first-hand and current voices in those communities?

This will become apparent as time goes on. No in-person visit of less than many days would gain you the information you seek or the understanding.

To not seek them out but to read their writings is the way. Listen to their teachings, observe their culture, and accept that their ways of today are filtered and distilled as their life on the land isn't what it once was. Their current ways have been adapted for today's cultures.

The ways of the Grandmothers are what we speak of and that is what they teach. It is written for all to read and learn.

Mankind is quick to point out the need for care now with the ecosystems. What is really needed is the protection from all levels of government, working together to ensure survival. Much money is spent on studies when it need only be directed to those who know to implement solutions. Not the scholars alone, but the elders of your civilization, the elders of each tribe of people on the planet, those who retain both the knowledge and the caring to make the difference.

Many are those who believe that the Earth will find its way back to full function—to health—this is not the case. The time is now to examine your collective consciousness and determine if there is sufficient care and concern among you for the plight of the planet.

As you observe the change of balance in the native indigenous communities and see the wisdom of the people extend to the bringing of higher education to the children, you can know that the past will rise again. History repeats itself and you are to watch for the resurgence of power in the First Nations peoples. When they reclaim their rightful place as stewards of the planet, there will be a gradual and harmonious return to wellness in your world. It is not too late.

(This will be a real David and Goliath story.)

Returning to the ways of the Elders and their Elders and generations before them in aboriginal society will show the wisdom to emulate for a healthier society today. It is the case that protecting and revering the land and caring for one another, knowing the plants for their wisdom and healing properties, learning of and emulating the wisdoms of Earth's animals—all these contribute to a society of peace and wisdom.

Whoa, this is a sentence to expand on please: "Learning of and emulating the wisdoms of Earth's animals." May you tell us more about the wisdoms of Earth's animals? (Many people don't imagine that animals have "wisdom" let alone basic feelings and emotions.)

Yes, and this is unfortunate. In the wild, Earth's animals, until some were hunted to extinction, knew how to survive on their own. Finding food, dealing with weather, changing landscapes and climate, all were managed through their ability to read their environment. Intuiting danger, sourcing water, protecting each other from predators and finding their place in the food chain— all was managed through innate wisdom of their land home. Family herds and moving throughout territories had boundaries, which they recognized and functioned within. Food sources were rationed, hunting instincts learned, protection of youth and Elders, migration strategies, all were learned and taught and abided by in order to survive and thrive. Pack leaders were respected and followed to ensure safety of the herd.

This is animal wisdom.

As we speak of animal wisdom, elephants stand out to me as beings in need of some special attention and awareness from us.

The gentle nature of this animal is a lesson for all, along with the family loyalty and protection of elders and the young as exhibited daily in their lives.

That they have a purpose and a pattern and a sense of peace while going about their daily habits. Not looking for trouble or threatening, despite their size, is another lesson.

Despite the locals advising against it, an African hotel was built directly on the path the elephant population walked to access their favorite fruit trees. The elephants were not angry or troublesome or deterred, and to this day they walk daily through the hotel lobby, in one side and out the other to find their fruit trees where they graze. They then return to their path through the hotel lobby and in this way all life remains peaceful and harmonious in that place.

That *is* a lesson.
And, how can those who care about them better protect elephants from ivory and game-trophy poachers?

With influx of monetary support to keep watchers over their territories and game preserves.

Laws are in place to prosecute and these augmented by outcry from Earth's people at the atrocity of killing protected creatures like elephants. Public shaming and large monetary penalties along with incarceration could be added. Public ridicule and shaming is high in efficacy.

I like your candor today, Pax. Preach it!
Speaking of public outcry, while it might be there, it's seemingly not very effective. Let's also talk further about the illegal poaching of elephants, rhinoceros, lions, and more across African countries, as well as the slaughter of wild Congo gorillas and over-fishing of white shark in the waters of Africa's southern tip. Many of these species are becoming extinct and some have such low numbers that they can be counted in the two and three digits.

A friend of mine, Eugene Cussons—a native South African conservationist and host of a popular TV show on the network *Animal Planet*—strives to spread the message of the imminent threat of extinction of many African species due to poaching.

The poaching of these animals is in many cases already illegal, and so how is it that this continues with little outcry from the world? (That is, in comparison to the threat of other species' extinction and various environmental issues that get vast amounts of attention.)

Greed rules, and those who sell ivory and other animal parts to China and other countries representing a consistent market will find those in government to protect their actions— 'twas ever thus.

It is time to enforce world laws, or create them, outlawing this practice *globally* and place enforcement tools where they can be used: rules and laws with teeth and severe penalties for allower and allowee. It can be done.

There is so much turmoil in your world that people don't know where to begin, which cause to champion, how to prioritize and define the parts of their monetary income they can direct to their choice and where need is great(est). It is a slippery slope now, on your Earth, and if the planet isn't repaired and sufficiently habitable, how can endangered species survive?

Perhaps the need is equal between saving plants and animals from extinction and creating clean soil, air, and water for them as well as humans. Sometimes the pendulum has swung so far one way it doesn't seem that finding balance will be attainable. There needs to be a division of the causes and when they are spread amongst the supporters, simultaneous healing may begin. The loudest voices will often receive most support, and now with the rising of the youth voices, they may be wise enough to understand that the division of causes among those crusaders stepping forward will be the way.

I have an affinity for dolphins, and I believe that they are wise souls with distinct intention. What is the collective

purpose of the dolphin species? I can tell that there is more to dolphins than we know.

Oh yes indeed, there is much more to dolphins than to be circus animals. This is an injustice and a humiliation for them, so don't do it.

These highly intelligent ocean souls have been responsible for saving lives and guiding mariners forever. They know and they show the way home for struggling vessels and they accompany them to their safe harbor. It is the case that without dolphins' intuitive nature and chosen cause to guide and protect, much loss of life over the centuries would have occurred.

For seamen who understand this, their intuitive calling to their Higher Selves for help out of a difficult situation on the oceans brings their dolphin partners whose guidance and sense of calm transmits to the mariners and the safe harbor is found. It is a partnership of old, and like many is a friendship offered but not always accepted by those non-believers.

That's beautiful and profound. Every year in Japan at a single event known as the Taiji Dolphin Drive Hunt, approximately twenty-two thousand dolphins are slaughtered for their meat, or, in some cases, stolen from the sea to be sold to marine parks. This despicable event is even more sickening when we know how dolphins wish to help and guide us. Dolphins should be sacred and revered. We really do, and *have* done throughout history, some very shameful acts.

Let's bring our talk back to First Nations peoples' wisdom.

To learn something from all cultures is advised, however for the purpose of your current thinking and direction, returning to history to see the future is best done with those who, today, function well in their societies, do not go to war, and resolve their differences intellectually.

To consider the First Nations, the aboriginal peoples of various world cultures, all can contribute. Do you see them showing respect to all people and animals, do you see them as a peaceful society treating all as equals on the land? We say these are the societies to be learned from. Those who treat the air and water, the animals, soil, and all peoples with respect are who you may emulate.

Greed and warring are responsible for the decline in quality of life and no civilization that succumbs to these is worthy of study. We speak of corporate and political greed being behind the decimation of natural resources in your world, on your planet, and to your people.

When we think of First Nations peoples, we tend to think of native Australian aboriginals and indigenous peoples of North and South America. Do you wish to speak specifically to the wisdom that we could gain from the ways of the Tibetan society? What about the wisdom to be imparted from today's tribe leaders in some African countries?

Tibetan culture is ancient and wise in healing modalities. Their reliance on the land for wellness continues. Their peaceful nature and intentions and respect for all are a lesson to be taken by all.

African countries are many and varied as are their ways. They have a common thread and that is their need for reliance on themselves for food gathering and production, their need to rely on one another and on their land for sustenance, shelter, and protection. Their resilience and trust in themselves to survive and thrive is strong.

As we endeavor to learn from our many wise First Nations and aboriginal peoples, I think we need a bit of advice: How do we dare ask for help from the First Nations peoples—now that we've screwed it all up and are losing the Earth—when we still haven't made the past right? How can we apologize to the First Nations people and who should offer the apologies when the settlers that took the land and decimated the peoples are long ago deceased? Current governments will very likely not give back any land. How do we begin to make this right again?

Your indigenous peoples are being compensated: there is the Truth and Reconciliation Act in place which is enacted and being followed. Lands are returned, the "Indian Act" (in Canada) modified, education and funding for it and housing improvements is in place, but not enough yet. The higher education of First Nations youth has led to stronger Bands and wiser Bands, and tables have turned. There is still far to go, but Residential School reparations are made and apologies also by government. Return of language and culture studies contribute to their strength going forward and working together now with Bands to ask their guidance in how to know and follow their past ways of conservation, brings mutual understanding. The wisdom shared will make the difference in your land and resource management practices.

The indigenous peoples are being *somewhat* compensated, yet I would guess that they are not satisfied with how they are negated, cast aside, and not respected and heard, especially when it comes to their efforts to protect the natural environments from oil drilling and water contamination.

You had said, "What is done underground by the oil and gas industry is a contributor to instability also: Mother Earth shudders at the intrusion."

Let's talk about that. Why does Mother Earth shudder at the intrusion of oil excavation? What is going on beneath the surface from a geological and technical description that is hurting Earth?

Weakening the stability of Earth with fracking and drilling is what is going on beneath the surface. Fill it with holes then expect stability against wind and weather? Not brilliant in the long term. As more and more boreholes are driven, the look of Swiss cheese begins, and we say you understand the stability of that for holding weight above.

The Middle East is known for oil, however, let's discuss oil excavation in North America as this directly involves First Nations peoples.

The Dakota Access Pipeline is some eleven hundred miles long and moves a half million barrels of crude oil per day out of the ground through North Dakota, South Dakota, and Iowa, and terminates in Illinois. This pipeline was built from start to finish in just one year (talk about high-level vested interest; we can't fix road potholes this quickly), and it was highly protested against by many First Nations tribes including the Standing Rock Sioux Tribe whose Standing Rock Reservation is directly next to the pipeline. They, of course, lost the battle, again.

Let's take a short trip down history lane because this harkens back to 1874 when General Custer's cavalry found gold in the Black Hills, part of the *then* treaty-protected land of the Great Sioux Nation.

The Sioux fought for their land, but then in 1877, the United States Government imposed the "Starve or Sell Bill". Another altercation ensued at a place called Wounded Knee on the twenty-ninth of December 1890, and Custer's Seventh Calvary slaughtered three hundred people from the Sioux (Lakota) Nation.

Now, here we are again. The Dakota Pipeline is the Black Hills Gold of today, and greed wins again. Can you imagine how disempowered The Sioux must feel? I guess that was a rhetorical question because I know that you can.

Those with vested interest don't see an environmental liability with the pipeline. That being said, I think everyone needs to hear it directly from you: Is the pipeline indeed poisoning the water sources for those living on the Standing Rock Reservation who report drinking-water contamination and water shortage?

What do you think? Water is required for the process and much of it. Leaching into the groundwater of spillage and contamination produced in the process is reality.

What is this pipeline's mental and spiritual impact on America's First Nations peoples?

It is one of disappointment, anger, indignation at being disrespected and a constant need to fight for what was theirs and should now be theirs, the ability to manage their own lands and keep peace with the ancestors. This diminishing of their rights as well as their identity goes on around the globe and is a genocide of sorts—the mass destruction of First Nation peoples' rights and sacred beliefs—it is disrespectful and injurious to them emotionally and spiritually. To be considered as unworthy, unimportant and generally of no value: what a place for a noble people to be in your current—and what you *think* of as advanced—world. More shame on your corporate and governmental groups.

And yet, they're not ashamed, as they should be. Our corporate and government groups will do just about anything to get that "Black Hills Gold" in all forms.

The Trans Mountain pipeline carries crude from the now infamous Alberta Oil Sands all the way west through British Columbia, Canada with a planned—yet highly protested—expansion to bring the black gold to a port at Vancouver, British Columbia to be loaded onto oil tankers and exported to the U.S. and other countries. The humongous increase in oil tankers is said to be three hundred percent more than current oil tanker traffic in the harbor.

The people of British Columbia and the First Nations peoples anguish over the potential annihilation of their pristine coastline due to the existing (and inevitable future) oil spills from tankers and the resulting impact on the crystal clear water, resident and transient Orca whales, the wild salmon they feed on, and other ocean life.

It seems that oil money always wins.

Pax, we feel like our hands are tied. The people do speak out. Yet, no one and nothing can stop the "black gold barons" and the power of profiteers involved and the ego of those in politics who will benefit through campaign contributions and voter retention by "supporting economic growth". We can sometimes feel hopeless because people in large numbers do stand up and speak out and it gets them nowhere as they are up against macro-economic control. Do you have any advice?

Ah well, it is the way of it now and into your future. That your people allow government and industry to continue fouling your air and water through the locating and drilling for and transport of crude oil, bitumen and the like is preposterous in your day and age with advanced fuels and heating/cooling methods in place.

What does it take for indignation to replace apathy? It has not yet been identified.

We should like to say the inability to breathe easily in your polluted air is generally considered to be a beginning. In your *very* soon time this becomes reality and your people will look around themselves asking, what happened and who did this to us? Reality is harsh and there will be complications in health and wellness for the masses in countries around the world, as there are now, but until those in North America, it seems, are strongly impacted there will not be generalized changing of hearts and minds to adopt means of halting and reversing your climate crisis.

That it takes crisis to get attention is a sadness.

Here's another sadness: not long ago, the Keystone 1 Pipeline in North Dakota leaked nearly four hundred thousand gallons of oil into the ground.

I'm mad, Pax. I understand that the Spirit World can't do the heavy lifting for us; you advise us and give us wisdom when we ask, but we are the boots on the ground and the only ones that can make the difference. And yet, the people *are* trying. The irony here is that the people who protest environmental atrocities are often the same consumers that drive all industry and all demand for such fuels. What I'm saying is that we're *all* consumers of products and therefore we're all part of the problem. So, here we are.

Pax, the big oil players and the petrodollar system will continue just as long as we need oil. What we really need— and I believe it's the only thing that will stop the madness—is

a replacement for crude oil. Do you see the vicious cycle that we're in?

We see and feel the crisis you are in.

We do not see so many faces standing up to make change for Mother Earth, however, as we have previously noted, many of those faces are attached to heads planted firmly in sand.

The seats of power grapple with these as becoming available and spoken of as superior, but the money still goes to and through and sometimes from the fossil fuel providers and those who preach this as superior.

I find it interesting that we refer to Earth as Mother Earth—in the feminine. What is the significance of this and what is the female role as it pertains to healing Mother Earth?

It has always been the female role to be nurturing. Now it remains the female role also of protection and repair of the broken, whether it be spirit or wellness, and it is hers to continue this on a large scale by taking the lead in growing awareness of the need. This need is to reject the present ways of industry involving polluting and creating of items for daily use that cannot be re-used therefore enter your garbage places forever, and teaching that better ways exist if the need for profit can be removed from the equation and those producers see the larger picture of Earth protection surpassing need for profit.

In your time and place you have great technology and the ability to create the means to travel through space, but you cannot extinguish the pollution, fear and hatred, crime and violence in your world today. For shame.

When is it time to go forward in peace and prosperity across the lands? Under the direction of the masculine-will this has not become a reality—the Middle East grows in violence. The time is now for abundance here, but the structure of ruling parties of government must change first—then it will be. As the sun rises in these places, so does the awareness. Women are to develop their personal power and proceed on the path to enlightenment. The future holds for them the wealth of power and enlightenment, which will transfer to their children and their children. The time is now for this.

All around the world the message is the same. The results will be the same in time. You will know the weight of the problem in time and see the future in the feminine ways. We see the future role of women mimicking the past: matriarchal society and respect for tribal elders, beginning with the wise woman who supports her people with her healing and teachings.

The reality is that most of the world leaders at this time are men. What is missing in the balance of this equation?

Today we speak of the inability of a great many men to communicate his wishes in the great wide world. Why are you still warring in the time when you could be speaking your minds and wishes for peace and prosperity in the world?

Men are capable of so much more. Go inward and ask for strength and guidance to find the way. The way is clear if you seek it. Go forward and ask for guidance. It will be there.

Our concern now for men and women against each other is the strength of one and the weakness of the other. Which is which, you ask? They both have strengths and weaknesses, of course, and where one complements the other, strength is realized. Where one duplicates the other, weakness is realized.

We ask, for now, that men and women who are joining forces to overcome the toxicity in your world, unite in the understanding that teamwork is necessary.

International politics are as troublesome now as ever. In the time of the pharaohs were spats and wars and greed and taking of lives. Now it is on such a scale as to be almost irreversible. Almost, we say, as it will indeed be reversed.

Thank God. So, there is hope for change?

Change comes through the forces of nature and will only be slowed, reversed, calmed, and set into motion for the repair of the planet when the leadership from elsewhere is put in place. The peaceful ones show the way—take the hand of wisdom and follow.

When countries are at war, the environment takes a backseat. How do people help the environment when they're still at a loss for peace, freedom, and safety from physical harm?

We are here to say that the impact of wars on the planet now serves to detract from peoples' intention to clean up the environment. It is hard to think this way when bombs are falling and killing is rampant over much of the world. Peace is needed in all areas. A paradigm shift is necessary to accomplish this. At this time, we ask for those not involved in the process of war to involve themselves in the process of peace and greening of the planet.

Young leaders now abound in the area of Earth protection and restoration. Their voices are being heard and their ideas are being taken to heart and preached by the younger generation. Watch these young leaders and hear their voices—they are sent from the heavens to show the way and it is to be heard and respected and understood and followed. No amount of ignoring the feelings of the growing masses of youthful change-makers will do—they are with you now and a role reversal is in place:

the young teach the old and show that *they have the wisdom of the elders.* That they are passionate about change is to the benefit of all walking Mother Earth today and those who await their own arrival.

Only through incredible effort from the majority of the population will this movement create the groundswell necessary to impact the planet. Yours is the mentality needed by the many: peaceful and unwilling to be anything but positive. This is the way for your planet. The peaceful warrior is an interesting phenomenon and bears exploration. We ask for you to do this.

The peaceful warrior—I like that. There was a book first published in 1980 titled *Way of the Peaceful Warrior* by Dan Millman. The book is an autobiographical novel wherein the author meets a wise old man names Socrates at a gas station. The author realizes much later that his enlightened guide was a spirit messenger. (A true story, according to the author.)

I see that the Spirit World still likes the term "peaceful warrior" and I do understand your much broader meaning and message here: a model for world peace and harmony.

Indeed, it is so.

What other ways should we be alerted to at this time?

The demise of many species now and in the soon time on Planet Earth forms a part of the Earth's plight topic. When species disappear from the food chain, all heck breaks loose, in your vernacular. The balance is disturbed, disrupted even, and there is no recovery.

It is clear that Mother Earth needs a full complement of animals, as prescribed to be there, and this lesson in print, Penelope, needs that focus. It is all one, really, as one depends on the other. There is a lesson to be learned from the introduction of fourteen wolves back into Yellowstone National Park. Be aware of the before and after of nature in that area as a result of reintroducing a missing species, a missing link in the food-chain and how it impacted and changed everything from plant species, other animal species, and the flow and direction of the river. This is powerful.

I had never heard of this occurrence in America's Yellowstone National Park, so I looked it up:

Beginning in the late 1800s, the wolf was hunted and killed off because they were eating cattle and farmers were suffering financial losses. Without wolves, the elk population grew out of balance. Elk overgrazed the land and decimated plant life including aspen and willow trees, all of which were critical to a range of animals including rabbits, bears, bees, birds, and beavers. When there were no more beaver to create natural dams, fish habitats were upset, and rivers actually flowed in the wrong direction. All of this happened because the environment was missing its apex predator. In 1995, a small number of wolves were reintroduced by scientists and just six years later, the entire ecosystem was returned to whole: plant life regenerated, bears and beaver returned, and birds flourished.

What a fascinating environmental decline and then repair, all from the removal and then reintroduction of the apex predator to the area.

Pax, may you please point out another geographic area in similar decline to which we have not yet attended or fixed; a place where we can impact a wonderful repair if we reintroduce a species or rectify a similar scenario?

As your planet continues to warm there are plains areas and there are jungle areas in contrast that are in trouble. In Europe central are areas where industry has stripped the soil, and animal populations are long gone. As the water becomes damaged beyond repair, all that had lived in it disappear and that which was fed by it, died. There is stripping of soil and pollution that will remain long after the industry kills the environment.

Areas such as this exist around the globe—man-made disasters they are, and it is for your civilization to decide what to do about it. Most become forgotten places and there is no incentive to repair.

Similar to Yellowstone Park, other areas in North America have been stripped of natural resources due to over-harvesting of what was native to the area.

It is for all of your people to look around themselves and identify these areas, then to determine a plan for repair.

To speak up and speak out on these topics is how the Yellowstone repair began and how those around the globe can be equally approached. One person at a time making a difference—this is the basis for a groundswell of change.

As we learn the ways to heal our planet, what is the best way for us to endeavor planetary re-greening?

Stop the killing of Earth's resources; then begin the healing. To do this in the reverse order is also correct. Without healing by educating the masses about the reality of losing your planet in the soon time, there will be no stopping the killing of air, water, soil, animals, and also people who cannot survive breathing the thick air and drinking the dirty water. Eating produce and meats raised in a dirty environment does not bode well for survival. It is a circle of despair on your planet at this time—see and acknowledge and act to repair, we ask.

A number of our scientists have said that planting billions of trees is the best climate change solution. Is it?

It is, yes. Trees filter and clean the air with their canopies, roots hold and nourish soil in place, leaves drop and fertilize, and bark sheds and feeds soil, as well. To provide habitat for birds and ground-dwellers is a purpose of trees and forests, to provide shelter and food, harmony in nature; it is indeed the need.

As forests are removed for commerce and animal habitat is lost, as deliberate scouring of Earth trees and foliage is repeated, again for commercial purposes (greed), there comes a time of non-recovery and non-reversal of damage accumulated. You are there in the very soon time—be aware and be warned. It is shortsighted at best.

I think that we sometimes wait for someone, some governing body, to tell us what to do. Many think that if the environment was in imminent danger, governments would step in and make systematic and systemic changes. And yet, we eat foods that are actual poisons to our bodies, all the while trusting that if they were bad, they would not be allowed to be sold. As far as the solutions to our problems, many of us leave it to the scientists and assume that someone will come up with the answers.

Look to your conscience, we say. How can you see what is, know *why* it is, yet contribute nothing to stopping the damage done every second of every minute on your planet?

We suggest *conscience* is the place to begin. To ask what footprint you are leaving on the planet, to ask what legacy for your children, this is the question.

Chapter Five
Food?

*H*ere's something that we do to our food every day: microwave. Do microwaves contaminate our food? And, do microwaves contaminate the environment? After all, there's one in nearly every home in "first-world" countries.

Well, it is the case that these *incinerators of food* are risk factors in your world today. Your environment suffers, as do your people, as these gadgets in use so commonly are not safe in the long term. It is a wonder they have not been recalled completely.

There is off-gassing and there is off-threading of waves of energy produced here and where do they go when the door opens?

You must also consider the ramifications of cooking plastics into your food in this process as plastic containers are common—it is a contamination overload and yet accepted as a way of life.

Some are sensitive to this more so than others, but no person should think safety comes with this process. It is a method in use now for many of your years and as the human body becomes weakened more and more by toxins in your environment, this is one integral to daily life and close to home—in the home—and could be removed.

It is a product of your society of immediacy and instant gratification and does no good thing for you, health-wise.

I just unplugged and removed our microwave.

You mentioned plastic. We use plastic for everything. We buy our food from groceries stores and everything comes packaged in plastic. Studies show that more than eighty percent of teenagers have traces of a synthetic chemical called Bisphenol A (BPA) in their bodies. Since the 1950s, BPA was added to plastic to create a tamper-resistant material and was used for many things including food packaging and medical devices. I'm trying to gauge *how* **harmful plastic is (with or without BPA) when in contact with food. Are plastics** *so* **harmful—life-threatening disease makers—that we should immediately purge all plastic food-storage containers and never again buy food packaged in plastic?**

Yes, and until manufacturing processes change, it is not a possibility to find all things necessary for life not packaged in plastic.

And, how about slightly different phrasing: if you were me, would you purge all plastic in contact with food, pronto?

Yes, for reasons stated above.

A set of glass food storage containers is going on my online shopping list.

To replace *all* plastic with glass is not workable. To replace plastic with sustainable and naturally occurring product is. We shall speak of this again.

I know we're talking about food, yet given your answer here, I suppose we should rethink plastic that is in direct contact with our bodies, too, such as clothing made from polyester (plastic).

For the highest of evolved beings—albeit, those that still require food to fuel physical bodies—what does food consist of, specifically, and how is food production best accomplished to feed large populations? Pax, you previously told me that a plant-based diet is what we must pursue in order to save our planet. Can you elaborate on this? Is it "wrong" to participate in the wholesale slaughter of animals and the eating of animals? Please tell us the truth because people are so very protective and indignant about what they eat, their very identities are tied to what they consume, and they will cite the Bible and their culture to absolve the suffering imposed on animals.

Looking to the past to find the future will show that plant-based diets evolved a specific form of human and this changed with an introduction of meat on Planet Earth. Those vanguards of advanced civilizations have come and gone and did leave their traces in the oral history of local inhabitants. They showed advanced (for the time and place) building methods, irrigation and growing methods, and study of stars to name a few. Mention of them can be found throughout early civilizations' drawings.

In advanced civilizations, there is no animal slaughter for the purpose of adding to diet. The cultivation of super plants, whether fruit or vegetable, in clean and nutrient-rich soil preserved by clean and nutrient-rich air and fed by clean and nutrient-rich water, is key. You have far to go but this is the goal. This is the practice in alternate universes on other planets. Trust in this and go accordingly.

Why do people eat meat when a plant-based diet was/is the way of our otherworldly ancestors?

Nomadic civilizations leaned on game hunting for survival as availability of plant sourced foods was not consistent. Survival depended on availability—another human need to adapt.

For full disclosure to you and anyone who reads this, I am vegan; I eat only plants. I say this up front because some might think that I have an agenda, and well, I do indeed deeply wish for mankind to stop eating and harming animals.

For many, meat eating is not just about nutrition, but also about taste and culinary arts, and it is integral to many cultures and traditions. How should we go forward in our food choices while keeping in mind the motivating factors of the environment, humane treatment, cultural traditions, and general wants and needs?

A contributing factor in saving your planetary environment is moderation and balance is found, both in use of soil and grasses, air and water, and what moves up and into the air from both sources. There is no one way—there has never been only one way for any length of time. Balance must be found and maintained. It is not suggesting a vegan diet or lifestyle, but more emphasis on plant protein and less on meat protein. This also serves to bring tolerance to mankind, not all of whom agree on any one way, as you well know. When it is shown that one works in balance with the other, and mutual respect exists for each philosophy, there can begin to be harmony.

What do you mean by "what moves up and into the air from both sources"? I feel like these words are key.

In your current food production, there is off-gassing and smoke, steam, and other side effects of processing, whether vegetable, animal, or mineral. We speak of the balance being found and maintained in cultivation and processing of these resources. Balance in all things is to be a desired goal.

What's just one example of what you see as out of balance in our food production?

For starters, driftnet fisheries are an abomination, a travesty of all that is good and natural and sensible. Lower the net and pull up every living thing within the area? When your lawmakers have the intestinal fortitude necessary to change this policy is when you may begin moving forward in your management. Until then, those who follow this way will have their way, to the decimation of all in their path. Get it together here people and see the light before it is too late!

For now, we say the end is near to the abundance you have come to depend upon. Right the wrongs and begin the replanting, reseeding, and restructuring of your harvesting procedures.

Could a plant-based diet for the world's population be the way to turn around our environmental crisis?

It would not address industry, pollution, corporate greed, or myriads of contributors to the environmental crisis. To have Earth's population become plant-eaters only is a simplistic measure which would take generations to accomplish: it is an ideal result but must be only a fraction of the overall change.

We have spoken of, and will in more depth, the return to ways of your past, including your aboriginal ancestors as being a contributing factor to the return of wellness to your Mother Earth.

Yes, you have.

When factory-farmed animals watch others before them suffer painful deaths in slaughterhouses, is there such a thing as the energy of fear and pain becoming trapped within the animal's flesh? If so, do we ingest these heavy energies when we eat the meat?

It is commonly known that the taste is affected by fear in the process. It is why some processors' methods are advertised as "humane" as the end result is more pleasing to the average person's psyche and taste is altered and more palatable in comparison.

Speaking of the taste of meat, Pax, what do you think of "cell meats"? These are cell-based meats that are being sold now and are "real meat" products grown directly from animal cells without the need to actually raise real animals. The products are grown in lab-factories and taste exactly like animal flesh because they are. While biologically it is "meat", it was never a body part of a living and breathing animal with a soul. This cell meat provides the same amount of protein as the flesh of the animal, and it tastes the same (for many people it is the taste of meat that they like, although in time, we might lose this need to taste flesh). In addition to zero greenhouse gas emission, no vast land use, and no cruelty or killing of animals, these products are said to be clean in that they are not laced with antibiotics, steroids, and environmental pollutants. It would seem that the downside is that the idea grosses out a lot of people. (I say that eating the animal itself should freak people out, but to each his own.)

What do you say about this cell meat, Pax? Is this a good idea? Is there a downside to it? Is it helpful for our environmental goals? Will this "lab meat" harm our health in any way?

This is a bizarre thought and a failing replacement for traditional meat as it is sourced. There will be scientific intervention to the extent it can be qualified as GMO, and this is to nobody's benefit. It is not a good idea and will take long to master and not have the desired outcome for those presently considering it.

Bad for health is speculative at this point but suffice it to say there is a limited market for this and the outcome is not successful. Those who wish to market this idea as the next best thing will have to be transparent in the overall research and development aspect, the production facilities, and people involved may not have training and insight, skills, and determination to make this organic and certified to the extent those who would use it would wish. Not the best it is shown in time.

Got it. I wonder: why the insistence for eating flesh when plant proteins are cleaner and healthier, and very tasty products are now commonplace?

I know you've already said that we should learn from animal wisdom, however most people believe that we are wiser and more intelligent than animals and that we are to have dominion over them.

Let's cut right to it: are we supposed to have dominion over animals and use them for our needs, or are we supposed to be guardians and stewards to animals and take care of them? And, I don't mean just for our pets, but wild animals and those that we call farmed animals like cows, pigs, and chickens.

How should we be relating to animals?

With respect, as we have previously mentioned. To believe that all things have a soul and treat them accordingly is the way. Whatever the purpose of that animal: companionship, food, or working and service—respect and kindness shown, as it would be to a fellow human, is the acceptable way.

To know that all animals have a soul brings to mind an interesting question: are there "famous animals" throughout history who were heroes among their kind or in the Animal Kingdom? If so, were they revered in some way similar to the way in which we hold esteem for extraordinarily talented and impactful individuals like German-born theoretical physicist Albert Einstein, Hunkpapa Lakota leader Sitting Bull, American civil rights icon Rosa Parks, or Indian independence advocate Mahatma Gandhi?

In a civilization where *animals had no masters*, perhaps. The closest we say are herd leaders who protect their families and organize them for travel so the old and infirm travel ahead with the young while strong and vibrant follow behind to take care of predators. Elephant families mourn their dead and protect their aged members from harm. Many species of mammals and birds form social and familial bonds and protect one another, so within those groups will be examples of extraordinary leadership.

The animal kingdom is filled with examples of heroics required to just get through a day, and the strength and leadership shown by the alpha members is quite extraordinary. They would say, not so, it is a requirement for continued survival.

Carole once told me about a particular horse named Blackie whom she talked to in her channeling work for animals in emotional pain. Blackie was a racehorse and she wasn't performing at her best—she was "off"—and so Carole was called in to communicate with her. Blackie told Carole that she knew the fate of other horses that didn't win;

they were sent away and had to leave their home. She was afraid and therefore put up a block.

Blackie believed that if she didn't get away from the starting gate in front of the other horses, she could not pass them to win or place. This distressed her and she felt defeated and unable to find courage to push through. Carole spoke to Blackie about her great size, excellent physical condition, and that she had all the attributes necessary to prevail.

They talked of the horses that were claimed after races and left the barn for new racing barns, and that it wasn't what Blackie should focus on as it could be avoided for her.

Finally, Carole asked Blackie if she didn't think she was good enough or capable enough to move beyond her fears and get past or through the field of horses that may have left the starting gate ahead of her. Blackie replied, almost indignantly, saying, "I am a big, strong girl, you know—of course I can!"

Within the week, Carole received a telephone call advising her that Blackie had won her next race.

Pax, may you please validate these feelings that animals have, including feelings of inadequacy, self-consciousness, and low self-esteem?

Anyone on your Earth who works with animals in kindness will know this—it is reality.

All right, so we now know that the acceptable way of living is to treat all animals "with respect and kindness shown as it would be to a fellow human." The fact is that we enslave animals in factory farms, yet it's not acceptable to enslave fellow humans. We eat animals, whether raised for food or hunted for food in the wild, yet it's not acceptable to eat fellow humans. We drown mice in laboratories to test the mental process of depression and the emotional process of giving up, yet it's not acceptable to kill or hurt fellow humans in laboratory tests. We use animals for their fur and skins, yet it's not acceptable to use human skins for furniture and clothing. I'm sure you can see where I'm going with this. This question is a little facetious, but I'm going for it anyway for both effect and more clarity: should we eat people (who are in abundance) as long as we humanly raise them and thank them for their sacrifice? (Pax, I hope you have a thing called irony, as my question is offhand yet also a sincere effort to clearly know the difference, if any, in superiority, pecking order, "use" for, or reverence between mankind and animalkind.)

There have been times, peoples, and cultures on your globe where cannibalism was the way. Was there superiority of any kind in this civilization—yes, but they still consumed their fellow man. There was a time in a race considering themselves superior to all where human skin was used for lampshades and other items, as there were thousands of captive and killed people of a particular religion whose lives were meaningless to this country of people who snuffed out their existence by the thousands.

Where there is conscience there is not this behavior. There is kindness and respect in its place. The eating of animals became a necessity in past civilizations of hunter-gatherers before remaining in one place and cultivating food became their way. Times change but not all norms of civilization change with the times. As the aboriginal people did, taking the life of an animal in the need for sustenance was done with respect and thanks to that animal for providing their life to save the lives of others. Without this, the practice is considered barbaric by many, and some fall away now from this practice in favor of plant-based diets. There will remain both, but the balance is shifting.

As there is not a way to show respect and kindness to our fellow humans by eating them or using their skins for our furniture, I'm going to conclude that the same goes for animals.

By the way, cows raised for food are responsible for twelve percent of manmade greenhouse-gas emissions: more than the entire aviation industry.

Well, there is a beginning now and a slow catching up to this reality. You will identify this need as being based on a combination of reasons. Saving energy in not producing animal-based diets, saving animal suffering, and returning to an agrarian society to save Earth's air, soil, and water from continued contamination of industrialization. You would say, "It's a no-brainer." This is returning to historical ways and bringing Earth back to clean and pure.

Without the added pollutants from processing of animal protein, the environment cleans exponentially. Therefore, to focus in this area makes strides forward in environmental impact. The cultivation of clean plants can be done anywhere on Earth, whereby the raising of food animals cannot. Eliminating the carbon footprint of the latter is a step forward in cleaning and greening.

Chapter Six
Super Plants

I 'd like to learn about highly nutritional vegetables, fruits, and plants used for medicine. However, first, we couldn't have a proper conversation about "Super Plants" without discussing the great redwoods of the California coast, perhaps the oldest organisms on Earth.

The redwoods—they're not *just* trees, are they?

Trees they are, yes, and protectors of the land also.

The energy they share and the air they clean, the canopy they provide, and the seasonal shedding and re-seeding offered— these are sacred trees and are to be eternally protected as the old-souls they are.

To feel the vibration of these redwoods, to know the cycles of the Earth while they have been standing, to understand the events they have witnessed and/or felt, all this makes these much more than how many think of trees.

Old-growth forests around the world have been and are being decimated; this is sacrilegious, and you are not to touch these stands of ancient ones. The resources once closely protected and guarded have become pawns for big business and commerce and have been traded for things of no long-term use.

This religious fervor about old-growth trees among some on your planet is well placed and needs to be extended to cover forests around the globe. It is they that filter air of pollutants and so much more.

Reality check people: without these forests, your consideration of cleaning your air will not succeed. In addition, you will have lost the wise-ones. We leave you to consider this description.

Thank you, that is quite a description and a direct directive.

I'd like to know about super plants and how we find them or develop them. Are super plants a technological advancement; plants to be created and grown through concentrated effort and science? Are super plants the way that all plants were before we started soaking crops in fertilizer and pesticide? You know, we now modify genetics to have apples that don't brown for weeks, and strawberries that are enormously super-sized.

The genetically modified growing *must* be reconsidered as a good idea. We say your people are aware of the seeding of illness in your children as a result. Your people must be aware of the percentages now of those who will succumb to common illnesses. How does this knowledge affect your people going forward?

I hope it has a great impact and that we wake up to what we're doing.

Pax, what are super plants?

In past times, all ailments were cured through the use of plant medicine. Shamans and medicine men and women in society studied all things growing and knew how to apply and combine for maximum results.

We suggest the term "super foods" is what was before pollution came to growing places and genetically modifying crops became popular for reasons of producing more and faster and larger and taking in more money as a result. Clean foods equal clean bodies and minds and renewed health. Where are you to find clean foods now—foods you can trust to be pure? If the soil and water are clean, is the air that surrounds the growing things? There is much to be done to ensure all things contribute to wellness.

"All ailments were cured through the use of plant medicine." Well, I can't tell you how wonderful this is to hear and yet it immediately brings some questions to mind based on my own experience.

I once had a broken spine in my lumbar vertebrae. In 2015, I had a lumbar spinal fusion with good results, I will add. Could plant medicine have fixed this? Or, before we go further into Super Plants and Plant Medicine, shall we qualify the difference between what are "ailments" versus other mechanical injuries or degenerative fractures, and some other diseases of the body in which plants are perhaps not the cure?

Plant medicine, as used by aboriginal peoples, was powerful and when combined and taken up a step by shamans, could be responsible for higher-level cures. If a bone was broken there was plant medicine to help the repair by reducing inflammation and pain, not directly to repair the break: this would be done mechanically with the added bonus of topical applications of ointments made from plants, and drinks and infusions made from plants.

Everything had a reversal in medicine.

Here's another example, can Crohn's disease be cured through the use of plant medicine? And, can asthma be cured through the use of plant medicine? If so, which plants for each?

These are issues of interest as your current pharmaceuticals are often derivatives of plants, as in these uses. Yes, these irritable bowels and breathing challenges are treated well with plant use—to open the breathing airways by inhaling the plant essence and settling the digestive tract by the chewing of soothing leaves while drinking the tea—these are the simplistic ways. These plants are known to those practicing homeopathic and herbal remedies.

To elaborate on your words, what plant can be used for those with asthma "to open the breathing airways by inhaling the plant essence"?

These are many and varied across your globe and in your forests—eucalyptus and peppermint, sage, and the leaves of nettles and plants dwelling at high altitudes, especially. These have been known, along with others, by your indigenous people throughout their time.

Mother Earth provides you with solutions to all, fixes and cures, building materials, and food and drink. Too much is taken for granted and too little is being appreciated, and we ask for your people to reverse this.

Do you know all the uses of bamboo?

I've been meaning to ask you about the bamboo plant. It grows very fast and some call it "The Miracle Plant". We have a bunch of them growing in our backyard and when I see them, I wonder if we are underutilizing bamboo.

However, in the last couple of decades we've seen many more products being made from bamboo—often a replacement to cotton, silk, or cruel cashmere—such as pillows, sheets, mattresses, and clothing. Bamboo is thermoregulating and naturally antibacterial. It's also used to make furniture and wood floors. I understand from our neighbor that the inside of the bamboo shoot is a tasty food similar to heart of palm. And, bamboo plants convert far more carbon to oxygen than do trees. What should our big vision be for bamboo's potential?

This ancient plant is a food source, clothing source, as well as providing uses in building materials and insulation. It is strong and resilient and grows at a rapid rate. Its use is not global yet, although as a decorative plant only it is widespread. As used to build scaffolding in the orient and Asia, as used to build bridges and structures requiring light weight combined with strength and weather resistance, it is popular and inexpensive. Your engineers might consider its use more in the Western world.

Are there other great uses for bamboo that we've missed thus far?

Use of this product's leaf for medicinal is also shown as therapeutic and has attributes for breathing and ease of lung function.

Okay, so the *leaf* of the bamboo plant can be therapeutically used to aid breathing. How is the leaf to be prepared or utilized: should we drink it like tea, or burn it with fire?

Oh no, to dry the leaf too much is to lose the benefit, so partial dry is best, like incense. This is to be imbued with smoke and the vapors open airways. It can cleanse like sage and even more therapeutic benefits come from this use.

Okay, not to burn but to smolder the partially dried leaves. I understand and it makes me think of a therapeutic sauna: placing hot stones on the semi-dry leaves would create a vapor to be inhaled without burning the leaves as with fire.

I'm very interested in your seeds of wisdom and I don't want to miss something big. Is there another plant or plant derivative of which we, the people of Earth, are not yet aware that has extraordinary healing properties?

Many, many plants around the world have not yet been utilized in modern times for the masses. Known to the locals, the aboriginal peoples through time as told from one generation to another, they continue their use for healing in place of chemicals. Together with the magic of traditional healers they sustain populations throughout centuries.

Is there the plantain leaf that has to be explored? Is there the inside of the peel to scrape and utilize? Is there so much more to be told by the elders? Indeed, there is. Is this plantain peel used for pain reduction and swelling? It is, and so much more to develop.

It would be a modern miracle (or an ancient miracle, perhaps) if we could completely stop using and abusing dangerous opioids and instead figure out how to utilize plantain-power for pain management and inflammation.

To clarify, is it the leaf or the peel of the plantain that holds the medicinal ingredients for pain reduction and swelling?

Inside the peel is magic.

And, how do we use it for pain and inflammation? Do we place the inside of the peel directly on a painful swollen joint, for instance? Do we scrape the inside of the peel and extract oils and make it into a cream? Or, do we dry this inside coating and make it into a tablet or powder?

Well, it may be used internally and externally for best results. The scraping of the inside of the peel will provide some thick product that can be used to coat the outside of the affected area and it can be improved further by wrapping a warm cloth around the area to hold this in place and relax the area—not hot, just warm. This will enable the body to relax and absorb. Repeat this until no longer necessary.

It may also be ingested as is, a spoon or two, to speed the process.

Magic, it is.

Thanks for the prescription. The plantain peel is very special, indeed.

There are uses for all the components, as is the case in many if not most plants. It is to know the uses and study them, and then apply as alternatives to pharmaceuticals.

All plants have magic properties when used to their intended purposes. As a natural ingredient, singly used, many have the capacity to work miracles and when used in combination with other compatible plants, barks, and berries, become stronger in their abilities to effect change.

It is your Homeopathic practitioners and Naturopathic physicians who train in the use of Mother Nature's offerings and they are the ones bringing forward the healing modalities from past teachings and practices. Look to them for solutions and alternatives to pharmaceuticals.

Is there a plant that can help with Alzheimer's disease? This would be a big help to our people.

Diet change and lifestyle change together prove to reduce the likelihood of this—it is prevention that is important. Now there is a solution to slowing advancement and this is diet considered, and we say the look toward prevention is key. There is much investigation presently underway to determine a path forward.

Is there a plant that can help with kidney disease? And, what plants can help with heart disease and stroke prevention?

The above queries can be reduced to lifestyle change and to look to prevention first is key. Focusing on repair, as many do, is to put the cart before the proverbial horse, yes? And we do not wish to travel in this manner, so we encourage your people to consider how they treat their own bodies as well as that of Mother Earth and her bodies of water, for example. To keep clean and fresh and healthy requires consideration of use—please remember and do so.

We do not wish to be specific about each one of these current dis-eases your people struggle with, but do want to ensure the balance is found between lifestyle and conservation of your Earth wellness. Our focus is on the large picture of Earth being poisoned and, in turn, poisoning her inhabitants. *These diseases you mention are the end result of it.*

Oh, Pax, can I ask you about just one more disease, please? Our scientists (and charitable organizations) have

focused a tremendous amount of time and money researching a cure for cancer. Is cancer cured through prevention alone, changing our eating and living habits, and cleaning up our environmental pollutants? Or, is a medical/pharmaceutical cure for cancer a possibility? (Otherwise, what's the point of all the research?) Can you offer any suggestions for a cure/help for cancer?

While the mutating of cells in the human body occurs for many reasons, this disease, cancer, is a result of numerous current-world environmental struggles underway. While your world grows in darkness of pollution and corruption, your people diminish in what they believe is control over their own lives; the damage is underway in the form of what you call stress. When you combine the negativities with the resistance capability, one will easily overcome the other. Localized or generalized cell mutations in human bodies are not only predictable but also preventable.

It is a study in internal dialog and trust and evaluation of personal boundaries that identifies what can be and what will be. There is no personal boundary established that should be ignored or crossed in the name of business, for example, or for the benefit of another when it harms the individual at risk. Too often the crossing of boundaries is allowed without so much as a warning or explanation of the rationale. Giving away personal power (to influence from outside of the person: family, friendship, business, expectations of the all) is the beginning and the ending. It is a travesty, this behavior, and one which your people do not connect with their personal dis-ease. It is time to wake up and smell the common thread in all this—each person controls their own life and should. When this is managed there is health and wellness and happiness.

Sometimes I get a feeling that you want to add something that I haven't asked. Pax, is there anything else that you wish to talk about here?

It is the case that the neurological disease Parkinson's is relative to your environment, did you know this?

It has come down through centuries and becomes more and more powerful and common amongst your population.

The combination of overgrowth of bacteria in your food chain is responsible proportionately, as is the pre-disposition among your people to it—sensitivity, if you will—to the causative nature of these bacteria.

From where do these bacteria originate?

It now is airborne and has originated centuries ago with the soil and an overgrowth of this transmitted to the surface where it ultimately became airborne. Previously it was drawn up and into crops of vegetables and fruits.

How are these bacteria recognized—visually?

The thing is, it is not, and at your time in the cycle of Earth it has become endemic and continues to flourish.

How can it be eradicated?

Cleaning of soils and treatment with neutralizing materials is the way as it is the root cause—the airborne spores will gradually eliminate as a result.

What is that neutralizing material?

Do you understand the physics of propulsion? If so, the use of this in a muted way to spray soils is a beginning. The product is a composition of CO_2 and ammonia, which becomes, when used together, a magnet for the spores and allows for neutralization. It sounds unusual, yes, and together with the intention to affect this cure, will do the job.

Is there a cure for people who *already* have Parkinson's disease?

There is the similar type of cleansing of the soil to be used in the body. It is an alternative to pharmaceuticals and treats the base of the problem with the combination of CO_2 and a derivative of ammonia. Your science can look at this and determine efficacy, but we suggest that the radical notion of this is to be considered, as there is not a present alternative. It is a flushing, if you will, of the body systems to clear and cleanse. There are alternate ways to dose and internally flush—it is up to your medical pioneers in this method to determine.

We suggest that the way forward now is to consider trials and offer those wishing to be subjects of this, the opportunity.

Ammonia: this almost sounds like it could poison the body?

You may think so and it may read this way, but your people of science will look at it with different eyes and understanding.

There are variables, yes, and for them to begin at this place in their thinking and go forward with derivatives is the way.

Thank you very much for this addition. This is remarkable information, especially for a disease that currently has no known cause or cure.

Many of our doctors of today are not trained to practice medicine in the way that you describe or in the way of the medicine men and women of our First Nations peoples. Once educated through the current teachings of our medical schools, most of our doctors never elevate their thinking beyond the pharmaceutical treatment of illness and illness management. Will the medical field as we know it become extinct?

Your medical practices are splintering into specialties and sub-specialties and sub-sub-specialties. This ensures continuation of investigation and treatment to a deeper level than ever before, and is a good thing. This, coupled with the rise of Naturopathic physicians will bring balance to the way people approach their wellness. Picking and choosing pieces from each will bring solutions.

Further, as time goes on and alternative medicine is recognized and covered by your health-care systems, more opportunity exists for the use of natural products and treatments for wellness.

Now that we have learned of a couple of plant superstars—the ancient protectors of Earth and plant heroes for medicine—let's look at the "Super Plants" to which you referred when you first brought up our need to cultivate Super Plants for food. You've been clear that "Super Plant" does not mean bigger, but rather it means pure and highly nutritional as intended by nature.

You will have no "Super Plants" without clean air and soil and water in which to grow them. We have spoken on this and it is a weakening now in your chain that foods do not have nutrient levels of past times due to these pollutants.

We are speaking.

We wish to say the time is now to move the soils of the world through the filters and this will account for the improved yields. We say the farms of the future will do this and all soils will be screened for toxicity; this will bring a totally new way of producing crops. It is now time to consider this change.

Pax, it seems to me that a filter as we know it would sift small pieces of debris in soil, but what kind of filter would screen for toxicity?

Toxicity comes in many forms, and we speak of chemicals that come from dirty air and water and sprays for pesticides. Your science has ways to neutralize these harmful pollutants, but they are no match for what continues to be injected into the equation. Until your air is cleaned of pollution and your waters not fouled with industrial waste, there is no hope for cleaning the soil on a large scale. Technology is in place and will be presented when earth-cleaning has caught up. How to begin this is to begin the shaming of industrial giants responsible for waste and pollution.

Well, I guess this means that "organic" fruits and vegetables are not truly clean and chemical free, but only that the growing soil had no prohibited substances for at least three years prior to harvest. Let's suggest here that our food producers adopt new labeling for organics, such as: Soil Organic; Soil and Air Organic; Soil, Air, and Water Organic.

Once we truly clean the soil, what can we do about the issue of polluted air as we attempt to grow Super Plants?

Without enclosed and custom growing environments with filtered water and naturally fertilized soils, there will not be the level of purity referred to.

Place a roof over clean soil and begin.

Volume 3
Do Unto Earth
Pax and Enviro-Tech
Gamechangers

"The only thing that scares me more than space aliens is the idea that there aren't any space aliens. We can't be the best that creation has to offer. I pray we're not all there is. If so, we're in big trouble."
Ellen DeGeneres
American comedian, television host, vegan, and animal rights activist

Chapter Seven
Contact

While this next question might seem extraneous, it's indeed one of our long-standing enigmas and so I need to ask you: In 1947, did aliens actually crash at Roswell, New Mexico; perhaps one of our friends from another galaxy? If so, what was their purpose or mission to be here rather than to only buzz by?

Buzzing by is what they did regularly, and for this craft to not make it beyond where it came down was an anomaly. It did land where people today believe it did, and the immediate action of cover-up caused the mystery that remains with you now.

Yes, there was knowledge by the government and military that contact was being made, very quietly, and the secretive nature of that was never divulged. Military engineers were building propulsion systems they felt could take them off-planet at a rate and to a distance previously not considered. They had help from the "visitors" and when this flight termination occurred it proved a disaster to that program.

The recovery of craft and personnel did take place, reverse engineering has been considered as motivation, as well as preventing civilian knowledge of the event. There is less secrecy now about visitors' crafts seen on your radar, but aside from that the mystery remains as intended.

(I'm stunned here as this brings alien existence very close to home in a very tangible way, yet decidedly I am deploying a journalism technique borrowed from cards: poker face. The reality is that our United States government still officially claims that the Roswell craft was a weather balloon.)

As motivation for what?

Motivation for engineers to get on with projects designed to take men to interstellar travel more easily. They had their own ideas and plans, but the ability to examine what came in from outside, unexpectedly, was a perfect opportunity to expedite the process.

Did any of the intergalactic visitors survive the crash? And if so, did the United States government keep them alive for a period of time?

Survival might have been the case for one, but the underlying thought of the time was to learn what made these beings able to travel as they did, therefore a certain amount of experimentation was carried out. Testing, it was, as you would test a body for its ability to function under stress. This did not bode well for the survival and it was not to be. Compassion was in place with some, but the process of testing took on new energy when the military might of the time was put in question and those who thought they could say they were enabled to travel intergalactically had to prove that statement. This escalated exploration of the visitors and their craft, and the end came for the visitor as a result.

I am sad for this visitor who died in our possession. I would like to say how sorry I am, on behalf of our people, that we did not help and care for this being who was alive after the crash and could have survived to return home. May you please tell me the name of this individual? Did the spacecraft's crew have families that mourned for them and miss them still (it wasn't that long ago)? Can I send the families a message, through you maybe, if that's possible? I'd like to tell them: "I love you. I'm sending thoughts of light energy to you."

As you have the ability to do so, you may send your thoughts, these thoughts to those close to the crew members who did not make it home. Names are not shared; names are not required in this process or needed for you to extend your sadness at this piece of history that played out in your country.

Can I also send my thoughts to our ET friends of a desire to collaborate with them, now? Friendly intergalactic visitors and their wisdom are needed now to propel our clean energy and clean travel forward. May I invite them to come visit me and help with the mission to heal Earth?

Certainly, you may invite them to collaborate in a telepathic communication. While there may not be instant response, know that if you "tune-in" to them and they to you, ideas will transmit. This is the way of it going forward. More may develop at a later time but for now, this.

I will send them my mind-made invitation, and I do hope that more develops at a later time. I'd be rather interested to meet some of our friendly interstellar visitors; to learn from them and to show them love.

Where are the bodies now of those who crashed at Roswell?

Burned, cremated as evidence was removed ultimately and records kept were also altered from their original form.

Was their spacecraft also destroyed or does any of this technology remain somewhere today?

Ah yes, pieces of this craft were recovered and transported to where they could be examined in detail. It was the need for reverse engineering that kept the secret. There is evidence of this and remaining pieces in secure and in locked vaults in the place where it was all stored originally. Much was destroyed but some know that pieces still remain.

This place is the United States Air Force facility in Nevada called "Area 51", correct?

Yes, and this place remains a safeguard against public knowledge of current projects to develop means of travel to space, and specifically to land and set up housekeeping on another planet.

What is the reason for secrecy?

We say there is consideration of national supremacy on your Earth. As there is much competition for being the first, it becomes about staking territory, planting the flag first and claiming the planet. It already is about divisiveness and supreme power and not about inclusivity and collaboration. There must be the need to be first to the target? This leaves out the option of doing more and better, sooner, and with less expenditure to any one nation. Unfortunately, this level of collaboration seems left to your children who understand the value. Of all the instincts driving your Earth people, greed appears high on the list.

Yes, we are a society largely motivated by greed, a desire to be better than or above others, and a thirst for control over others. Frankly, it's embarrassing—how ridiculous we must appear to our enlightened ET visitors and onlookers from the Spirit World.

Let's please finish our talk about Area 51 and why the clean-tech knowledge from our interstellar visitors has not been utilized.

There was a sense of fear surrounding this project; fear that more visitors would land, and the knowledge of the time was that the military was no match for what might come. The 1947 landing was a crash—it was felt that if it was followed by a landing of intact craft and crews, there could be no equality in resources or abilities. Fear, again, was responsible for much of the overriding beliefs and actions of government and military officials, as they expected a warring group of extraterrestrials to descend and take over Earth, beginning with the corner inhabited by Area 51. Had these officials thought of a landing and meeting of visitors and hosts as peaceful, and simply interested to learn the fate of their craft and crew, history would show a very different outcome. And, of course, the spinoff is that where there could have been collaboration and learning from the visitors about how their propulsion systems worked and how the construction of their craft could be replicated, there was a missed opportunity. How many decades did this set back the space travel program? Unfortunate, it was, that those in command functioned in fear. This is a lesson for today in your world. To not fear the unknown, but rather respect and take from it what is beneficial while giving what can be shared, is the way.

These visitors who crashed at Roswell: what is their home planet called, and in what galaxy is it located? I can imagine that there are—still—many beings and races of peoples from many planets in many Universes. Is this true?

Yes, this is true, and be aware that names of planets and galaxies that you may know are not a part of this discussion. All things do not bear divulging, as all things are not named, as is your planetary custom. We shall keep this for another time and place.

I just had a thought: Pax, are the friendly visitors who came to help bring us advanced technologies and then crashed at Roswell our relatives—the very same ancestors who so long ago assisted to deliver us to Planet Earth?

Not at all as there are numerous interstellar visitations underway.

The visitors in this experience were of a further galaxy and this makes it even more curious that the craft malfunctioned as it did. It is the case that they were from distance and did not intend to stay.

So, they were of a "further galaxy" to the ones from where we originated when we were starseeded to Earth. Are all interstellar visitors friendly?

Yes, indeed, and their intention equally friendly and their wish to observe and interact also. There was a higher purpose to this mission. We say it was known they were to visit that day and there was a plan to come together for information sharing. Your military knows this and declassified records, still well buried, will show this and more.

Area 51 it is said, is the place where communication with other planets was being attempted and where craft that could make a voyage into space was in development.

That the visitors chose to contribute technology was a consideration, but did they? It would have been a friendly intention, if so. And have others done so previously, or since this experience, we say it is so.

You say that the United States government was attempting communication with other planets, and that this was being done out of Area 51. Were they successful in the communication attempts with extraterrestrials in that they got a reply and the meeting was planned by both parties? Or, were the communication attempts received by the ETs and they basically just showed up in response?

It was known, yes, as there had been two-way communication and that technology pointed to the fact there would be a landing at Area 51.

Earlier you said something that I must go back to. You said: "The visitors in this experience were of a further galaxy and this makes it _even more curious that the craft malfunctioned as it did_." Of course, this is a very good point. These ETs made it all the way from another galaxy only to make an error so close to a safe landing. That makes no sense at all. (It hasn't gone unnoticed by me how very clever you are with giving clues while insisting that I come to the thought and ask the question. I'm understanding your way: the golden path is a choice and we must seek to find and ask for it to be given.)

And this brings me to ask: Did the United States government crash the ETs' spaceship? Did they _deliberately_ shoot down the craft?

Again, the greed and warring nature of your people caused them to react in fear and down the craft in order to steal its secrets regarding technology.

To welcome these visitors with love and acceptance would have brought full disclosure, as was their intention, but instead there was action of the lowest order by your military. *To live and act in fear is the lowest denominator of human interaction* and this was prominently displayed. It will never be completely known what might have come of this had there been an equal exchange of respect and knowledge.

It is a sadness to us that your society doesn't appear to have progressed far in the time since Roswell. At no time is there this type of behavior among other populations or the Universe in general. It is too clear to all that much soul-searching must be done, and change made amongst your civilization before you become a peaceful society to be welcomed elsewhere. You have the ability, but we do not consider you have the time or *will* to make yourselves over into a society in consideration of the bigger picture of maintaining the health of your environment now or where you may wish to relocate. You are where you are for now and until your higher thinking and acting is established.

Oh. My. Goodness. We crashed the spaceship at Roswell. *We crashed the spaceship at Roswell!*

This is a terrible, terrible shame. And, I'm baffled at the timing of the formation of the United States Air Force which was established as a separate branch of the U.S. Armed Forces in September of 1947; the Roswell incident occurred four months earlier in June of the same year.

Additionally, coincidental (or not) it is that the first surface-to-air missile (SAM) went up around 1947 and by 1950, SAM tests and launches were in full swing. I wonder (as historians

might wonder) if the SAM was made after and as a result of the encounter at Roswell or if it *was* the weapon that took down the ET craft. You said that this ET visitation was known to the U.S. military, and so my question is: Was the U.S. military making preparations in advance of the ET visitation, planning in a way for this event?

As it was known this visitation was to take place, so was it known that it would be useful to take down one of the visitor craft for the purpose of taking the secrets to how it functioned. Your Earth people were not nice, at the time, about things such as this. They functioned in fear and this is what informed their decision-making process pertaining to the Roswell visit.

Premeditated, it was, and this is the reason why no further interest in visitation to Earth exists on the part of peaceful inhabitants of other host planets.

Oh my.

Did the home-planet people of the ET visitors know what happened—that this crew was shot down? Was there a way that this information was communicated all the way back to their home peoples? Or, did they just go missing and mysteriously never returned home?

Theirs was not the only ship arriving at that time, therefore the outcome was known to their home people. Communication between them is instant, as thought, therefore your way of considering how they could or would transmit this news differs from their reality. There was knowledge of the event, yes.

This is something that I missed or didn't ask: there was more than one spacecraft involved in the Roswell incident. How many crafts were there that day? Two, three...a dozen?

Eight crafts in all intended to stop but not all did, of course.

Apart from the craft that was shot down, did the other seven crafts just leave Earth that day and return to their home planet? They didn't fire back? Did they try to help their fallen team members, or did they instantly exit when our people became violent?

The small fleet that was present was planning to visit—this became a non-event when the military intervened and the rest is history. Their way is to not interfere in a situation such as this, not retaliate, and at that time their protocol was to depart immediately. Those other visitors left the area.

I'd love to imagine what they look like. I can't ask about the appearance of *all* extraterrestrials—given the wide variety of beings from many interstellar places—however, I would like to ask you about the appearance details of those beings who crashed at Roswell. This is one of those points of curiosity for our peoples and also it will be a revelation when this description matches the records that we will uncover in time about this incident. Therefore, what did the Roswell Alien Crew look like: how tall were they, what was the color of their skin, what was the shape of their head and eyes, and so on?

These details are well recorded by those who witnessed the event and we suggest no change to their descriptions of small body, large head and eyes. It is of no consequence now in your time.

We say that the visitors who came and stayed, *unintentionally*, were not alone. Others who come by are also similarly located while others from afar also keep watch. There will be opportunity to meet again and the full picture will become clear.

When?

At this time your people are not ready, nor will they be for generations, perhaps. There is no willingness on the part of off-planet visitors to make contact with those who would be hostile, fearful, warring, ready to monetize the event, and otherwise untrustworthy. These things your people currently are, and those who would make contact, especially.

Do the aliens have red blood like humans? (Some of our movies portray them as bleeding green. I guess we think of green when we think of aliens.) It's a novel question, yet I'd like to ask anyway.

Too much Hollywood we say. It matters not what color the inside when it is the outside that would not be accepted. Do you not find in your world today that you all bleed red, yet it is the exterior color that determines acceptance? Your people have far to go in realizing that eggs come in many colors but they are identical in the yolk.

Well said.
Did the Roswell ETs wear clothes—perhaps a space suit?

In their function as flight crew, there was need for specific attire, yes, and that was it.

Would they have been able to breathe our air, or would they have required their own breathing equipment for this visit?

Your atmospheric conditions were not a match for their needs so their ability included transport of what they did require should they leave their flight vehicle.

Had the crash not happened, how were they planning to communicate with earthlings? Could they speak English, or would they have used mind-communication, or would they have used a sign language of sorts as a universal communication tool?

Telepathic communication is their way. While they were capable of mimicking your language, it was not their choice to do so, but rather that those they communicated with should rise to the level of telepathy.

I've asked a lot about Roswell because it's America's most famous alien-encounter mystery. Interestingly, in doing an Internet search, I see that the overwhelming majority of UFO craft sightings are reported in the U.S.; more so than in Canada or Denmark or African countries, for example. Is there a reason for this? Are interstellar visitors more interested in the United States than other countries and areas around the world?

We will say that these fly-bys are in the areas mentioned not due to greater interest but as there is greater population density in the U.S. over Canada, thereby resulting in greater frequency of sightings. That is all.

The interest is in civilization on your planet, which is not determined by nationality. As we have previously stated, the visitors buzz by to see how civilization is progressing, *if* it is progressing in the broad sense of the word, and off they go.

People all over the world will read this and so I'd like to be equitable in my questions. If I were an extraterrestrial, I'd be doing quite a bit of buzzing by China and India—places densely populated and busy in their development of technology and communication modes. Yet, I couldn't find stories of ET or UFO sightings in those places. As you have said, the ET fly-bys are happening everywhere, but then, what's the reason for little to no claims of sightings in these countries?

Ah yes, if it was technology that interested them, they would look in these places. However, whatever technology is there is quite primitive to the visitors.

When we say they buzz by to see how civilization is progressing, it is civil-ization in question. There is a use of this word in your language, being civil to one another meaning polite and helpful and non-threatening and reasonable in action. This is a gauge, not development of higher technology—for that they can provide guidance. As long as your peoples are warring and acting in ways designed to benefit self-interest not the greater good, it is a moot point how advanced in technology they are. If your leaders are corrupt, so are your people and if they are not corrupt but do not speak out against higher corruption, where is the division?

When we report the visitors see nothing they want so don't stay, it is into this morass of corporate and political corruption and greed they wish to avoid going. They do continue their watch, ever hopeful.

There was a claim of a UFO and two humanoid aliens spotted in 1965 by a farmer at Valensole, Alpes-de-Haute-Provence, France, and the event was dubbed as "France's

Roswell". There was also a rumored close encounter of a UFO by another farmer in France in 1981 at Trans-en-Provence, Var. May you please speak to these; were they truly alien crafts and beings?

While there was almost proof of the sighting in 1965, it became legendary for not becoming provable. Nevertheless, the local people believed something has been there that didn't belong.

In the later 1981 close encounter, it was just that, and was there something, or was there not? We say there was the belief strongly that the area had been disturbed by something other-worldly, but it was not to become fact.

While each was reported as an alien encounter, it was not so. For the local people to believe it was did not sit well with the military in the region and we say no further reporting was investigated.

UFOs are described as "flying saucers"; why are they disc-shaped?

You will note that they are not all disc-shaped—these differences are reported by those who see them on radar and, from higher in space, perhaps in close range. Aerodynamics will be a contributor to design, as will size requirement for specific use. Uses vary as do shapes and that is just the way of it.

Thank you for all of these details. I believe we've had a thought-provoking talk on historical alien encounters. I'm so very curious about it all and our readers will be, too.

Is there contact today from friendly interstellar visitors with the current United States government and/or other countries?

At this time in your U.S. government evolution, the friendly interstellar visitors you ask about are standing down from visitation for anything other than observation. It is a time on your Planet Earth—*globally*—that the energy of warring and negativity in general is bringing consternation, in a small way, to those who might visit, as they refrain and allow your people time to regroup and heal.

There can be no forward motion of a people when the people do not agree on the direction of that forward motion. It is a pivotal time for your future wellbeing.

Chapter Eight
Oil and Water

I'd like to explore some future technologies and advancements that can help our environment by replacing harmful methods and materials.

Carole recently mentioned to me over coffee that some decades ago you told her that people shouldn't be smoking tobacco, but rather we should be using it for our home insulation. May you please expand on that?

Ah yes, there are many uses for tobacco leaves, one of which is insulation against heat and cold.

What we said then was, "Focusing on tobacco use—it is a chief cause of decline in health for those of your world population and leads to the inhaling and taking in of other substances that harm the body and environment in other ways.

For the children to begin this evil is criminal; it should be removed from their sight, reach, and knowledge. Legislation against the sale and use of tobacco will be. It's hard for you to imagine this now, but it comes in the soon time.

Money derived from production and sale of tobacco is a large segment of the national income and is directed to politics in a big way. This connection is not lost on the people. Also not lost on the people is the need to put a stop to this, but how?

We ask for the industrial leaders to find another use for tobacco and the income will not cease, just originate from a different segment of the market. Has it been considered that tobacco leaves can be used for insulation in buildings? Find this connection and the next wave of invention begins.

Moving forward in time we say the non-smoking environment creates renewed health for all and the new uses of raw products keep happiness with the industry. It is a win-win situation."

You were right: this evolution of thinking and acting did come in the soon time. Much has changed and the non-smoking movement is vast, although too many still do smoke and we have not yet begun to invent new ways to utilize tobacco. However, I have a feeling that tobacco leaves for structural insulation will now be explored.

You said, "There are many uses for tobacco leaves, one of which is insulation against heat and cold." What are some of the other good uses?

Packaging for transportation of goods benefit from the insular properties of tobacco.

Okay, like for food service deliveries, medicine, and so on.

Also, there are rubber-like components to be found within the strands of the leaf and when associated with sporting equipment, uses can be beneficial. In shoes, particularly, there is a benefit and industry may begin to expand into this area.

You have me thinking of ski boots, winter gear, and more. What is another resource that we're using the wrong way?

Hemp is underutilized. It is a natural resource and renews itself at a rapid rate. Those items now made of plastic type materials can be created through the use of hemp.

What is the reason this resource is being overlooked? Is there greed within the industry that allows the use of man-made materials as containers and other larger items that ultimately go into the landfills and oceans? We say there must be, and the time is now to investigate.

Hold the presses. So, everything that we are manufacturing using plastic can be made with hemp? Well, now, this will change things. From this day forward, if we could swap out all plastic (polluting and non-renewable petrochemicals: crude oil) with a hemp alternative (a rapidly renewable natural resource) to create the same needed containers, tools, and medical equipment and such, much of our environmental pollution would *instantly* cease.

I've read that hemp is a carbon neutral material because it captures CO_2 as it grows and does so at a rate four times faster than trees. To hear that hemp can replace plastic is a huge tip.

So then, what *is* the reason that this resource is overlooked? It sounds like the truth runs deep and may be laced with nefarious ties, perhaps even with subsidies or other payouts and corporate codependency. Other than the manufacturing companies who make plastic, who else is

benefiting from the perpetuation of the use of plastic and the continued pumping out of plastic products?

As the saying goes in your society, "Follow the money." It is rather like the pharmaceutical industry, yes? Your natural resources provide food and plants as medicine, but the majority shareholders in pharmaceuticals do not release this information.

Plastics remain the standardized use material for much in your society from containers to furniture to building materials. This has remained the go-to slice of society and now that ideas and attitudes are changing, it is time to know the resource of hemp growth is there. To mobilize the growers, to empower the growers is a beginning. Do they stand up to major manufacturers of plastics? Do they compete on an equal footing; a level playing field as it were? We say not in your today, but as they are empowered by society asking for alternatives, it will come to be.

We have the power, is what you're saying?

Do you know that all change begins with an idea followed by a voice and an intention? Yes, and this is the need now in your world before more time has passed. To blow open this information and share with those who care about distress in oceans currently covered with plastic is the beginning to change.

What this litter and plastic pollution is doing to fish and other water dwellers is just plain criminal, we say, as it need not be. What are you thinking, you manufacturers who know the error of your ways? We say you think of profit only—how do your children and grandchildren remember you if this is your legacy? For shame.

Now is the time to make amends to the Earth and society by offering to change your own manufacturing equipment to accept the raw material of hemp and transition your process. Now, don't you feel better about your contribution in this manner? Mother Earth thanks you.

As we are having this conversation, I did a quick Internet search for alternative materials to replace plastic and there are many suggestions ranging from mushroom root to cornstarch. After some looking, I found that hemp is known to some and being used—although *not* widely—as a plastic alternative. I read about a company that uses cellulose from hemp to make products using a 3D printing technique. Is this the way? (It sounds like a winner to me.)

A process of forms and filling is simple enough using the liquefied cellulose product and is lower tech than 3D printing. The liquefied extraction of a hemp component, cellulose, will be pourable and malleable and an alternative to the artificial components of plastics. Also, it will return to Earth whereas plastic will not.

I'm also learning that there currently are "bio-plastic" products such as cups and other items that are made from vegetable fats, corn starch, woodchips, recycled food waste, and so on, that are labeled "biodegradable", "compostable", and "plant-based". And yet, there is rejection of these among some environmentalists for a couple of reasons: Firstly, it's said that they actually do not break down—not for many years. Secondly, if the bio-plastics accidentally end up in with plastic recyclable materials (due to similar appearance), they can ruin the batch of recyclables because they cannot be processed along with plastics.
How well and fast does hemp break down when it's used as a plastic alternative? And, is hemp different or better than these other plant-based plastics that have been introduced?

As organic wastes are recycled for use as plastics alternatives, and as hemp is included in the configuration of the material make-up, so it can become a new and organic material which will satisfy environmentalists as to its ability to be strong in use but return to earth when discarded. The use of these materials together ensures a fully recyclable product with no fear of contamination of any sort. There are fears of the unknown here, and so long as manufacturers do so with ethical intentions, all is well.

The hemp is but one organic material, as has been mentioned, and its organic nature fits the profile of worthy components and it is the case that other seed and nut byproducts contribute their strengths and fibers to the equation and the end result is strength and clarity and the ability to degrade in recycling or composting even: both are required for variety of consumer uses.

There are popular tourist attractions frequented by organized tour groups, where, as part of their travel packages, the tourists are given water bottles throughout their day of sightseeing. These water bottles are distributed by the millions every day, and many of these countries either don't have recycling policies, or the bottles just end up in the trash, regardless. Every single day, millions upon millions of water bottles go directly into landfills. Imagine if all of the companies that make plastic water bottles changed over within a year's time to using hemp for manufacturing instead. That one change alone would make a tremendous difference in the global pollution crisis. Is it a fairly easy and likely shift to seamlessly move from plastic to hemp?

Wholesale shifts like this are not easy from an economic perspective. It must be shown that costs are workable and that the resource is plentiful, and also that the public rejects the notion of continued plastics use. Like plastic bags being rejected, this is a target to remove plastic bottles. It is the users to target. The bottled water companies who purchase them, the drink manufacturers who purchase them by the millions—these are the targets for selling the idea of a renewable resource that grows at a rapid rate, not a chemically based plastic. Public demand and public rejection are powerful incentives in corporate decision-making.

In addition to plastic's payload of environmental pollution, there are the health impacts of our daily contact with plastic that we spoke of earlier. Plastic is used to make everything from the cups we drink from and the containers we store our food in, to the teething rings, bottles, and bottle nipples that our babies suck on, to the toys we play with from infancy through adulthood, and even those that our pets chew on. There are some brands of individual tea bags that are made from plastic which inevitably shed plastic fibers into our drinks; it's everywhere. Not to mention, polyvinyl chloride (PVC) is widely considered the most toxic of plastics, and yet it's a building material that runs throughout our living space like veins. We seem to know that chemicals in plastics can leach into our foods and drinks, and yet we're still using them and serving them up to our beloved children who are too young to decide if they want that poison in their systems. Oh, crikey, and yes—think of medical plastics like IV bags and what is really being pumped into the veins of our sick!

Beyond plastic in contact with food, may you please speak plainly to the health ramifications of our plastic use?

It is the sadness of your time that duplicity exists to the extent it does. Why do your people put heads in sand and not acknowledge danger where they know it to be? Is it for convenience of the consumer and growth of wealth for the manufacturer?

Why is there no disclosure of truth? Even as your pharmaceutical industry discloses potential side effects of drugs, which, if truly listened to and understood, would shock and scare the average person away from their use, but it does not. It is a time of ostriching, we say, and your humanity has no chance of survival while in this position.

Do you wait to be told what is to be next in your journey to planetary wellness? Do you not act until told how to act? You have past civilizations and cultures that succumbed to this ostriching and leadership took a dark turn, as did the behaviors or lack thereof sometimes, of followers. It was a dark time and a sad time and a seemingly to-be-repeated time. Woe unto those who plant head firmly in sand while the way to survival is being shown.

Plastics use is one area of your time that will be read about in history books and not understood by the enlightened societies to follow.

It is shameful and toxic and the off-gassing from plastics in household use is of a high level, one that shows itself in increasing toxicity and dis-ease amongst your peoples. Do not think that chemical imbalances in the brains of children are unrelated. When did the epidemic of this become noticed—was it coinciding with the wholesale replacement of glass with plastic in your homes? Think on this, people.

We have many issues to tackle and you are gifting us with the wisdom to do it. I'm sure you know of the two gargantuan floating islands of plastic rubbish currently in the north central Pacific Ocean. We're very aware of them; we've even given them names: "The Great Pacific Garbage Patch", which includes the "Eastern Garbage Patch" between Hawaii and California, and the "Western Garbage Patch" between Hawaii and Japan. Oil (plastic) and water don't mix (or shouldn't), so let's look at it.

I've read that while some people are thinking up ways to collect these islands out of the ocean, we don't currently have a good plan (or perhaps the resource or interest) to successfully do so. Do you have a suggestion from the Spirit World?

There is the awareness of plastic collection floating processing platforms currently in use on your oceans. They have been developed in recent times and are making a difference now, however more of these floating platforms are needed to be created and deployed around the globe. They were developed in your western world and available with enough funding to produce and purchase. Their evolution is underway and yet the current iteration is also very efficient and removes tons of plastics as it works.

All right let's see when these floating platforms are fully utilized, and the project is accomplished.

As we discuss water, it's in short supply on this planet and I don't understand why that is the case when I see oceans full of water. Why isn't desalinating saltwater to make potable water the solution?

Desalination methods exist and are in use but not widely on a large scale. We suggest to not think grandly of making fresh water from oceans using your *current method* of desalinization.

Yes, our known methods of desalination are distillation (water evaporation and condensing) and reverse osmosis (pushing water through a semi-permeable membrane, yet against water's natural tendency to equilibrate the minerals as opposed to removing them). Both methods are expensive. The former is expensive to heat and then chill the water, a downside that outweighs the benefits. And the latter requires a ton of electricity to push water through a filter. Although, in Kenya there is a pilot project that uses solar energy to power the desalination process.

What are we not considering as a solution to a lack of clean and drinkable water?

More focus is to be placed on preserving and increasing the fresh water that exists on the planet. How to accomplish this? It is a holistic approach, don't you know? You must preserve your forests and reforest where needed. The progression is reintroduction of wildlife to fill out the ecological system; birds and bees and wolves and beavers; herds of deer and grazing animals; fish returning through clean streams and rivers. Putting the land back into balance is key.

All imbalance causing climate change needs addressing; this is a beginning. None of it is effective in creating balance if air, soil, and water pollution continues at current rates. People of Earth, you have a choice to support future lives, or not.

It's better to fix what we have and what has, throughout time, sustained us and worked perfectly. You spoke before of systemic repair of our Earth ecosystems using the example of Yellowstone National Park and the total system imbalance when the wolves were killed off. It is enlightening to learn that ecosystem repair and balance is also an answer to the replenishment of our freshwater sources.

Out of curiosity, how do otherworldly advanced civilizations get their water?

Vapor catching and exchange is a common method. Life and needs are different as are requirements as you know them.

Maybe this can be applied to help some of us now?

What needs are on other planets are not Earth's needs, so focus where what is needed *already* exists.

Let's look at a place like California where the water supply shortage is considered critical; where the need for water cannot wait for a decade of ecosystem repair. How can they get more potable water in such places, faster than ecosystem repair will provide?

Other methods are in use now in your world and methods of cleaning saltwater to become clear and fresh water are well known (by some). It is for your people to advance the use of this technology to clean water in large quantities. You have water, California has ocean, and there is no reason to bypass this when technology exists.

Can you speak to the nature of this advancement in the technology of desalination?

The new way is a space-age technology in use currently to create clean water. Do some hold this close to themselves? Yes. Do some wish to share this with the developing world? Yes. Will it come to be that the technology is shared for humanitarian reasons?

We wish to encourage those with the power to release their methods for the survival of people, animals, and plants. Crops for feeding Earth are decimated in drought. It can be avoided.

Oh, Pax, this is important. I referenced California because I live in the United States, however the water shortage issue is much more dire in other places in the world such the major world cities of Cape Town and Mexico City, to name a couple.

This issue will become life-or-death for many. May you please further identify how saltwater can be made fresh? Do you have any out-of-the-box wisdom to share?

You have not considered the desalination *of old*.

A "neutralizer" exists that will clean ocean and all water of bacteria, dirt, chemicals, and render it suitable for sustaining life. It is found in nature and available to your people. It is an extract of tree soil, useful now and going forward *if it is harvested with respect for the land.* Think on this.

What kind of tree's soil; does it come from a particular tree? Does the tree give something off into the soil that is the magic ingredient?

Your forest floor provides nutrients dense in healing properties, especially in your old growth forests—another reason for preserving these sacred areas. Your First Nations people understand the breadth of healing properties found in nature and in these old groves of history-holding redwoods. The redwoods have watched your civilizations prosper and fail and return to try again, all the while cleaning the air and holding place for animals and birds in safety. What lies beneath and around them holds healing properties and, again we say, if harvested with respect for the land. This entails respect for standing trees, their roots and canopies, and careful extraction of appropriate for use amounts of soil.

Indigenous peoples and foresters are to be consulted.

Yes, you called them *"the wise-ones"*! The redwoods are only found in central California up through southern Oregon. Is this magical tree soil to be shared with other countries? While they have lived for thousands of years,

the redwoods live on land that today is designated national parkland, therefore "owned" by the U.S. government. I'm afraid that our people will not be able to resist stripping this resource to profit from it. Is there a way to reproduce the saltwater-purifying ingredient within the soil of redwood trees and therefore leave the redwoods be?

We say that as with many other developments, reverse engineering can accomplish this. The magic is in the soil and the accompanying and resulting magic is in the application.

Your engineers and scientists can extract for testing and consider the ingredient to duplicate. To share with the world, as and where needed, would be a goal.

Pax, do you know that this can change our world and save lives? Of course, you do. More than a billion people around the world lack access to clean freshwater (truthfully, California's water issue pales in comparison to the issue in countries like Yemen, Kuwait, Libya, Jordan, plus the Western Sahara and more); one third of the world's population experiences water scarcity at least one month per year, and for many it is every day of the year. Thank you. Thank you!

I feel like we need additional protective legislation in place beyond the existing Redwood Act (1978) before a single redwood is approached for this purpose. Secondly, it sounds like we need to form a task force of indigenous peoples, foresters, engineers, environmentalists, and water specialists.

We are here to say the future comes in stages for your planet, both positive and negative, and this is the repeating of history. There is to be utmost concern now for your climate and ecology as it has been under attack for so long the recovery is perhaps not to be complete. It is never too late to begin the healing and we direct and encourage your Earth people to get on it, now.

As the air needs cleaning, begin with reduction of pollutants from chimneys and stacks heaving filth upward—for shame you should know this already.

The natural inclination of nature is to repair and re-grow when given opportunity, so stepping back from the harm-doing and allowing Mother Nature to take some deep breaths is the way. As a field lying fallow until the next planting allows the soil to rejuvenate, we ask you to expand this to all of the planet's soils and waters and air—just think on it and bring it down to smaller increments and begin.

To not be deterred by the perceived enormity of the task is the key. When we say waters, begin with one stream, one small rivulet and clean and protect.

Chapter Nine
Future Devices

*L*et's get a sneak peek at our tech devices of the future. I suppose we should begin with where we are now.

Along with all of our wireless devices today must also come a fair amount of electromagnetic field (EMF) radiation. In particular, we think of EMF from our cell phones and what this might be doing to our brains and organs as cell phones sit in our pockets and are held to our heads for sometimes hours every day. We suspect that cell phones are "frying" our brains, although we still use them. How harmful are cell phones to our brains?

The continual pressing of this current to the head is a fascinating trait of your people—it is not a wonder then that as user generations age there will be seen an influx of symptoms relating to early diminishment of mind-power as well as physical power. There is the relationship there that has resulted in debilitating the person in ways not previously seen. Neurological connections can be traced and without doubt be pointed to cellular phone use as causative.

Some experts say that cellular networks such as 5G wireless communication emit powerful radiofrequency radiation
and are sickening people, causing cancer and microwave-
type burns, damaging DNA, and causing premature aging,
etc. May you please speak to this technology and the "pressing of this current to the head," as you put it?

In the now is mass communication via cellular devices, satellites, and means that travel your words through and over wires
and cords and wireless networks. This is a global mess, don't you
know? Imagine your world without this electromagnetic mess
cluttering the airways. And this is the way of the future.

There is to be clarity and not chaos, there is to be pure and
intentional communication and not the messing with interruption of signals and pirating of messages and intentional barriers
being set to willing and clear purposeful communication. At this
time there are barriers to purity of intention as well as efforts to
communicate those intentions globally. There are so many fences
to climb and patterns which may be disrupted—it is a travesty
now of pirating versus purity. Your world communication is a
mess.

Recently, a friend tipped me off to a mineraloid stone
mined from Russia called shungite. It is claimed to provide
protection from EMF radiation, and shungite patches for
cell phones are now available. Yet, I've also read that shungite might have some negative side effects. Is shungite a useful material for EMF protection and what else can you tell
us about EMF exposure as it affects our health?

Well now, this returning to the past to fix the future continues, yes? As this mineral is useful here you may also consider the

damage done to mind and body from continual cellular telephone use. It is not just frying the brain that is problematic.

Oh, no? Do tell, please.

Combine that with the lack of awareness of the outside world in ways common to past times, consider the inability of children to converse and communicate with spoken words—this in itself is a travesty—then it is learned they are being poisoned by their devices. How uninformed can some people be through their own neglect of investigation. The shungite mineral itself is useful, not harmful, but contributes to the belief that harm is removed through its combination with electronics, while it is the electronics themselves contributing to the dissolution of wellness on your planet.

It becomes the easy way to plant a child somewhere with an electronic device to keep their attention; meanwhile it is a distraction rather than a learning tool when used this way. We anger at the picture of the next generation of learners becoming robotic in their need for electronics and lack of need for human interaction, in person. There should be limitations on use of behavior modifying devices—electronics.

For those who need to use a phone for business or to keep in contact with friends and family far away, is a shungite patch attached to our cell phone one small way that we can protect ourselves from EMF radiation?

Whatever is needed for self-protection is to be done, yes, and also the need for constant communication in this way is to be considered as questionable. There was a time when the need was not present and the world seemed to turn, as it should.

While we understand the need for instant gratification in most things among your peoples is high on the scale of needs, time will show that insufficient knowledge of what is accepted as required for successful and happy life may be not all of that in the long term.

Never mind, it is a sign of your times and this too shall pass.

There is something else coming to replace our current cellular phone technology—that's what you're hinting at, isn't it?

To function *as they are now intended*—there is an alternative, yes, and it involves a design modification that eliminates the way charging is managed.

Cellular technology has not considered the health connection in development of power sources. There is no need for this always-on way of being.

Well, well, well: a cell phone charging modification. I'd like to wrap my mind around how this alternative charging would be done: how does it work, Pax?

One development that will be of interest is a considered power source that takes into account the personal health and wellness of a chronic user—it is to be addressed. It is the use of the method of charging that will change with the type of battery installed. The need for electricity to charge is replaced with light such as solar—it is a beginning and options abound. This is the place of where your satellite communication remains the way, and these signals will be received and replace the battery as you now know it. This method revolutionizes the industry as current battery types can be problematic and cause damage to not only health and wellness, but also environment. Greater global dependency on connecting is answered in this manner.

Change comes and you will approve.

I can just see all of our experts in communications technology working more rapidly on these new directions.
What is the next evolution in replacement of current cell phone technology?

Communication in your soon time looks different from your now, and in your far time does not require external devices. Think on this.

We have stated the way of your future is telepathic communication and this is what you shall work towards.

This is exciting, to say the least.

Penelope, moving ahead in time, we see the communication method being telepathic alongside tiny instruments that do all for you. Understand that this is acceptable and in the soon time come prototypes of what will be then common. It is the best of times and it is understood that commonsense is required with advances, and to understand those that will benefit mankind and instill in each other the knowledge that less is more in terms of equipment.

Can you tell us more about these tiny instruments that do all for us? What do they do for us? Do they work like a cellphone in that they operate by an electrical signal transmitted by radio waves?

These tiny instruments as we have called them are what you will use for communication and programming of all your earthly needs by satellite transmission. You will not only communicate with each other your plans and movements but advise your means of transportation and your household gadgets what you want of them, and when. It is a command post, if you will, that you speak to and the voice recognition takes it from there. It is your way to make all life movements trackable and all needs monitored via this device which fits into the palm of your hand or is wrapped around an arm or wrist or hung on a belt—it is the object that manages all life needs.

You will be glued to it.

Does this device also evolve—as it seems that all technology does—and if so, what will its future become?

One day it can be so tiny as to be implanted under skin and you will not need the external device. Each person will be chipped for identification and this device is also a transmitter and receiver for communication. It is useful for all things you presently carry in your wallet and cellular telephone and replaces all. It's quite simple, really, but speaks to a higher level of control if utilized incorrectly. It is intended to simplify life.

If the device were to be imbedded under our skin, how would we operate it and interface with it?

Telepathically is the way, as it will be for all things.

It will be mobilized by a thought command as your instruments of today are in speaking a command to contact a person or open a door or activate music, all pre-programmed and some not, but voice-activation of today becomes thought-activation of tomorrow.

Wowzers.

Do you approve or disapprove of the chip under skin?

It seems a natural progression and the inner-strength and knowing of how to function in these times becomes a glorious quest for many. This is the way of your future and the determination is if *you* approve.

We understand it is to be, and that when used for pure purposes will benefit your people. As with reality there are nefarious purposes of control that could be enacted. Your people will understand this and have options for the use of their personal chip—you approve it and you control it. We state it is to be the way and that is the story.

The micro-chipping of humans is something of which we've heard and read. This concept of chipping everyone would replace everything from paper currency, to medical records, to tax filings, and criminal records, etc. It would basically hold all records and identification of each person. Many people say this is what was described in Revelation in the Bible as the "sign of the beast", and "the anti-Christ".

Was this the chipping forewarned in Revelations? And, is this story in Revelations true or did we misinterpret it?

As you understand that the Bible book was rewritten more times than were counted and interpreted by those writing at the time, this story was the equivalent of the present-day science-fiction tale. Many ideas were visualized and considered while the influence of outside was in action—this is one and while visionary, is not to be feared.

If this story is to be believed by your people, it should be understood you will have generations of "beasts" and "anti-Christs" to come. Interpret that.

Hmmm. I'd best leave that for our theologians.
On a somewhat related topic, what do you think about globalization?

Consider the big picture and one's neighbor country or continent as to be respected and protected. To live locally in terms of commerce and agriculture is meaningful to the future of Planet Earth. It is time to scale back the reliance from afar when the way of self-sufficiency has been discarded. This came of a lazy attitude and is now to be replaced with reliance on self and community.

A reversal of the ways of purchasing and giving away of personal power is to begin. This must now revert to self-empowerment with your people, a regaining of your confidence in your ability to provide and succeed.

Rely on yourselves for your future—it is your power to reclaim.

Volume 4

Do Unto Earth
Pax and the Crossroads of Our Survival

*"The climate crisis is a spiritual crisis
for our entire world. Our solutions must
weave science, spirituality, and traditional
ecological knowledge with technology."*
Rose Whipple
Environmental activist from the Isanti
Dakota and Ho-Chunk Nations of
American Indigenous Peoples

Chapter Ten
Planetary Energy Tumors

*P*ax, are you enjoying this conversation? I am! And, it interests me to know, do you *enjoy* experiences and the sharing of wisdom? Is enjoyment a thing for you?

We teach, we share, we collaborate, we enjoy, yes.

Do you "travel" for enjoyment? My husband and I went to Miami this past weekend to check it out, see something different, and have some fun. Do you visit other galaxies, universes, or spacetime locations for either "business" or pleasure?

We are amused by this notion. We are not in need of travel, as we exist simultaneously where thoughts take us.

Thanks for humoring me. Now, back to our "business" (which is actually a lot of fun, I think).

In my first book, prior to our talks, I mentioned a theory that I had channeled from my Higher Self consciousness about large energetic masses, or tumors, of both light and heavy *viral energy* upon the Earth that we have created and are creating by way of large pockets of love, hate, joy, fear, and all of our light and dark actions and intentions. Pax, can you validate this?

Energy tumors, well yes, Penelope, this is all over your world at this time, to the extent they can be seen from space. You need to focus on this as the world, as it is at present, is aware of heaviness and great negative change, but what to call it and how to endure or relieve it? Penelope, you have the term and the description, you now need to share the way of relief.

The heavy viral energy tumors can be seen from space!?

To be visible from space means literally the feeling of the energy radiating from those areas, not a visible-to-the eye cloud. Palpable would be another word for visible and this is the true meaning. For empaths who see and feel energy, the density of energy in those areas is palpable.

We've talked about the physical damage to our environment in that we are the cause of extreme pollution, global warming, and species extinction, to name a few issues. May you now please speak to the *energetic* damage mankind has done to our planet, such as the byproducts of heavy energy events and actions and attitudes—energetic tumors and scars created by war, indifference, religious and cultural intolerance, hate perpetuated throughout many generations, the on-mass pain and suffering commonplace to the wholesale slaughter of animals, and the many global impacts of heavy viral energy on-scale?

These dark energies have existed always on Planet Earth. They remain in place but can be dissolved by light energy, by love and intention to raise vibration in places previously damaged. Love always prevails, and focusing love energy in or on people, places and things, animals, plants and soil, water and air, along with consistent effort to heal in those ways possible, combine to bring healing and wellness. It is the intention that makes it real.

If we put concentrated intention and light energy on these heavy energy tumors by having many people simultaneously focus their light energy on them, can we heal these pockets of heavy energy through our viral intentions?

Oh yes, this is how it is done: concentrated energy heals.

When you gather together with intention to heal—focusing energy on a specific area, group of people, energy mass, dark intentions and beliefs—and bring the healing light into focus on those targets, energy change occurs. This is palpable and this is real. Effectively moving the mass of dark energy into the light is the result.

You must also know that the epidemic of mental health disease on your planet is dark energy at work. Those "sensitives" pick up, feel in all ways, dark energy and it envelops them. The descent into inability to function as a result is what must be addressed.

I believe that many forms of depression are not a "mental health crisis", meaning they are not a problem with the brain or a chemical imbalance in the brain, but rather many forms of depression are a "spiritual health crisis", meaning the depression was created by an immersion into heavy energy for a chronic period of time. Also, that to have a longstanding sense of lack of purpose can also create depression. These are energetic/spiritual crises that can be cured

by energetic/spiritual therapy: Light Energy Immersion Therapy. What do you think of this as a philosophy?

Yes, this is a truth and cause for much of the mental health crisis currently experienced by your people. Sadness and emotional trauma result in dis-ease of the soul and spirit and show as depression on the quiet side and violence on the other.

Many therapies exist, the most common being drug therapy: we say this is a shortcut in the system and only masks symptoms, doing nothing to find the source so healing may begin. It is a sadness in your system that sufficient time is not allotted to the individual in need.

Natural remedies such as light therapies, as mentioned, are effective. Sunshine in an artificial form does repair emotional lows in people sensitive to seasonal change.

Removal of dark energies, family strife for example, is a beginning of the journey to wellness. It is not a quick repair; it is a slow repair, which leads to wellness.

Your First Nations peoples have the right idea in their delivering a person *back to the land to find themselves*, to find their spirit, has been their way of accepting that person's journey to wellness is managed by their extended family of support and love. They are then welcomed back into the circle.

Nature immersion—yep, when I was depressed in my youth, I could have used about three months to marinate in and equilibrate with nature. (Recently, people started calling this Forest Bathing.) What else should we know about depression and heavy/dark energy?

Those *severely* affected by dark energy are the ones responsible for crime, mass killings, and acts of violence that they may say originated with voices telling them to do so: voices in their heads. Consider this is a possession of sorts, that this energy that affects others slightly or not at all, when felt by one sensitive to it, becomes a guiding darkness, the opposite of "guiding light," in this person.

To set about moving these cells of dark energy away from your Earth atmosphere will be the beginning of healing in all ways. Those who are energy sensitive will be lifted from the grasp of what they don't know or understand but do experience negative thoughts and feelings from.

To move energy, to lighten energy, and to change the balance of energy is to bring about a change in your world in ways not previously considered related.

Yes, it is the way.

I'm inspired to help enlighten the energy on our planet and anyone with light intentions can join in this effort.

If we set about moving these cells of dark energy away from our Earth atmosphere, will the dark energy then negatively impact the space outside of our Earth's atmosphere?

The method of removing this dark energy is to neutralize it so it is away from your Earth, yes, but no other place; it is gone.

To ensure our readers are clear, is this dark energy at all the same or related in any way to what exists in space that we call Dark Energy or "dark matter" or antimatter?

You speak of anti-gravity things. What we speak of here is simply energy—human created negativity—and is readily neutralized by humans.

Let's talk further about the global viral contemplations for Planet Earth? It's one thing to gather people in large

numbers to focus light energy intentions on a piece of land or a person or an event with the goal to enlighten—cleanse with light, dissolve the darkness—such as a tumor of dark energy at work, however it seems quite next-level-consciousness to *move* cells of dark energy away from our Earth atmosphere. (I envision our comic book character Superman mightily flying upwards from Earth and into the outer planetary atmosphere while carrying a gigantic ball of dark energy.) How do we accomplish moving cells of dark viral energy away from our atmosphere?

Creative Visualization is a process by which attention is focused on an area or thing and intention placed with it. In this case, the mass focus on an area covered with dark energy, with the intention of neutralizing, dispelling, eliminating, vaporizing that energy—while *visualizing* it being there, then beginning to clear, then completely clearing—holds the power to do so. You may dissolve a cloud using this method—try it.

Ah, yes, you mentioned this before and so this past weekend, while lying on the beach, I tried to dissolve a cloud using my thought power and it worked! Part of me was not surprised because you told me it would work, and the other part of me was like—*holy cow, I just dissolved that cloud!*
We mere earthlings are not used to thinking this way; that our thought power can move or affect something in the physical world. And yet, it worked.
You have my attention, Pax. How does it work?

Intention, pure and simple. It is the placing of intention behind a thought.
We discussed this earlier and you have put it into practice.

As we have previously stated, the use of intention with thought is responsible for great things, from building pyramids to curing one's own dis-ease. This is well known in your Earth time and practiced by those who trust.

This is going to be vital in healing our world, I can tell. I'd like to keep going in a lesson in creative visualization and conscious creation. You've told us, "When the student is ready the teacher appears." Well, I'm here to learn. May you please give me a next step or assignment beyond dissolving a cloud?

Dissolving clouds tests only your belief in self. The use of this creative visualization extends to all needs on your planet. Consider creating wellness from dis-ease and consider creating peace from its opposite—all things are possible when your intention is placed where need exists; you speak your intention and see and feel the result. It is *your belief in the result* and *the visualization of the result* and the *feeling of having and being the result* that is the exercise.

We share the how and you decide the why and what.

This is indeed very empowering. Although, if we found it as easy as this sounds, we'd all be manifesting our "whats". Many people have heard and read about these methods and there have been a few popular movie documentaries that promote the concept of which you describe. What else do we need to know in order to learn conscious creation and visualization for manifestation?

That people have not learned the earlier lesson means only they have not chosen to learn. We say that to look to the above, again, for explanation may be useful: all things are possible when your intention is placed where need exists, you speak your intention, and see and feel the result. It is *your belief in the result* and *the visualization of the result* and the *feeling of having and being the result* that is the exercise.

There are many books on visualization, attraction, manifestation, affirmations, and conscious creation. There's even a book, originally published in 1978, with the exact title *Creative Visualization* by Shakti Gawain. It was a pop-culture phenomenon at the time. (At least it was in some areas and with some audiences.)

We've had a lot of time to incorporate these lessons and to become a more empowered people, yet it's still not mainstream thinking or practice.

In my viral energy work I recommend the concentration of thought-energy to heal people and disruptions in nature. I have a colleague who did some light energy work in Japan to heal a man's land where nothing was growing and the animals were dying. She led a group who encircled the water well at the center of the negative energy; it worked, and the land was healed. Incidentally, this friend is of the opinion that Egypt and New Zealand are also in need of energy healing for various reasons.

What land or pieces of land do you see as sick or in need of energy healing?

Your Mother Earth is in distress globally. The choices of New Zealand and Egypt are interesting.

My colleague visited New Zealand and while it's a land and people of extraordinary beauty, she witnessed that too many people are hooked on the drug fentanyl. She felt it as a place in need of healing.

We suggest the basis for these choices is underwhelming and a deeper introspection may find evidence of a need throughout the Middle East. Generations of doom-filled regimes have led to endless dis-ease in that area as there is no growth or refreshing of energy in place. Distrust and hatred and greed and warring have contributed and now it is time to bring the greater good to the area. Separation of cultures has been the way and in order to heal, there needs to be inclusion. To send out healing energy here and as chosen, New Zealand, is a good beginning. What you will find in the former far outweighs the latter, however. For a variety of reasons, there is need globally, some regions more deeply than others, so you may systematically circle the globe focusing on specific regions as you go.

To heal from greed and hate and intolerance and racism and discrimination is a goal.

You will be supported by the Universe in this.

The Middle East—yes, this makes sense to me and is a great place to begin.

Another friend, who is an intuitive, said that she feels a palpable repelling force from Egypt-energy. Yet, I know other people who are stimulated by the energy of Egypt and experience it as very enlightening and attractive. Is there one particular energy indeed present around Egypt? Also, is there undiscovered ancient wisdom at Giza, such that we would benefit to focus on uncovering it and then learn from ancient people's wisdom found there?

Ancient wisdom is found in many forms, and some energy is dark energy. Any civilization of that age will be imbued with good and evil, light and dark, and uncovering artifacts from those early times will have all these attached. It is for the archaeologists who know this fact to protect themselves and work areas while uncovering past mysteries. There are baffling happenings surrounding those who do this work in certain ancient sites, and no other explanations exist for the negative energies and fates that befell some workers. It is the way of it.

How will the Universe support the work to heal the world by way of concentrated healing energy intention? (I have to say, it gives me goosebumps to hear you say that the Universe will support me.)

The Universe will support by bringing to our writings the masses of people looking for guidance in how their thoughts and intentions can result in Earth healing. They need to gather together and have a leader who will create the format for mass healing gatherings.

As your media formats are established, they will touch people around the globe and result in a critical mass creation, the power of which is unmistakable. It is the logical next step from your first book and the Viral Energy Institute and then our collaboration and sharing of purpose with this following. It is mystical and magical and a place of peace and purpose for the many.

This makes me very happy. How do you envision or see these "en mass healing gatherings"? Will we do this in person in venues like sports stadiums, or will we connect with people through television and radio broadcasts, and online through cyberspace?

Initially, these gatherings are through your cyberspace as it is getting the most with the least effort, the least upheaval for people, and the communication this way leads to splinter groups in person as time goes on.

The magic of television is to be considered, as this becomes a splinter group as target markets are considered in order of preference. There needs to be connection of the most numbers in the soonest time, so this combination is to be considered.

Consider it considered.

Going back to the cyberspace gatherings and in-person gatherings, I feel like the Universe is already working to get this project rolling. I met a very talented singer, a vocal artist from France, Erin Kann, who creates beautiful tracks of music and vocals that act like medicine to repair body organs and disease by way of healing sound vibration. She calls them Sound Balms. We have collaborated on a custom Sound Balm titled *Earth's Voice* as the track for a guided meditation—Global Viral Contemplation—to heal Mother Earth and to aid people all over the world in accessing their Higher Self wisdom. Erin has worked with a bio-energetician and an astrophysicist to verify her methods of healing and enlightenment through sound vibration.

Do you see merit in this project—healing sound vibration in focused energy intention work for Mother Earth?

Of course, this is to be.

The ancients knew sound energy and its uses in healing (as well as warring at times: certain frequencies can make people quite crazy if used for extended times and can shatter glass).

Some frequencies are healing and enhance meditation—the Om vibration and sound as example. Sound therapy and in your current place, music therapy, which is a derivation, works miracles in certain applications. This is yet another tool to use in the healing process.

You must know that playing sounds of musical notes and vibrations increases plant growth, crop yields, soothes people and animals, and brings peace where heard.

Chapter Eleven
Earth Speaks

I've read that Earth has a magical energy grid and that energies run through ley lines around the globe—straight lines drawn between various historic structures—and that these ley lines were recognized by ancient ancestors to provide energy for enlightenment. I've been to two places that are said to be ley line vortexes: Mount Shasta in California, and Sedona, Arizona (there are four vortexes in Sedona: Airport Mesa, Cathedral Rock, Bell Rock, and Boynton Canyon), and yes indeed, I felt a powerful vibration. While I won't share an exhaustive list, some other ley lines or ley line vortexes that I've heard about are: the Great Pyramids of Giza, the Stonehenge Circle, the Great Wall of China, the Nusa Islands, the southern tip of South Africa, the tower of Glastonbury Tor in England, Es Vedrà on the Spanish island of Ibiza, Chichén Itzá on Mexico's Yucatán Peninsula, Mexico's Mayan ruins in Tulum, Maui's Haleakalā volcano, and of course there must be more. Are these ley lines a real thing, and if so, may you please explain what they are?

It is the case that ley lines are found encircling the globe, your Mother Earth globe, and as they intersect there are power centers where the believers congregate for healing. Many experience great change and many experience great insights, and all experience something whether recognized at the time or later, but the experience is enlightening in different ways. Higher consciousness is achieved and clear thinking and feeling and visions are a result of spending time near a vortex. For some, the power is too great and physical feelings of unwellness occur—for these sensitives it is a need to distance somewhat from the power center. Those lesser developed on their spiritual path may feel little until the cumulative effect is noticed.

The power is there for the enlightened.

We are here to say these are indeed the places where mankind should be concentrating energy. It is at these sites that collective consciousness and personal consciousness can be greatly impacted for the better. The positive energy at these sites has been gathering for centuries and can't help but affect pilgrims who visit there.

Well, this is intriguing. How should we be utilizing these powerful ley lines?

The awakening of the mind to the potential for change is the first step. Understanding the details and understanding the power is next. Respect for these places must be present in the hearts and minds of visitors. Change will occur when in the presence of the energies.

Ley lines do exist with all their potential to positively affect those in their presence. Make the trek and find out.

In times of old, Earth's peoples knew of these places and traveled on pilgrimages to be healed and changed in many ways.

The idea that they need only visit and believe was appealing, and it is the case.

Today there are believers and non-believers, but the fact remains that those who visit these areas are changed. On the inside is the movement of the water in the body—it is the gravitational pull that makes the difference. See it for yourself.

My dear, Pax, I'm going to have to ask you to please expand on this: "On the inside is the movement of the water in the body—it is the gravitational pull that makes the difference." I get the gravitation pull on water idea; it's like the power of the full moon and other astrological phenomenon. What I need help with is *why* this movement of the water of our body composition affects our inner-power-charge, empowerment, healing, and enlightenment?

It is empowering in its awareness of self and Self being increased and energy being catapulted to the highest levels known to a person. It parts the clouds so that truth and possibilities are brought forward to the knowing. Infinite possibilities are seen, and the mind is opened to life's next steps. The journey becomes clear.

When in these power centers, all life opens to view, and each person's experience differs but is the same in that a shift takes place in personal energy.

I would then say that Mother Earth is interactive with us, she shares her energy with us, she's a living energetic organism and she speaks to us in many ways.

Does Earth have emotions? Does Earth cry or mourn for her sickness and diseases? Does Earth speak to us somehow: in the wind, in whispers?

Well yes, all of this you suggest is the case. And Mother Earth has emotions and currently begins to show them in not the subtle ways of past. Where She has whimpered and cried in past, your Mother speaks now in floods and fires and eruptions and earth shifts and typhoons, tornadoes, and hurricanes.

If you can think of this, the anger pockets in place around the globe, those black spots of dark energy, they transmit to your Earth people with sensitivities and the need to punish, showing themselves in mass killings and acts of violence of all types.

Is this, too, the manifestation of pockets of "viral energy"—large tumors of contagious energy?

It is a contagious *viral energy* mass of punishment taken up by those who think they can cure all by violence. Being infected with this dark energy fuels their need for validation and they escalate to what you see in your world today.

Here's what I've discovered through years of viral energy work: It is through our dark intentions and actions that we create the dark energy, and then the dark energy creates more dark (negative and heavy) energy and actions. (Or light energy creates more light energy, of course.) And, this occurs through a viral movement of energy—both light or dark energy are contagious and also transfer passively, by osmosis, simply through immersion in and around such dark energy.

Is this all correct?

Indeed.

Dark energy is of your people's creation and grows as it is taken on by people sensitive to it, resulting in negative acts which perpetuate the cycle: more is created, and more is held in your space and time. Wholesale healing is needed—intention to clear this energy can be undertaken by people alone, or in groups around the globe. To pray for peace and pray for healing energy to replace dark energy is the way.

It seems that worldwide there's been a higher frequency of mega-sized storms, fires, tsunamis, and earthquakes.

Consider the arrival of fire and tornado. Consider the almost constant pummeling of Planet Earth now by natural disaster. Is this not a warning; a heads-up to your population at this time that enough is enough, and acts must be cleaned up and new ways of thinking begun and acted upon? This is the intention. How it is received determines your future. Your peaceful forward motion in time is dependent on decisions made by your people and your leaders now.

The places most affected are somewhat peaceful locations; places that appear to hold more light energy vibration than heavy energy vibration. Of course, appearances might be deceiving. Are the locations of the Mother-Earth-Speaks natural cataclysms the same locations where our greed and violence and other dark actions have created masses of dark energy? Or, do the eruptions show up in non-dark-energy related geographical locations because these places have vulnerabilities or weaknesses, or is there another reason?

That these vulnerable areas of Earth continue to be troubled by natural disasters is a combination of reasons. Mother Earth has been damaged and hurts, resources have not been well managed to the extent the area is vulnerable, and what happens underground is also causal—fault lines being one.

Some might say that ravaging the places of people showing great wealth and great narcissism and great self-interest sends a message. Contrasting that is the damage to people who do not fit this description: it is Mother Nature stating it is time to move off this land. Your Earth has been badly treated and this can go on only so long before Mother Nature shows you the way to her regained wellness.

Those who rise from the ashes will continue to do so, claiming the land over the constant reminders that natural disaster continues, sometimes annually, and what does it take for the message to be heard?

It is also to be considered that the First Nations peoples of old, very long ago in your time, *when removed from their lands sometimes left an energy field around it* that led to it not being inhabited by others for long periods as unfriendly experiences such as nature would show, were too often experienced. Is this the case in California? Is this the case when Moana Kea erupts, and her sacred self is shaking? Is it?

I say you are giving us a rhetorical question and that it is in fact the case in California and the Moana Kea volcano in Hawaii.

Should we leave these energy fields in place until First Nations people are returned there or they themselves lift it, or should we all work on the energy to turn it into energy that is more hospitable for life in these places?

Oh, now this is a question. Would you decide it right to override the actions and beliefs of those who consider these sacred lands? If there were to be an en mass healing and shifting of energy, it would best be undertaken with the blessing and participation of those who placed that energy for their purposes and beliefs. To go against those beliefs, albeit with good intentions, would add to the burden on that land.

Knowing this, I would only wish to undergo a mass healing *with* the blessing and leadership and guidance of the peoples who placed that energy there.

Do the present-day descendants of those peoples know of these intentionally placed energies?

Oh yes, and it would be considered their traditional territory and protected as best they can from the encroachment of tourism and those who would take from the land without respect. This is not a good thing to do.

Old energies remain in place and are to be considered and respected.

Understood. Maybe one day these energy fields will be lifted, *if* that's what those First Nations peoples decide. Although, it sounds like these energies are still needed to protect the land from those who still haven't the heart and mind to care for it with respect and love.

When we were talking about the ways of the First Nations peoples, we had a discussion about the Dakota Pipeline in America and the effects on the Standing Rock Sioux Tribe. Here's a thought: could the Sioux Nation place such an energy field around their sacred land, thereby deterring the success of the Dakota Pipeline (an energetic kink in the pipe, so to speak)?

Indeed, this could be, however, to be destructive would not be a positive step. It is the way of this to educate the invaders in history and tradition and try to work together in respect and harmony. While this is a lofty goal, efforts continue to enforce what rights the Sioux have while bringing awareness to the world of the bigger picture—the protection of sacred land so as to not injure themselves emotionally or anger ancestral spirits.

In Brazil, tremendous chunks of rainforest have been cleared to create space for oil palms. Also, in Indonesia, the harvesting of palm oil is damaging the rainforests and decimating wildlife including orangutans. When tallied back in 2017, over fifty thousand orangutans on the islands of Borneo and Sumatra had died because of palm oil deforestation. It's heartbreaking and unacceptable, yet it's accepted. Do you know, Pax, how many of our products contain palm oil? These include food products, candy and snacks, cosmetics, biofuel, animal feed, pharmaceuticals, and industrial-use items. We are mowing down forests so that corporations can take this natural resource. How can we protect the indigenous animals and natural habitats and ecosystems?

Despite your outrage at the ramifications of growing and harvesting this crop, it is a dietary staple.

And so, what's the solution?

We suggest the humanitarian aspect of this be taken to the governments of the countries involved, along with an alternative offered in harvesting methods and buffer zones left for animal population solace and survival.

What can you tell us about the great Amazon rainforest burning? Are forest fires set on purpose to clear land to raise more cows for export commerce? Let's narrow in on the big

one of recent times: were the very destructive Amazon fires in 2019 set on purpose?

This is an extreme example and not to be repeated, but fires are often set in the Amazon rain forest by farmers—to create grazing land is a need for some. Fortunately, the growth there is so rapid that the jungle can take over cleared areas in short time and reforestation is managed. The area is habitat for many animals and also growing area for cattle and crops. They exist in harmony, usually.

To pray for return to health of this Amazon rain forest is helpful.

How critical to Planet Earth's health is the Amazon?

The rain forest is critical to the health of the planet as it is responsible for cleaning the air to a very large percentage.

Let's talk about the bush fires in Australia that are devastating wildlife. What is the cause of these historic fires and why are seasonal bush fires worse than ever?

Some fires are man-made, and these are no different.

Agricultural farmers versus sheep farmers, always contradiction in rationale and need for land use.

Some who clear land for planting do so with controlled burning which can become out of control.

The climate, high temperatures in Australia have been relatively constant, but even they grow more intense in this time.

Pax, I'd like to follow up on what you said: "Agricultural farmers versus sheep farmers, always contradiction in rationale and need for land use."

How does this contradiction between crop farmers and sheep farmers relate to the cause of these fires? Have some fires been deliberately set in some sort of a battle of the farmers, or to sabotage the other? I'm trying to figure out the connection between these two types of farmers to the fires.

When the indigenous people clear land for farming and to keep firebreaks in place, they do so by controlled burns. There can be accidents when due to wind and weather a fire becomes larger than intended—there would be no intentional damage to the Earth created in the name of protection and prevention.

When non-indigenous farmers do the same, the results can be expected to be similar. The sheep take growth down to the dirt, which is not appreciated by the agricultural farmers, and the sheep farmers continue to need grazing land for their flocks and there is a push and pull ongoing. Neither would knowingly harm the land so that it could not recover. This would be disputed by some, but those who need healthy land to support livestock and crops are wise in the ways of conservation.

Fires in Australia occur each year during their hottest months. During the 2020 fire season, the fires covered six times the land and forests of what was burned by the 2019 Amazonia fires. More than half a billion animals perished in the 2020 fires in Australia, and many experts say the number is much higher. The loss of thousands of koalas has been called "a national tragedy" by the Australian government. It seems that there is a growing link between climate change/rising temperatures and why these fires rage on no matter what initially sparked them.

Pax, what do we need to know about Australia and these bush fires?

This is not the way of the ancients in this place, as they managed control of their soil and bush over their time of existence. They see the future of this now and are deeply saddened by man's inability to manage the resources.

If these fires go into the ground and find the coal, it will spell even greater disaster and that, over time, results in the inability of that portion of Earth to support life.

OMG—the coal!
Australia is the world's largest exporter of both coal and natural gas. The ground is rich with coal and the mines that bring coal to the surface are concentrated in about the very same places as the fires; no one is talking about the potential for the fires to reach the coal supplies.
We need to sound the alarm.

It is a crossroads now for this continent; a place of determining future, or not, for healthy life on that soil. Desecration is the present situation. How repair is managed determines habitability in future.

I wonder if we can call in outside help. Is there anything our interstellar visitors could do to help?

We say that the way of this connection is to not interfere in what mankind—the Earth inhabitants—have created. What could be remains unknown and what will be, the same.

In times past the people would gather and pray for rain. Now your people don't understand that they have the capability to set their intention to this, people around the globe, and by the power of their intention and prayer, bring healing moisture to this suffering region. It is so simple and so not practiced—the power of intention and prayer together make mountains move.

Let us all pray prayers of thanks and gratitude, send up light thoughts and pure intentions and visualize rain quenching fires. May people around the globe unite in prayer and thought intention for the continent of Australia, and for peace in the world, healing for people in peril, and protection for animals in crisis. Let's send thoughts of love and peace to people and wildlife and farmed animals.

We are here to say that the next generation of your Earth people bring change and repair and higher vibration to your Earth—there is hope. Now is time for those in power to listen to the youth as their idealistic and pure intentions and guidance pave the way to this growth. Trust in this.

Chapter Twelve
A Crisis of Climate

*W*hen we were discussing mysteries of the Earth, you said something that I now want to go back to because your words bring up the exact argument made by climate change deniers. We were talking about sunken civilizations and you said, "If you ask about remains of previous civilizations, then yes, very much, as over time the seas have risen and coastal inhabitants and villages have been taken by the tides. It is a repeating event now on your planet as the seas again rise and those nearby are and will be impacted by loss of land and lifestyle. History repeats itself in climate change, ice ages come and go, warming and cooling cycles, and life goes on."

And so, those who say that anthropogenic global warming is a hoax or fabrication will say that you are making their point. I know numerous people who think this way. Just yesterday, I had conversations with two separate individuals about the environment (the environment is "trending", top-of-mind, and all the rage—literally) and both of them said that they don't believe in manmade climate change. To say that I felt frustrated is an understatement. I held back my reaction and instead asked them *why* they don't believe it.

In a nutshell: they believe the Earth merely goes through natural cycles. You have confirmed these natural cycles.

Science can show the statistics of this.

Okay, let's look at the statistics.

In the United States, the National Aeronautics and Space Administration (NASA) says that climate change is extremely likely and is "greater than ninety-five percent probability" to be the result of human activity. Their data shows measurements of atmospheric carbon dioxide from ice-core samples that date back eight hundred thousand years ago. To see a line chart of climate over these many thousands of years, it looks like numerous evenly sized waves and then, starting in 1950, a tsunami with its crest not yet realized.

The Intergovernmental Panel on Climate Change (IPCC) could not be more clear that we are sitting far above pre-industrial levels and that this is human-induced warming, which correlates to the Industrial Age: cars, factories, grossly scaled meat production, deforestation, and other factors of human pollution—all elevating greenhouse gas emissions.

Planet Earth has cycled through warming and cooling over the millennia and what you experience today is not a natural cycle. It is a speeded-up version and a deepening of severity version and a possibly irreversible version of what has gone before, certainly from the standpoint of continued human habitation. It is what it is.

Your science has documented ice ages and their beginnings and endings, warmings that followed, and the repeat—this now is at a level of severity never before experienced by your Earth.

However, many people still don't believe the latest data. What do you know that even our data doesn't that might prove to climate naysayers that global warming of today is caused by humans and not just natural cycles of the Earth?

For anyone to see the fouling done by your industry of air and water, soil and all things growing as a result, and attempt to deny the correlation, shows them to have heads firmly embedded in sand—a pity and a travesty and you know who you are.

Until awareness comes, Earth continues to foul and your people will go—"to where?"—they will be first to ask. Theirs will be the last seats on the bus to forgiveness and safety.

Could an asteroid collision cause an ice age and/or major climate change on Earth, as many believe? Has this ever been the case?

It could and it has and could once again. It is the beginning and the end of what is and what will be. Cataclysmic it is and not in your immediate future.

To be crystal clear, are humans creating our present-time crisis of climate?

You are doing so, yes, and it is always humans creating and recreating, destroying and recovering. Retaining status quo all-is-well would be a consideration, yes?

Your people's continued focus on self and not Earth is responsible. You know this and steps are being taken by some to change. Too little too late has been the case in past; do not let it be so now.

And, is anthropogenic global warming a real and imminent threat to human survival on Earth?

Well, yes, and it is known to your leaders as well as your people. We have discussed the ways forward toward solution. Get on it, people, please.

On behalf of your Mother Earth and all who rely on her, we ask for action.

For those who believe in Earth's cyclical nature but do not believe that we are in a new era of anomaly that is far out of balance to the former natural cycles, for those who do not believe that this major blip in the data is directly tied to industrial age human pollution—what message do you have for them?

Wake up and smell the pollution in your air. Go to the ocean or river and drink the water—go ahead. Do you find clean and pure or do you simply reject the idea of drinking from your oceans and rivers? Look at the soils in your agricultural areas and see pollution there from chemicals plus polluted air and water—how do you feel about your food growing there?

It is a case of opening the mind to reality; of seeing what is.

I'd like to ask you about the city of Venice, Italy which was not long ago affected by high water that hit seventy-four inches; the highest flood water in fifty years. However, even greater water levels were recorded in Venice in 1966. So, what was the cause of the high water back then?

Tidal action being affected by moon activity combined with severity and length of rains all play a role—many natural sources touch results such as this—there will be more and all are somewhat different in their origin, but the result looks the same: flooding, high water to levels unprecedented.

Some people say that they know we are polluting the
Earth in a terrible way, and yet they still believe that we're
only partly responsible for climate change. They also believe
that the Earth may have had past natural events such as
volcanic eruptions that caused the greenhouse effect and we
are just contributing a small amount. What would you say to
those who say, "I don't believe that we 100% created climate
change,"? Let's be as clear and strong worded as possible.
These people don't believe the data. What can you tell them
to prove it?

Let us not spend time attempting to prove to closed minds
what they don't wish to believe. Let us, instead, address the partial responsibility they agree to and begin there to clean their
way of living to reduce pollution in their own lifestyles.

That they agree to some damage; let them agree to some
level of fixing and repair of what has been done. This should be
a place to begin with all who take some little responsibility, or
large portion—do your best, each of you, to repair the damage
you see.

Of course, you don't need to read our latest IPCC reports,
yet how do you know that we have a global warming crisis?
Pax, how does the Spirit World sense and detect an out-of-
norm and unnatural rise in our global temperature?

We are not a gauge of temperature; we are a gauge of what
is, in the overall on your Planet Earth. That your reporting of fear
and requests for assistance in diagnosing and repairing Earth damage comes to us through thoughts and prayers is our entry into
the overall knowing of your presence in this time and place of
fear and not understanding the way forward, as it is with all things.

So, when we send up prayers, they come to you? May you please share how it works when we send up prayers and they are received by the Spirit World?

As the heaviness of energy and emotional un-wellness on your Planet Earth impacts your people and your environment, it is known to Spirit and felt.

When people pray using the name of a deity or divine one, you still know and feel their prayer?

That you do not pray to us does not result in our inability to feel the energy coming up from your people. Some pray to deities and some pray to Mother Earth and many saints and protectors of civilizations past and present—the energies transmit like ripples on a pond and are felt far and wide. There is an awareness and as we are included in the requests for healing and sharing of solutions, we become a part of the team as it were.

And what does the Spirit World team have to say about the state of our environment?

Moving ahead in time we see your world glowing—this is not in health but in excess heat. Now is the time to take steps to stop global warming.

Your world is in for a crisis of greater proportion than is now believed. It is a crisis of climate and rising waters. Too soon there will be a realization that the time is now, the time of it being too late to fix. In some geographic areas that is the case. In others on higher ground change comes to ensure life goes on, but it is still ignoring the underlying cause.

Industry money has been known to support politicians who then assist in lowering standards for industrial waste and contamination regulation. This game must not continue. It is for these kingpins of government and industry to know they are using the global population as a pawn in their game.

Who are the "kingpins of government and industry" to which you refer?

Industry and political leaders, CEOs, bankers and those who control the federal reserves, for example—the top 1% who rule all through allocation of and receipt of $$$.

How do you allow so few to control so many for so little in return? This is a travesty and must stop. Where is the social conscience of the many? Standing up and being heard is the only way to begin the end to this practice. Unite and make the difference in your world.

We wish to speak of the change in the minds of your people as being the need, and we wish to speak of the change in structure of your governments also being a need. We speak of how and when and why.

The time is now to advance the movement of love throughout your planet. The power of love is what will move you through from decline to ascent in all ways.

How does one clear-cut a forest when one loves the trees and the animals who make them their home? How does one overfish the oceans when one loves the purity and cleanliness of the waters and the life it holds? How does one treat the planet as a garbage dump when one loves the earth and the grasses and the flowers? And how does one allow for pollution to the degree you experience, when one loves the freshness and purity of the air and the birds who fly in it?

Renew and recharge and replace the man-made pollutants with the purity of the planet as it was created.

It is in your hands now. We charge you with the responsibility of cleaning up your own mess. Only your generation, and we repeat, Only Your Generation, can make this difference. To wait longer is to step over the threshold into the place of non-return, non-sustainable, and non-renewable. Can you live with that?

No, Pax, we can't.
Please imagine that you are looking into the eyes of the most powerful leaders on this planet today (those individuals who have the ability to change policies)—what would you say directly to them?
You have the floor.

Without integrity and true belief in change and the relaxation of need for supreme power and the motivation of greed among your leaders, no healing of your planet is to be.

We wish to speak of this need and the way forward to achieve it. To go forward without regard for natural resources is to sign the death warrant for the planet. Harmony comes easily when greed is left out of the equation. Do you understand this? It is greed that motivates and causes acquisitions to be of key importance. When those acquisitions involve taking liberties, rights, land, from others, it is not appropriate, healthy, or cause for celebration. It should be seen as bullying from great heights when carried out by countries, gangs, and big business. Step aside from these human conditions and look toward the elevation of consciousness and actions. It is time.

It is our message to your time that the end is near for your Earth. Go forward in the knowledge that as you sow, so shall you reap.

Mankind is not listening to the signals in nature.

Ours is the purpose and ours is the intention to put forward the truth and the lessons from galactic history that will bring heightened awareness and resolve to bring peaceful change to your Mother Earth.

What would you like to say directly to our people?

The future of your planet is in the hands of the children and the elders, and that fusion creates the answers. This fusion is beginning now, but it is to be publicized and pushed and palpated and postulated and practiced. It is to be recognized and, rather like the dunes, looked over to see what is behind it and in front of it, and we say that equals energy. That is the energy of the old and wise coupled with the energy of the young and idealistic; a wonderful combination. As tribal elders sit in circle and speak their recollections and ensure their oral and written traditions and histories do not disappear, this shall be the way of the current elders of civilizations, countries, regions, business, etc., so that each area of expertise is covered and there is someone there to accept their knowledge for the purpose of storing and cataloging and sharing.

It is to be recognized that the true worth of a person is what they will give, and now we ask for the giving of time and energy, interest and talent to protect that which will take your people into their next pathway, that of going back to the future or going forward into the past.

Much like our signature which is the sign of infinity, this is the path to take—forward becomes backward becomes forward again. Past, present and future all in one, this is the secret and this is your path.

It is the reliving of the old wisdom and the relearning of the new—yes relearning. Nothing new is ever new—it is a repeat of past wisdom that has been left out and forgotten. There is no new information. *When discoveries are made you may consider that they were in use in other planetary systems before Earth was a player.* Yes, this is the truth: someone has done it before and thousands of years ago as well. So, when your intellect sprouts wings and flies into the realm of what you thought not possible or even imagined, wrong; it was and is and will be again. Yours is to resurrect the old and call it new. But we know the reality.

While the world takes a few more turns, we wish to say that actions speak louder than words. To this end we wish to inform that the best truly is to be for your society. There will be change and growth and making the best of each day and planning for world peace becomes at the forefront. This comes about through change in national leadership and quiet and strong revolution among the people to the end that no sub-standard leadership will be tolerated. This begins now and grows to mammoth proportions resulting in leadership moving from corruption to clean and clear thinking and acting for the common good.

We ask for all mankind to adopt the ways of the aboriginal peoples whose stewardship of their land kept it for all their generations in the condition of pristine wilderness. This is a beginning for the next phase of your history that will show the intention toward wellness for all. Practicing this brings wellness to all, to the globe, to your resources and environments, and begins the healing you know is needed. It will be your resurrection from the current path of low actions to the higher good being sought and achieved. This becomes a bright star in your people's evolution.

Vibration of the planet will change with the collective consciousness of the people, of course, and why do you think otherwise? Your world is impacted greatly by the thoughts you put out there, as are your bodies and minds and the plants and animals. What you think, you radiate, and what you radiate, you are.

That simple. We are here to ask the people of your world to look within. What you see there is a microcosm of what you experience outside of your self. Think on that and correct it.

Yes, we are here to say the time is now to be aware of what you each can do, in your way, to halt the progress of decimation of your planet. Do not think each of you is powerless against tyranny and against developers, and against tree-cutters, and all that comes your way to interfere with the continued well-being of your race and planet. Light always wins over darkness.

Each person is imbued with power—more than is often thought. As individuals, you have power and as groups of individuals, even greater. It is for you to understand that banding together for the common good is what will make the difference.

The best of the best are working to save your world—why not become one of them and make your own contribution.

Change is coming as quickly as you can make it.

Volume 5
Do Unto Earth
Pax and the Path of Purpose

"I recently watched an interview with the astronauts who, back in 1968, took the iconic photo that's come to be called 'Earthrise'. I marveled at the ecstatic joy they must have felt at their first sighting of our blue home suspended in the vast, dark firmament. How small we must have appeared. How fragile our existence. How enormous our potential."
Oprah Winfrey
American TV host, actress, producer, and world-renowned spiritualist

Chapter Thirteen
The Life of Life

*P*ax, today it feels to me like I just watched an electrifying movie and at the very end, the next sequel was revealed. Now I get to watch the story unfold and I'm grateful and committed to this next destination of our journey together.

As we get going, I'd like to ask you a number of questions that have long interested humankind. When I looked up "Questions You Would Ask God", these were among the top queries; curiosities that are shared by many people. Here goes—

Why does light always win over darkness? How is this a certainty?

You may shine a light into darkness and it will illuminate what is there, previously unseen before arrival of the light. Darkness will not extinguish light in the context of this discussion. As more of your people become light-workers, the balance tips in favor of goodness and wellness for your planet. These are the new breed of scientists plus many more of your Earth people learning they can make a difference and will be part of the solution now.

Why do bad things happen to good people?

Who is to say what is a bad thing for another? When there is not a way of knowing what that person's life blueprint is, there is not a way to determine for them if an occurrence is a bad thing or a good thing. Remember this.

Why do bad people often get their way?

Is a "bad person" a ramification of what others deemed good people did not say or do when they should, a result of others' lack of forward motion in manifesting what should be, according to them? Is it lack of empowerment, weakness, or just a lesser amount of corruption?

When what is deemed bad by some is met with a sufficient amount of good, as deemed by those same people, physics would have it that there is an impasse. Do you understand this lesson? The simplicity of it is that without resistance, whatever pushes forward continues in motion.

Yes, I do understand this.
Many people want to know why the Spirit World won't step in and stop suffering caused by cruel or greedy people. Why is suffering *allowed*?

That people wish to hand over responsibility for your current world situation to the Spirit World indicates a lack of willingness to accept your role in creating this world situation. Do not consider your creation of a mess is the responsibility of others to fix.

We ask your world population to understand there are con-sequences to your actions—*an action has a reaction*—and yours is to repair the damage you have actively caused or passively allowed to be. It is yours to undertake the next chapter in this story.

This, of course, is reasonable—that we clean up our own mess.

Let's look at this question about suffering, not as related to our environmental crisis, but as related to historical atrocities such as the Holocaust. There were millions of people praying for a divine intervention—praying for years, even—and in the end, some six million Jews were murdered by the Nazis. That being said, I hope that this is a fair ques-tion: why could the Spirit World not intervene to help?

The division between chosen directions by those on Earth and those not is the answer. One does not interfere in the other.

That world powers initiated an action is for it to play out in history. There does not seem to be a reason but in fact the reason is there.

For your history to show the steps along the way from begin-ning to end of this you refer to is to put in place the example for the world to follow going forward—what to see and experience that teaches the reasons for avoidance in future.

We see this is currently underway again and being watched *but not disallowed by your population.*

An example was set in this that took many lives and this example is to teach the future.

As it is being elevated now in memory, it is to have a resur-gence of emotion among your people and reintroduce and rekindle the will to *not* accept this in future.

It is happening—be watchful.

Oh Pax, please do tell us more regarding this clear warning.

In the world today, sadly we are largely bystanders of many acts of extreme wickedness in many countries, including but not limited to the mistreatment and mutilation of women in some religions; the crisis of "ethnic cleansing" genocide of the Muslim Rohingya people in northwestern Myanmar; the civil war in South Sudan with its brutal killings and rapes; the deadly conflicts in the Central African Republic between the Christian militias called the "anti-Balaka" and Muslim groups, rising to a level of genocide; and atrocities by Arab militias against non-Arab peoples in Darfur, a region in western Sudan.

Much of the genocide occurring in present times is taking place in African countries, and like the Holocaust these are the outcomes of religious and ethnic divides and hatred.

I must mention one of the biggest and most profitable criminal businesses in the world that is also one of the most prolific and yet little-known (or little discussed) horrors: human sex trafficking and the global sex trade, and the fact that at this very moment there are more than four million adults and one million children in forced sexual slavery worldwide.

Of these and other acts of barbarity, to what do you refer when you speak of the Holocaust in warning us that "this is currently underway again", and "it is happening"? Which of these many horrors do you see escalating to the level of the Holocaust?

We speak of divisiveness among populations and individuals by race, color, religion, gender, anywhere there can be one group of peoples denying another equality. This is the Holocaust reference and how that began.

It is underway now among some races and countries and they deny equality to those who do not look like them—a resurgence of the Aryan Race *mindset* extended throughout your global societies. This is as dangerous as it ever was, and more so now in your age of electronic communication where misinformation spreads in nanoseconds.

Please use the example of the Holocaust to help us understand that "light always wins over darkness".

When people take positive action against what they see as negative, it is light over darkness.

That nobody stood up then to disrupt the negative movement allowed darkness to rule.

It was not that light was lost or failed; it was that light was not shown to the dark.

Inaction and blind following without question was the cause.

What is the true nature of mankind? Are we good or bad by nature?

Consider the nature of a baby at birth, a child growing; innocence is the true nature. This is what begins, what is intrinsically yours: purity of intention.

It is what is taught, what is learned that makes the change. Is racism intrinsic to the baby, is greed and a tendency to corruption, is cheating and bullying a part of the baby, or is it learned behavior? You decide.

What caused us to move away from our true nature?

Influence. Influence of those in control of life and commerce and learning and building and growing relationships—these account for change, these influence change.

What must happen to allow a child to grow into maturity without these influences taking over? Self-empowerment and confidence and trust in self—these are the needed barriers to the destruction of purity of spirit. Is it the case that these are also learned behaviors? Is it more to the point that these attributes are within each person at birth and are lost as the child grows in experience? Yes. This is it. Each person does not learn these traits, each person is born with them and either retains or loses them based on nurture. Parents and the "nature versus nurture" aspect of humanity will determine if the child becomes an adult with confidence, compassion, empathy, good humor, forgiveness, strong work ethic, and an abundance of care and concern for all nature and mankind. These are all found within the individual's DNA and are either lost or retained as life progresses. The soul arrives in purity.

Does the Universe operate only by physics or does it "think", make choices, and so on?

It is our joy to share what is of benefit to your Earth people. From time to time we must ask that you accept what is without the minutia of understanding that comes from dissection such as this. While philosophical in nature, the thought is a psychological one of contradiction and comparison.

In this case there are secrets to be uncovered, mysteries to be explored and grand information to be known and tested. Life goes on and the world takes many turns while awaiting this series of events. For now, it is fair to say that when your space exploration is taking place this too shall be further explored.

We suggest that the understanding of all things heretofore left to imagination is to continue while your mankind works out the implications of trying to manage their own lives on your planet. With your present inability to do so, more attention could be paid to the peace on Earth policy and the love thy neighbor policy and the true nature of mankind-coming-to-the-fore policy.

It is time now for your people to look within for their peace and use this time to reflect on what is and what could be. Managing life on your Earth has not gone well of late, and it is time to turn your efforts in this direction.

This is true.
What's the purpose of a person's life?

What is each soul's purpose as laid out long ago and agreed to on each go around?

For some the meaning of life is to gain control and financial wealth, yet for others it is to heighten their spiritual wellness and strength of character, to teach the ways of the Higher Self— never the twain shall meet, but there are myriads of meanings in between. To each his own it is.

At that soul's inception is the blueprint determined for each life's purpose. This is a contract between the Universe and the soul to guide the way to future growth and wisdom, wellness, and greater movement toward enlightenment.

Between physical incarnations is there a processing of our life and a process for preparing for the next incarnation?

This determination is made by each soul considering return, and is the continuation of their journey toward enlightenment, toward completion of their blueprint for life and lifetimes. There are journeys to take resulting in contributions to global wellness or following the course of one life to ensure it is on track to wellness, and amazing gifts to share and experiences as well. To regroup in the Spirit realm prior to return includes the choices and the preparations for what is to come. Some wish immediate return and do so by choosing to be an unborn baby in their family, returning that way to bring love again to the circle. Others have much healing, both physical and emotional, to manage before considering their next adventure on your Earth—it varies.

It sounds like a soul comes back fairly quickly after death, that is if they don't have much healing to undertake between lifetimes. How thrilling that we could bump into a loved one or know them again in another incarnation. Is it *common* for a deceased loved one's soul to reenter the physical plane at the same time that we're still here?

It is not uncommon and is dependent entirely upon the lessons remaining to be taught and to be learned. It is a possibility and results in healing by way of those remaining becoming aware of the new soul in their midst having remarkable abilities to trigger feelings and memories and healing. Always there is a higher purpose.

Is the choosing of a "life purpose" a formal event, like a meeting in the Spirit realm?

The Universe celebrates all growth toward enlightenment. However, as the soul's progress is dependent on its own timetable through its development, the transition is a personal one.

Life is a choice, don't you know?

Does this mean that *everything* in life is a choice?

Indeed, it is, beginning with choice of parents to enter the next lifetime and everything throughout that lifetime. What comes will come, and how it is reacted to is your choice. Think on it—each time you make a decision to go or do it has been a choice.

If an illness is presented, how it is reacted to and therefore the outcome is a choice. To accept or reject the realities of life influences outcomes, and each decision along that path is a choice.

Free will equals choice, and those with limited free will choose to be compliant or not. All choices, and those with choice are empowered to control outcomes.

What about terminal diseases—if a person had terminal cancer, can they choose their way out of it to health?

Choice began with the acquisition of the dis-ease as a component of the chosen life blueprint. Remember this.

Do we choose our death?

The blueprint for life that one creates for themselves and their next incarnation includes the ending of that lifetime.

All is a choice, yes, and pertains to the lessons intended to be learned and taught and shared. It is the contract one makes with one's self and the Universe for that period in time; their presence at that place in time.

Death is a beginning of the next chapter in a soul's progress, the next lessons in a next incarnation. It is a process—a soul's journey.

Is there a time when it's too late for choice?

Once the contract has been made, we say it is, it becomes the way forward. There is this trajectory of life that is patterned according to the chosen steps along the path for the lifetime.

A person capable of changing that trajectory is a rare one and would require much personal work to determine why the path was chosen, what was to be learned from it, and why a deviation would be appropriate. Regarding the pertinent past lifetime, to recognize the signposts for this journey would be needed along with forgiveness and openness to acceptance of the what and why of it.

Regarding karma, do we keep coming back until we "get it right" or learn a lesson? Or, perhaps there are no "lessons", there is just what we choose to create?

Karma—this is an interesting discussion, as it is known by other names in other realms. What is the common thread is the action of it, the magnetic pull to continue a lesson or right a wrong or contribute what was withheld and so many opportunities lost are wanting to be revisited and rectified.

It is a self-imposed state of being and is very real.

Pain is caused by lost opportunities and it is the way-of-correcting that exists in order to not only do right but create peace within the self that is needing release from the wishing for other outcomes. It is a process and a valuable set of lessons and repeating with new knowledge and clear intention to contribute good where it was previously lacking. It is a blessing to all.

Apart from finding a good hypnotherapist for past life regression, is there a way to review a past life that is helpful to a current lifetime?

We wish to state that there is a difference between past life regression and hypnosis therapy. One can take place without the other.

Meditation does it for many, so consider the deep and guided meditation which takes one through the process of reviewing life and lifetimes with the intention to visit the one pertinent to present life blocks or challenges. This can be managed at home through the use of guided meditation recordings. It is effective and can be therapeutic and liberating.

Is it possible to reach a level of "consciousness attainment" while in the physical, whereby a soul decides to (or graduates to) remain purely spirit?

Remaining in pure spirit is a choice made on the other side. There are those souls who do so, preferring to remain to welcome and to teach and to communicate as we do as guides. Stages and processes and passages of time determine who is what and where, and the why is determined by each.

I'd like to talk about our transition between all of these lifetimes that our soul experiences.

My dad had a near-death experience many years ago. He described floating at the ceiling of the room and looking down on his limp body in the hospital bed. He then said that a tunnel opened above, and it had walls of gaseous grey clouds that were slowly turning like a vortex. At the end of the tunnel, far ahead, he could see a doorway emitting brilliant yellow-white light—an actual doorway.

What is this experience all about? Why a tunnel? Why a doorway at the end?

Each person sees their own version of the way to their heaven. It is not a universal vision except that there is a bright and welcoming light. The doorway, of course, is a universal recognition of an option, another dimension behind the door perhaps, and if you choose to open the door, another place to be.

Oh, so these are symbols, compelling for each person and for all. And, what is "the light" at the end of the tunnel?

The light is the welcoming arms of those loved ones who have gone before and are now present to greet them when moving from body into spirit. It is love energy to envelope them while transitioning into spirit.

Your people must recognize that the common denominator in these near-death experiences is that there is another place to be, and that heavenly place, as described by many, is in the light that draws them forward. It is where they will be welcomed and brought into spirit, if they choose to make that journey. If they are not yet ready, they will return to the body but retain the feelings and visions of that magnetic light which is filled with love and acceptance.

That's a peaceful and comforting vision.

Many people live their lives as if getting "*there*" is the goal: the ultimate achievement to arrive in the Afterlife with an unscathed soul and to, at last, relax in that place of eternal rest and peace. As if holding their breath for the finish line, many believe that "Heaven" is the reward and goal, and the whole point of making it through a grueling physical lifetime. Yet, if it were indeed a *choice* to return to physical, why wouldn't every soul choose to stay in spirit form in the Spirit World?

It is the message of much organized religion that life is to be lived in excruciating purity in order to enter the gates of heaven, or known by other names—the final reward. It is the journey that is as important, if not more, and to be considered its own reward.

To remain, between incarnations, in spirit form is to deny the continuation of life with family and friend groupings chosen to re-enter for purposes of completing cycles of transformation within those groups. Continuation and finalization is important, returning to teach and to learn through a choice of parents and family groups is what many long for. To learn what more can be gained through human form that can contribute to the overall wellbeing of humankind, it spreads beyond small family thinking and toward global change.

It is our wish that your people understand that they have unlimited potential on your world stage. We do not see this as a widely understood innate ability and it is our wish to inform now that to each there is a season, a reason, and a lifetime to become what is in each heart.

We have *unlimited* potential in our world? Through your last passage, I'm getting the impression that the physical dimension is not a test or penance or a hardship—as some might think—but rather, it's an opportunity and a sought-after adventure and the "stage" where growth and spiritual evolution plays out.

While we are in-between lifetimes, are we fully empowered in our potential before we re-enter the next physical incarnation? And if so, when and why do we forget that we have unlimited potential?

Not always—there is healing to be done, as stated above.

Unlimited potential and the having of it—is it forgotten or is it not instilled in children as they grow? And for some it is denied or scoffed at or simply not supported by parents as an option. For those downtrodden *themselves* it often is not a concept that their children can overtake their accomplishments and proceed through life with a positive attitude while accomplishing their goals.

There is a choice of parents that will or will not support the spirit in its relocation into a lifetime and the level of challenge it will encounter in trying for heightened wellbeing. It is a crapshoot at times, and at others, well planned.

Well, well: I am surprised to hear that a soul's next lifetime can be a "crapshoot" and not always well planned. I mean, come on, a soul can be in an Earth lifetime for many decades; wouldn't anyone want to plan such an adventure (at the very least to plan out the inborn circumstances that will aid the soul's purpose and spiritual evolution)? Why are some lifetimes given less planning consideration?

You must understand this is entirely dependent upon that soul's choice. Lifetimes are determined to provide opportunity to teach and to learn as well as to reconnect with known relatives for continuation of a journey. This is one factor, another is to arrive as soon as possible to jump in once again to Planet Earth and join a movement, such as climate change, with the intent to make a difference and improvement. The chosen parents or family is not the key ingredient in the decision, and as a result could go either way in terms of support. Understand that differing motivations result in differing pathways—it is the way of it.

Do souls ever choose to return in the next lifetime to a different planet and peoples other than Earth?

An interesting consideration this is. Our suggestion is that souls may return to Planet Earth civilization or remain in spirit for brief or long periods of time. To decide to shoot away to another unknown life journey is not the way.

We do not say this will continue as the norm as changes in Earth people's lifestyles come, as interstellar travel by Earth people becomes regular, and as what is to be found is found and changes the way of your living; all things are changeable.

What is to be found is the ability to relocate and travel and these options are presented as available to those open to this change and challenge. It will form a part of the journey to the next age of your people.

Pax, if we didn't have stress, guilt, regret energy, and environmental pollution, how long could the human body last? How long do we have the *potential* to live?

Think of clean air and water, clean food and clean thinking and living without angst? A century or more would be quite *average* without the body growing unwell. This time may come again. It is a far journey, however, from present day world situations to a place of purity and longevity. All is possible—you should begin the journey. Trust in yourselves to know the way.

May you please give us a succinct sentence or two of what life is like in the Spirit realm for those souls who have crossed over?

Loving, learning, teaching, support, growth, return, release, joy, welcoming, progress toward the next journey. Love is the over-riding sense of being in this place on the journey: a jumping-off point for the next lessons.

I have so many questions for you. Like—where do our pets go when they die?

Your Earth people have an understanding that the Rainbow Bridge is the place of gathering their souls while they await the arrival of their earthly guardians when they pass over.

Personally, I'd rather think that my sweet kitty, Sabrina, who died at twenty-three-years-old would come back as another pet in my life. I don't like the idea of her waiting for me, especially if my soul decided to rather expeditiously come right back to physicality. Is there another scenario of our pets reincarnating and living again in our current lifetime?

Be aware that this time at the Rainbow Bridge is filled with happiness and play, enjoyment of youthful activities.

Your choice to return quickly or not is not a major concern as there is no linear time to be felt and when you realize this it changes all.

In the blink of an eye many lifetimes on Earth have come and gone while the pets play on.

Does the animal soul *evolve* through lifetime incarnations as people do?

This is a question not often addressed, and it is the case that it can be.

Do we make agreements with our pets as to how our souls will journey together?

That you may journey again together is a choice, an agreement that may be fulfilled with a meeting elsewhere in time of spirits.

Where do other animals such as farmed animals go when they die?

There is a need for peace and harmony for them, as some have not enjoyed that in life, and this is a consideration as their final chapter on the Earth plane.

Do farmed animals of any kind reincarnate?

It is based on a willingness of that animal and does not seem to be the norm, as stated above.

Let's say that it is their final chapter as a cow or a chicken, for instance: where does that soul go after physical death? Do they get to now enjoy the peace and love of the Spirit World?

In the pastures of peace, indeed.

The term "Spirit Animal" has been used by First Nations and indigenous people to indicate that they feel a connection to and bolster energy or powers from a certain animal or species of wildlife. Is there such thing as a Spirit Animal and is there a sharing of strength, traits, or powers between a Spirit Animal and a person?

Most certainly and it is recorded in the history of your people. It is the spirit of the animal that holds the strength, the power, and results in many people trying to emulate the powers of their chosen animal spirit. To do so brings enhanced abilities both physical and spiritual.

Chapter Fourteen
Tap Your Cell Memory

$\mathcal{P}$ax, we have much to explore in understanding our innate abilities. To go deeper, may you please explain cell memory?

While the mind gives many signs and signals also, it is the Higher Self involvement of the soul memory that brings knowledge, information, and guidance in nanoseconds and tiny particles that combine to form a picture of what is to be, in feeling or knowing or vision—either way it is a protection to be acknowledged.

I'd like to understand the "tiny particles" that you speak of in this context.

Oh yes, this is the information highway of the Higher Self advising the self, the body, and the mind of information needed to proceed in safety. It is the knowingness that comes with experience and memory—cell memory. It is to be recognized as such and acknowledged and attention paid, as it is the early warning system in operation.

Not all benefit from this Oversoul of care—to be blessed by your knowing of its presence—for your well-being and protection.

What is the "Oversoul"?

We have said that this Oversoul is your Higher Self consciousness sum total of past lifetime experiences on which to draw for current day information needs. Your link to this wisdom is within you, of course, and is accessed through your inner wisdom search engines (this is to resonate with the youth) and with your asking to connect.

You have the wisdom of the ages coursing through you, in your soul, which has traveled with you through many lifetimes and carries the wisdom and experiences of all of your lifetimes. Through accessing your memory banks, you can learn and grow and understand, and grow into the wise individual you have the power to be.

To not acknowledge these cell memories that affect your lives in positive and negative ways is to disallow the growth from knowledge of what has gone before; who and where you have been and the strengths and challenges you bring to your current lifetime. These are to grow with and understand they will elevate you to the place of understanding your lessons in this Earth school, this time around.

To recognize the lessons is step one, to follow your plotted course of learning is next, and to be open to following this path guarantees the process is to flow well for you. Remain open and watch for the signposts along the way. The rainbow brings the opening of the gate and the clouds will line the trail.

You have a golden highway on which to travel from your place of asking to your place of touching down in the knowledge/energy storage vault. Anyone can access this place within their Higher Self—it is there and awaits.

Is "the rainbow brings the opening of the gate" mere beautiful imagery or is this a real thing that you can tell me about?

We say the "rainbow" represents increased awareness and trust in oneself.

As in your world, a rainbow is reportedly to show the place of a pot of gold at its end, this we say identifies the time and place of growth in spirituality to the extent that it can be equated to finding gold.

Clouds lining the trail represent a tangible feel of walls defining the path for each of you, and their somewhat solid composition ensures you do not step off your path when you recognize the difference between the positive of the rainbow and the potential of negative in the clouds. Roadmaps they are, and quite recognizable for their guidance we say.

Very nice—thank you.

Are there a finite number of souls in the Universe and those souls just keep getting reincarnated? Or, are brand new souls created? And if so, from where do brand new souls come? And, if new souls are created, does it follow that some souls cease to exist, or is creation just a matter of more and more, such as exponential growth? (*Whew!*)

Ah well now, this is the question of the ages and those souls continuing to travel through the ages are the dear ones to us. As experience and knowledge grows and is shared, the wonder of it all expands and grows also. There are new beginnings and there are endings, and each has its place. As a soul's journey completes there is a diminishing number and as a new sprouting comes there is an increase. How does the new soul sprout, you ask? It is *seeded* and occupies a place for which it is destined. The seeding is the wisdom of the ages presenting the next step in a journey for worlds involved and people involved and becomes a new beginning from which grows progress and continued evolution of the process.

We have a long-standing philosophy that says that energy cannot be created or destroyed. Given that souls have "beginnings" and "endings", it would seem to me that energy is indeed created, and energy is indeed destroyed. What do you say?

Energy is shifted and warped and stretched and twisted and expanded and contracted and occasionally hidden, although it remains a presence. There is never only one way in the Universe. It dissipates and flares and becomes all-encompassing while diminishing to a candle flame—it will not be defined as one way.

What is causing the Universe to *exponentially* expand—more and more and faster and faster in its expansion?

Energy: internal and planetary at the core, energy. This continues movement as it shows itself and will continue as the fire within the core of your planet continues to burn. This creates energy which must be accommodated, and as you magnify the core of your planet by the number of others in existence, the energy must go somewhere, yes? To occupy the existing space was the idea, and as growth reaches the edges of that space, something must change, or catastrophic ends come to what is within. To pre-empt that, space expands to match. There is an expression about "expanding to fill the available space." Where you think that came from?

You are saying that the creation of more energy causes the Universe to expand. Therefore, energy *can* most definitely be created, and it is. This is extraordinary information, especially since our scientists do not know why the Universe is exponentially expanding. It expands from within all areas (not only from the point called the Big Bang). In fact, the outer reaches of the Universe expand even more rapidly than sectors of galaxies that are already fully developed—which makes sense with what you're telling us because expansion occurs as new creation happens.

To be sure, is this recap accurate?

Indeed, it is accurate—would we tell you a story?

There is much to know and grow within your science, and we contemplate the outer edges of reality as the place where some seekers like to spend time. Others who look for basic and intellectually understandable and provable theories are missing the opportunity to step out of their comfort zones and explore the ethers—herein lie the answers.

Out of our comfort zone and into the ethers: I like that. It is curious for most that our cells hold the memories of all of our past lifetimes and the wisdom of the ages. Being that we're speaking about memory, is it just the cells of our *brain* that hold this "cell memory"?

Oh ho, not so we say. The repository for cell memory is *all* cells.

How can we access this cell memory, and, well, *remember* it?

This is not the way of it to remember all as it would be detrimental given there are negative as well as positive cell memories.

As the need arises to remember reasons why an emotional challenge, for example, needs understanding, it is accomplished through accessing one's Higher Self in going within. Some meditate, some use other means, but accessing one's inner wisdom and knowing is the way.

If the "coding" of all memory is held *in our cells*—as opposed to in our minds—then is it possible for scientists to find this memory-content within our cells: to see this movie of soul memories and wisdom? Basically, can it be measured or found by science?

As long as science remains far removed from spirituality there is little likelihood of this meeting. There is no measurement available now for this esoteric substance.

All right, all of our cells hold all of the memories of all of our past lifetimes. This is quite a library of wisdom for those who learn to access it.

Does our cell memory also contain wisdom that might benefit us in terms of healthcare and the possibility of new medical exploration?

As you know, a salamander can grow a new tail when needed, as the body remembers what was there before and recreates it. Isn't that a thought that can bring science to a place of growing new organs and limbs on the human body, as needed? Science is, in fact, addressing this need now, and in laboratories around the globe are fascinating discoveries being made on how to sequence nerves to instruct the body to do the very thing: grow a new arm or leg, finger or liver.

It is a matter of time only.

I am against testing on animals, and so may you please explain a method that we can use for experimentation to make this discovery *without* using animals?

In your now the "need" for answers for humanity precludes the wish to not include animal testing.

Pax, I'm empowered in my purpose and one of my roles is as a vocal protector of animals, and so I feel that I can say to you that I cannot accept that answer; not even from you. The reason is that many humans are so selfish and devolved in consciousness that they test on animals in the most torturous and heinous ways. This statement from you (without crystal clear clarification) can be misinterpreted by the many who have no respect for the lives and pain of animals, and who would only use such medical miracles to monetize a product or process while having zero concern for animal suffering. Please keep in mind that, upon hearing this information, some humans would proceed to cut off the arm of a fully conscious chimpanzee, cat, or dog just to see if it grows back, and then they would study the tortured animal to determine why the limb didn't regenerate.

It is time to think outside the box in terms of experimenting— if it breathes, it should not be subjected to laboratory testing.

I'm glad you made that clear. Can we find an alternate suggestion then, please?

Here's one: I live in southern Florida. I see salamanders every day and they're not hard to catch (ask our cats, Max and Andy, who find lizards daily while playing in our screened lanai) and yes, if the salamander loses its tail, it can

break free and carry on with its life, unharmed. Can our scientists catch only salamander tails and then release the animal to freedom? Would that be sufficient to test on? Or, can you gift us with the knowledge of a future method?

In medical science today there is a diminishing appetite for animals in labs. There are other ways being defined now with DNA sharing and 3D printing and you know science has these means to adapt.

Three-dimensional printing? This is a mind-expanding moment for me. Are you saying that an organ, body part, or an entire body model can be 3D printed, and if so, that truly efficacious medical testing can be done on a dummy-human?

Indeed, this is the case and underway in your science. While it appears now that this is in the initial stages, behind the scenes are experiments on the printing side of development which are awe inspiring and bring your Earth people close to the ways of your off-planet cousins. They, of course, can clone and recreate a body almost at will—it is old school there. You have far to go on this journey, Caterpillar. (But yours is the right track).

That the world needs to take a few turns before much more is unveiled is a good thing—we think those who read these words and are involved will understand their need to rise above greed and corruption and protect these developments for the betterment of mankind, both physically and philosophically. We leave this discussion for your consideration.

We marvel at the tenacity of your scientists to find the way, as they will, and integrity must be top of mind here as this is serious business, this "cloning" of humans, which is to come in a mainstream manner.

At this time, making a salamander tail or a human organ is a given. So much more to come to benefit mankind—we should like to see that the developments soon to be unveiled are intended as a benefit and not to monetize a finding of science.

Well, yes, as I'm sure a new human organ would fetch quite a price from those who can afford it.

And, I can't let your mention of *alien* cloning slip by. I'd like to better understand the concept of cloning and see if we can share some moral guidelines, if you will. When ETs clone a body to harvest new body organs and parts, would the clone not have a soul of its own?

A reminder that the cloning of a body is not for the purpose of harvesting organs—there is no need for this as organs are created at will and require no bodily host.

It is the case that pieces and parts are made as needed and there isn't a container with soul involved. It's much more simple and not philosophical in nature that this practice exists. It has become the norm in advanced society where advances are such that your worldly practices appear primitive.

There is no moral component, as you ask; it is a matter of repair and replacement parts, much like your automobiles. That is all.

Then, if organs and parts can grow back, what is the use of the cloning of an alien being?

Cloning is for particular purposes involving new models, much like your automobiles where updated features are researched and then developed. There is always a purpose.

Like what? What's an example of a purpose for cloning?

A purpose would be to introduce a feature allowing for developments aimed at the greater good for all. Off-planet ideas and ideals and the continuation of community in the big picture—there are reasons which in time will be known.

Chapter Fifteen
The Power Within

$\mathcal{M}$any years ago, I watched a movie called *The Power of One* (1992). It's a film about a boy in South Africa who positively changed the life of an entire village. Like the title of the movie suggests, the message was that one person can make a difference, and this ideal made an impression on me from a young age.

As a result of practicing my impact and the power of my intentions, I do believe that I can make a different in the world, and that each and every person can do so, too: we just have to have the intention, and then act.

We are here with you today, Penelope, for those people who need a nudge in the direction of understanding their own abilities and acting upon the knowledge that they are powerful—if they believe they are—and able to accomplish all that they dream of.

We have seen the best and now we see the worst on your Earth plane. We have witnessed, we have listened to excuses, and we have failed to see attitude change among those in power and in charge. It is those at the upper echelons of power in business, in industry, in government, who contribute the most in damage, while the masses who contribute the least feel disempowered to make improvement. We share how to change that balance, make those responsible, accountable, and empower the average person to hold them to account.

The ability for mankind to speak about their opinions and act on their inner strengths and beliefs is lacking in much of your population. We see that guidance is needed for those in need to find their way to their own personal power. There is much to consider for people on this journey to self and Self, and we say the first step is in sharing the knowing that each person has a Higher Self to access.

In living the creation of your own reality, you each contribute to overall change in the world. The shift of energy from negative to positive moves the balance, and change occurs. It is the way of the past and the way and hope for the future.

To all who share curiosity of yesterday, today, and tomorrow, they will find answers and more questions within these pages. To question more rather than to adopt what has been put in front of you as fact—this is the impact. To consider options and alternatives and not be accepting of all you are told without a query—we do not preach but rather we invite deeper exploration of fact.

To study this book, page by page, is the way as a quick read does not seem possible. To study this content becomes then a study of philosophy and physics, of metaphysics and religion, of astronomy and self-help, and further, the study of empowerment which enables all else. This is our greatest wish that your world's people become empowered and strong and take on the planetary repair now in desperate need of leadership. Do unto Earth; it's not too late, but we ask your people to "*get on with it.*"

We have much still to learn. Let's continue our talk.

We should like to point again to the wise ones of past times who circled their people and taught lessons of conscience and caring and working together to keep all people healthy and fed and educated.

We wish to say that moving ahead we speak of the need to think differently and act differently toward one another and your planet. When you understand this need, improvement comes.

What does it take, Pax, for people to understand this?

In order to reach the change needed to save Planet Earth, each inhabitant needs to be that change, yes? Be the change you want to see.

It is their journey to self that is needed, and specifically the journey to Higher Self. For most, they do not understand the difference and we are in place to show the way to put feet on the path to wellness of Self, and self. This is the lesson now for your people.

We speak of greening the planet and clearing pollution, but until your people have cleared their own clouds and purified their own thinking and living, they aren't likely to look further afield to do good.

We shall begin within, then work to with-out. Yes?

Yes.

We are here to show the way of change for Earth people, to revert to their history and their peaceful ways as taught once, and through this to find their way back on their journey to Self; the Higher Self. For Earth people to understand the difference between self and Self, their Higher Self, is a step toward understanding there is more to them and their daily lives than they imagined and brings the curiosity and need to learn more and grow more into what each can be. On this path comes wisdom and awareness of what is and what can and should be in life on Earth—this is our direction at this time.

Many people today feel disempowered to make change or to "be the change".

Yes, we say the attitude of, "Well, I can't make a difference," must stop.

It is for everyone to understand they can make a difference and it is up to them to act on this belief and share this belief with others who may be in doubt. Whatever the situation in the world where people are trying to be their best and do their best, it must be remembered that each person can make a difference.

When grouped together, of course, the crowd power takes on its own capabilities and much can be accomplished. Realize that the first few steps are the hardest and when they are taken, the snowball effect comes into play and the power of the people is felt.

Be aware that the power of the people begins with the power of one.

To clarify for our reader as we begin to talk about empowerment, what's the difference between *empowerment* **and the** *Higher Self?*

One keeps feet on floor, and one is a journey to inner wisdom—not even close.

Okay, good. We'll get to Higher Self; let's look first at empowerment.

The word empowerment indicates the empowering of a person, an inner strengthening and emboldening which enables that person to live their life to its best and attract that which serves him to his highest and best good.

This is a popular topic for us, especially now. Many people want to live their best lives and practice self-confidence— they want to know that they have a voice and something to say, and, most importantly, that they have the courage to use their voice, speak their truth, and follow it up with action.

Pax, because you are talking about empowerment in a book titled *Do Unto Earth*, I have a feeling that our empowerment has a much bigger purpose than what we currently understand in terms of its usefulness for our best-life or personal motivation.

What could be our future outlook if the majority of our world population got this message and became truly empowered?

The peace that comes to the globe is palpable and brings with it another type of world and lifestyle. Greed and corruption are things of the past. Errors in judgment are made in small ways that are corrected quietly and peace in the heart spreads to peace in the Universe.

When people look back on your civilization and on the wars and skirmishes and non-war conflicts around the globe, they will shake their heads and wonder how archaic that was and how people of this time could be so narrow-thinking and acting.

Narrow thinking will be our legacy; that is a shame.

Now you think world peace is a silly thing to think could actually be; not so. Remember to move in the direction of understanding that world peace will be. Feel it, it's palpable. Act like you are already there. Feel the feeling and spread the feeling and each do your part to bring peace into your lives and your environment.

I'd like to get your opinion on some debatable subject matter because it pertains to the images and awareness of world issues that we take into our minds and consciousness. I'll give you an example: I became a vocal activist for animal welfare because I faced the reality of issues that are very hard to see and to know. My belief is that if animals have to go through such torturous lives and deaths, then at the very least, I will allow myself to know the truth of what is happening at the request and demand of humankind's whims and appetites. (Think of the fur industry where frightened foxes and tender chinchillas are electrocuted. Or, the way in which alligators are staked and skinned—often while still alive—because cutting their throats damages the valuable skin used for boots and handbags. Or, think of the wholesale slaughter of twenty-three million animals per day that occurs on our planet just for food; a number that has greatly increased in the wealthier countries in recent years.)

When I became aware of these horrific truths, I became an activist and a voice for animals. This also naturally led me on a path to become an environmentalist and it helped prepare me for my part in the mission that we share. This awareness has formed my life's purpose in ways and depths.

On the flip side of all of that is the advice by some that one should not expose one's self to such "negativities", and that our goal should be to only envision and hold the images of what we want the world to be. For example, we should only hold positive thoughts and not seek to know those compartmentalized portions of life and the ways in which

we get our consumer goods. While I believe in the practice of envisioning and focusing on the good, with tunnel
vision we would have no environmentalists, humanitarians,
or world-changers of any kind.

May you please speak to this and help to unpack our
social/moral responsibility? And may you also speak to the
beauty in living a life in purpose and on-purpose—if only
we are aware and awake in the world?

Each person is empowered to change themselves and their
world, some locally and some globally. Those temperamentally
unsuited to strife and activism in person, many choose to write
their concerns while others are suited to crowd speaking and
crusading. Each has value.

In order to change what is felt unjust, one must know it; so
burying head in sand does not contribute well. Awareness is one
thing and moving forward with change while protecting one's
self from inner hurt is possible. There can be crusading without
immersing one's self in a scenario—levels of involvement exist,
and each must choose theirs.

Knowledge is power.

In discussing empowerment, perhaps we should consider
how dependency can be disempowering. For instance, receiving
too much help and becoming dependent on outside resources
dampens one's ability to know their potential and true power.

Would you concur and do you have wisdom to add on
to this thought?

Of course it follows and the study of finding one's inner
strengths has been much discussed.

As we have stated, all begins with believing the self is worthy,
and knowledge of self in terms of wishes and wants and strengths

and leanings and cravings as well as fears and phobias and disbe-lief and unwillingness to consider certain ideas are fence-posts along the pathway to inner strength or weakness. Each has the ability to choose.

Free will is limited only by self and the associated lack of trust in self.

No lack of self-empowerment should exist, but it does, and this reduces the availability of perceived choice.

All is possible when *trust in self* is in place.

Having touched on dependency, these lessons of trust in self and empowerment lead me to mention independency. I would like to point out that we are in an interesting time where many people are getting married much later in life as compared to generations past, and some don't get married at all, instead choosing to devote their time and passion to careers or purpose pursuits. What are your thoughts on this and is it okay to focus on our own spiritual development, talents, and passion-pursuits as a fully involved dedication?

You will not lead you wrong.

We are here to say that the nesting-syndrome practiced by many of your world will come to an end. There is to be a large event, taking place in the northern hemisphere, which will alle-viate the need for this, and the many will change their habits.

Oh, do tell. What is this large event; this metamorphosis in the northern hemisphere?

What we see is single people and lots of them. We see profes-sionals who have opted to remain true to their professions and their self-study and growth internally, and not combine their lives with partners and/or families and children. The new age of strong and single professionals begins now with the feeling that there is much work to do globally. The need to focus on it is too intense to share oneself with a relationship called marriage and the resulting offspring which take the focus away from world repair and interplanetary travel.

Follow your heart if you are one who has been feeling this pull and you will find your passion. This is key: passion and destiny come together most often and it is for you to recognize this and allow it into your lifestyle.

The best of the best comes from each person when they leave room in their lives for their light to shine brightly from within. This light is ignited when one does what one is put on Mother Earth to do: to create, to bring their gifts and talents to the forefront and shine their light onto the world. Think of it: your light can shine so brilliantly it will illuminate the world. So, recognize this and allow it to rise brightly and be the halo around yourself and your gifts to the world.

Of course, we both know that individuals can successfully follow their passions and purpose whether single, married, or married with children, but I get your point: people are feeling freer than ever to make that choice for themselves and to choose time and space to live their deep purpose.

We are here to speak with you now on the state of affairs in your world as it applies to self-preservation and self-motivation and self-empowerment: all very important topics to the people of your time. Now it is for you to realize that there is much work to be done on your planet and that all of these are needed by your people in order to begin and continue and complete the work necessary to ensure successful preservation of your lifestyle and your people.

You're not messing around here, are you Pax?
Empowerment should be much more than a genre of books, workshops, and seminars; it should be a collective philosophy. It should also be something we teach our children and should be as commonplace as learning about the alphabet, reading, mathematics, and walking and talking for that matter. Do you agree?

We say the reality of your need today to rise above what people consider their personal glass ceilings and break through by way of developing trust in personal power. This is the way of it.

It is for us to point out that while many have been raised in the belief that they can accomplish what they set their minds to, a great many have not, and further to that have been schooled in the belief that they should not aim too high. This is no way to instruct a child in the belief in Self. For those who don't subscribe to this philosophy, rather they believe that the sky is not even the limit, the stars and moon are theirs and more.

The likelihood that children born in your world today will live in another solar system or on another planet is to be considered. We have discussed that at your present rate of planetary destruction, you should be thinking of alternatives to call home. Given that this is the case, it is necessary to consider personal power and focus on its development within as a topic of study in school. We don't believe it receives sufficient focus.

Structurally, the school systems are in trouble, as is the human race: too much emphasis in the wrong places. Come on people, wake up and smell the failure of your systems.

As your children in school are taught reading, writing, and arithmetic, or variations on those to suit the times, these children must be taught belief in themselves, trust in their own abilities, and understanding that personal differences are to be explored and enjoyed, not treated as a reason to mock or exclude on the basis of color or economic status, dress, or language. Inclusivity and mining the depths of knowledge of each culture and language is the way to grow these children into trusting and self-empowered adults who view differences as strengths and interesting ideas to consider. *United Nations* of individuals as children are found in schools and their differences should be celebrated while drawing wisdom from the history of each culture. It is through this amalgamation of cultures that the cream raises to the top and the working together of all for the highest purpose becomes reality.

It is good that children are taught academics and sports and music, but please don't forget personal development, personal power, trust and belief in self, expanding consciousness, and those studies that instill in the young that they have unlimited capabilities and should know their imaginations can take them anywhere they want to go.

Pax, as we seek to evolve, where do we go from here?

We suggest that moving ahead with empowerment now is a good thing as most humanity lacks the strength of purpose required to become speakers for the planet at this time. We also wish to speak more on collective consciousness and the harnessing of that. While Universal Consciousness should also become a topic, it is the collective consciousness that helps people understand they do not stand alone in a protest.

Let's look at them both. This term might be self-explanatory, yet what do you wish to share about "collective consciousness"?

When we refer to collective or collected consciousness, it is to describe the critical mass of those who, when combining their thought powers to make a change, can do so with relative ease. It is the empowerment of these individuals to know that when they place their intention on an outcome, and together send their energies to that end, magic happens and, as we say, mountains may move.

It is power of the people in their unification behind a need and a creation of desired outcome. There is major change that can be made when group consciousness works to bend the spoons of what they see as wrong. This is a metaphor for the ability to send their energy, for good, and create the best possible outcome as intended.

What is Universal Consciousness and how can we access it?

This is Source energy, the Universal mind, the wisdom of the ages—all there to be accessed. Much like our wisdom and energy, as we have stated, it is there for the enlightened and anyone can access it. We channel together here and now, but others may also reach up to the Universal energy for their own learning. We do not restrict our wisdom nor does the Universal Consciousness restrict access to those seeking. It is the reason for being, to share, to be the resource and to carry the records of all that was and all that is, making this knowledge available in love to those who go within themselves in contemplation or meditation and seek to receive.

Excellent—consciousness is a resource pool that we can tap into for wisdom and empowerment.

Does consciousness have a tipping point, so to speak, whereby if x-number of people were to hold a belief/knowingness, then that wisdom or idea is virally spread through collective consciousness?

If tipping point means that it takes a specific number to activate the collective consciousness, then not so. The power of one is magnified by as many as are present and grows from there. Small beginnings may result in a growing of an idea and growing of the manifestations of these small ideas into global change. Never underestimate the power of one voice.

You said: "We also wish to speak more on collective consciousness and the harnessing of that." Let's be sure to cover the harnessing part. How is collective consciousness harnessed?

Well, it is the case that it is the power of collected consciousness that is harnessed. When masses put their thoughts and minds onto a topic, combined with an intention, proverbial mountains may be moved. It is the raising of that energy to a level where the blending becomes the power and the holding of that energy in a place of intention for a common outcome gives it the teeth, the power, and the ability to make change. It is the way and it is too often overlooked by your people. Everyone has personal power and if it is magnified by themselves times the many others in the collective, amazing outcomes are created.

I'm now more accurately understanding what empowerment is and just how powerful and important it is. Our empowerment as individuals is our confidence in the idea that we can create change as individuals and that many empowered individuals together are power.

If you can dream it, you can do it, or it can be done.

Chapter Sixteen
Clearing Clouds (In Self and the World)

*I*n earlier conversations, you've tipped us off to the need for us to clear our own clouds before we can rise to our Higher Selves and/or affect greater change in the world around us. What exactly is clearing the clouds in self?

This is where the trust comes in. Just go toward it (your inner voice and higher calling) and do not listen to detractors who can dilute enthusiasm and change the course of one's feet along the pathway.

Who are the detractors who can dilute enthusiasm?

Family is often the strongest detractor for people who hear a higher calling. If it is not traditional it is not respected in many circles. Hogwash. Do not listen to this—if the world leaders who are untraditional—scientists, composers, and artists—listened to this drivel, where would your world be today?

Yes, this is true about the undermining of our dreams by one's own family, but *why* is this the case when family should be one's greatest supporters?

Unlike friends, family members will feel entitled to control the path of one of their own. If it does not meet with their approval or prescribed philosophy, it will be contradicted, and attempts made to change the trajectory.

Friends have more respect and will talk and guide and listen and offer thoughts and opinions, but with love. Not that family doesn't act out of love, it is usually the case but the need for conformity confuses their thinking and actions and results in enmity where there should be understanding: a sadness always.

Interesting, family members might have a need for conformity within the family beliefs and culture: I hadn't looked at it quite this way—this is helpful.

Allow faith in one's self to rule. "I rule" is the mantra. "I rule in my life." "I am number one"— "for if I do not develop myself to my full potential, how can I inspire others, children, family, students, etc. I must learn my full potential and find it." This is what makes a fulfilled person and one who contributes to society in the strongest way possible.

Each personality has their strengths and challenges, and it is for each to recognize this and begin the journey to Self, casting aside doubt and reaching for the stars and moon. Someone said, "Reach for the moon, then if you miss, you'll still land in the stars." We think this appropriate.

Do not be held back emotionally or mentally or physically. Trust in your Self and follow your heart.

As we strive to exercise our voice, to live in conscious creation, to act in bravery, and to trust in our own self and intuition, what else should we allow to drop away as we "clear the clouds" in our thinking as individuals in terms of our personal lives and interpersonal relationships?

Well this is a good thought and to each his own. When a goal is identified, whether it be personal or for the good of all, it will be felt, and anything entering the field of personal power that is detrimental to the achievement of that goal will be known, identified, and deflected.

To not allow in those roadblocks placed there by detractors, is the way. One must understand one's own personal power, trust in it to take them to the finish line and deflect interference where it is felt and seen. Much like a sports game, there are those propelling forward and those defending and blocking the intended goal, and only one will win. You choose which you will be.

We are here to say the time is now to understand that moving ahead in one's lifetime in happiness and abundance is dependent on living up to one's potential in one's heart. When a person does what they love, they love what they do, this makes for a happy and fulfilled life, which attracts abundance to the person as they are functioning at a high-level of vibration and attracting goodness unto themselves. Without all these components in place, when one or more is missing, a person is not fulfilled and therefore not completely happy: in this state there is consternation and an undercurrent of dissatisfaction leading to disharmony in the soul. This frazzles the life cord and causes it to vibrate to a lower-level, bringing disharmony and unhappiness to the person.

The long-term result is the person being unfulfilled and resentful of a life not well-lived, and resentful of others who they perceive are holding them back from their dreams by virtue of expectations placed on them for work, child raising, marriage requirements, geographic location, or other. It is a self-perpetuating situation causing one to spiral downward. Very destructive is this.

You got my attention with "life cord". What is the life cord?

Each of you comes into a lifetime with a plan, a blueprint, an agreement for what you bring and are to learn: this is your life as it is intended. We refer to the life cord as a visual so you can imagine if there is a kink in the cord, or an injury to the cord where it is made thin or burned or cut, that life interrupts and does not go according to divine plan. The plan is the agreement that the soul makes for its evolution through learning in the next lifetime chosen to live. Lessons are to be learned and taught through closeness with the people chosen as parents and family in each incarnation. To disturb this means to begin again in the next lifetime together, *if* this is the chosen life lesson to be learned and healed between them.

Can a person get to a point where the reasons that their soul originally chose another soul with which to journey— for instance a parent(s)—have been fulfilled, and they can now choose to cut off access to the person that continually harmed and sabotaged them? Basically, can there be a time when our soul-business is done with another who hurts us, and is there a best or correct way to officiate such a completion of soul-work, karma, or soul-travel together?

Our surprise at this question is coupled with a sadness for those who continue to accept less than deserved and consider it duty.

It is for your people to know they do not give away their power, and then in that place of being, find their own happiness or productivity.

To divest yourself from that which no longer serves you is the way, whether it be a person in the role of parent, or an old sock if it no longer contributes to your wellness and happiness and inner peace, especially if it does the opposite. If that sock has a hole in it or that parent rejects your being and refuses to accept you for who you are, then in aid of continuing your mental, spiritual, emotional, as well as physical good health, you may cut the cord and release yourself from the constant barrage of criticism and turmoil that contributes to your life. This is hardly a question of being polite or honoring another person: it is protecting your self and rising to the mission and purpose for this, your lifetime.

Why are you and what are you to become and contribute to your world today? Do you have the inner strength to make this journey and fulfill your reason for being? Will you take back your power, your inner strength of your own convictions? Or will you succumb to another's demands and shrink from the purpose you so dearly hold true and wish to commit to? In your vernacular we say it is a no-brainer. We support the truth of following one's heart and trusting in one's self—in this way, you will know the answers to these questions and make the choice that best serves you and your world to which you want to commit your powers.

The decision to sever the tie, cut the cord, is yours to make, each of you, and it is yours to return power to yourself and speak your truth in kindness. There is no one way or right way, there just is the way, and that is to go within to your heart and feel what is to be right for you. That you feel your soul journey together is complete comes from within you.

It may be that it is just this lifetime experience that terminates in a lesson for both sides and the soul journey continues to new lessons in the next time together. To not throw the baby out with the bath water is the way; as one lifetime of conflict is met with lessons, do not consider there is nothing more to be learned. This is a lesson for one needing to take back their power, and a lesson for the parent as well. Which one learns their lesson? Which one grows from it? Time tells all.

Aha! "Clearing clouds" is a practice in our empowerment. This has come full circle—you're good Pax!

It feels right to clear our clouds by speaking our truth in kindness and to take back our power from those who would attempt to undermine or disempower us. It also feels right to keep an open mind as it relates to these ties; perhaps the whole purpose of the relationship is to at last become empowered in one's own Self and to cut, *not the life cord*, but the giving-away of one's empowerment to another's expectations at the cost of the spiritual evolution of both people.

Thank you. This perspective is both freeing and beneficial.

And, I might as well ask about romantic and marital relationships too because there are countless people who feel stuck in unfulfilling or tension-heavy relationships: how does one know when they should continue trying to make it work because they have soul-work to do together, and when should they exit the relationship in order to end the fighting and hurt?

It is the inner voice and inner feeling that tells this story. How does one react to the thought of staying versus leaving? This is the heart feeling and the cell reaction, not the intellectual thought that guides.

When the feeling of trepidation overwhelms the feeling of hopefulness, this is the signal that the end is come for this relationship. That there may be soul-work left to do is not sufficient reason to remain if that seems overwhelming. The soul-work will remain for later in the lifetime or it can be taken on in the next meeting of souls together in another lifetime.

If you agree that we are ready to move on, let's discuss clearing clouds in our world powers, politicians, governments, and industry.

You have said that you would like to speak about industry money supporting politicians and the deregulation and lowering of standards in terms of environmental protection. When industry funds politicians, they do so to sway them to their benefit and monetary gain. What a vicious cycle it is.

As I see it, one solution would be to completely ban political campaign funding, period. Instead, a new system could be instituted where each viable candidate gets the same allotment of funds to promote their message. This would eliminate the potential for such favors returned and the keeping-happy of corporate donors and industry supporters. Do you foresee this as a potential change in our government system, and an effort that the populations should focus our attention on?

Penelope, to the extent that your people have willingness to consider this question, it would be finding approval. However, the reality is inherent: greed and political aspirations overtaking where conscience once was.

I wonder if these individuals can become enlightened and inspired to change, or should it be our goal to unite to

ultimately unseat them because their intentions are not able to evolve as fully as is needed in this generation?

Looking at the controlling powers at the very top of banking and industry, plus the many corrupt politicians in all levels and departments of government, is it "out with the old and in with the new", or should we attempt to raise them up in consciousness to do better?

Unseating them, yes, and do not anticipate this to become reality within this generation. This level of entitlement and control is not easily released. No amount of intention to fill their heads with what is good for mankind and the planet will likely result in contrition to the extent they change their ways. Ultimately, via attrition, they will be replaced, and new beginnings can be undertaken with new thinkers and those who see the big picture for your world renewal.

Yes, I suppose it will take some time to turn over all of the bad apples in the banking industries, government, and corporations.

Pax, you have said that we need to unite and stand up to the powers that be in industry and government, and that you would tell us the "how" and "when" and "why". I think we've covered the "why". Perhaps you can give us a look at the "how" and "when"—is it time to start discussing this here and now?

We do not speak of warring and overthrowing government here: we speak of education and information-sharing and teaching of better ways that do not harm the planet.

I've come to know that war is never what you advise; as you've said, the "peaceful warrior" is the way for peoples and countries to talk through our differences.

As far as the Tetris of our government structures, there is much to discuss. What do you wish to speak to first?

There must be solutions given and alternatives offered for the ways you see that are detrimental to your world. This applies to construction and industrial waste mis-management, fish farming and so many questionable decisions made that line the pockets of some and wreak havoc on resources.

We wish to discuss the ways in which your people have put their own needs above those of others, particularly in the corporate world and, shockingly, government. There is much lining of pockets for personal gain and little lining of food bowls for the poor. This will bring continued negativity and dark clouds to your world and focus must be placed there. There are also to be options given as solutions and direction for change.

It is to be noted that as powerful and corrupt leaders in your countries continue in power, your people have given away their individual power to make a difference for the better. Your citizens are to recognize two situations: one, those in power tend to be corrupt and wishing to build their own riches, and two, your people have given away their own power to reverse this and bring change to industry and government through higher expectations and using their votes in all ways to do so. This is the beginning of change. If you do not give support to a person or thing, it loses power. Act on this for a beginning, then continue to grow your power as change comes.

Advances will be experienced in all areas and it is noticeable that those in the greatest need of self-confidence remain lacking while those not lacking continue to advance. Why is that?

Those lacking confidence don't want to expose their insecurity; it's a symptom of our current era of artificiality.

Admitting that one is in need of a backbone is the first step and then allowing the fullness of time to pave the way for acquiring one, that is the way.

The people of your Earth are at a crossroads now but within just half a generation their new crossroads puts this one in a diminished light: to move ahead in technology or to advance philosophy is a question. As the world of the future splits in two, it becomes apparent that the philosophers are gaining and surpassing the technicians. And this is the way of the future. Advancing on the discoveries between now and then is the way of thinkers and educators who believe that the peace not war stance is desirable. Adhering to this mantra becomes the need for many.

As we understand the need for many to release their former need to conquer and rule other nations, it becomes clear that the laying down of arms and the taking up of books and peace banners is difficult for some and impossible for others.

It is certainly impossible when one is missing a backbone. This is why our self-empowerment is so important, huh?

We ask for those affected to understand that there is great need for this as bullets whiz by and bombs explode, taking young lives along with them. It is unthinkable that this brutality and barbarism should continue. Look to the future and understand that the first rule of peace is: do no harm to others and treat them as you wish to be treated—that old golden rule says it all.

In ancient civilizations was the time of "greatness" revolving around attack and conquer. Some time passed before it became clear that speaking of differences and resolving them amicably, not fighting, is the civilized way of the more highly evolved to reconcile differences.

In some countries there will never be a wide distance between the need to invade and conquer and the actual doing of same. Otherwise, the remainder of the world understands the benefit of speaking and bargaining and understanding the needs of each other and working through turmoil, allowing it to settle into peaceful accord is the highest ability there is, so that all parties are pleased with their lot, this is the gift.

Take no prisoners. Take no arms against others. Take only the wants and needs of others into account when attempting to resolve differences—this is the way for peace to reign and mankind to flourish.

You have been making a very straightforward point, and that is that our government leadership is directly tied to our success in saving our planet and healing our environmental crisis. And yet, your even greater and more profound point is that in order to clear the clouds of government we must first clear our own clouds and activate our individual personal power in addition to acting on our collective responsibility to be empowered. Am I getting this right?

Yes.

What we wish to speak of now is the way in which the greening of your planet must go together with the greening (enlightening) of your Earth's people in that they look toward expanding their vision to include seeing their higher capacity, their higher probability for success when they come from a place of love within themselves, and this is how they treat all people and places and things.

We are here now to discuss the way that your Earth people disinherit their attachment to your Mother Earth. In this attitude they feel no responsibility for her care and feeding. How is it that they can look the other way while casting about plastics and caring little for where it all ends up in your landfills?

Now we draw the parallel between the raising of human consciousness with the resulting improvement in the life and lifestyles of your people. Do you see the need for life and liberty and freedom for all? Do you look at the way countries and cities are not treating people as equals? Where is it written that the mighty and rich may run roughshod over the more hard-pressed for survival and meeker citizens they pass on the roadways? This is not the way to move forward in harmony among your people.

There are places in your countries where people of color have been persecuted, and not popular are people of some religions and people from countries other than those powerful and thinking they are the greatest. This tyranny is to cease, now, and if it does not there will be chaos. Look to world history in the last century alone to show how this comes to be when those who see it do not speak up.

It is a dangerous situation beginning now to repeat.

You are pleading with us to remember the 1940s and earlier political upheavals, aren't you? (The tyranny of the Nazis from that era comes to mind, as does present-day communism in Russia, North Korea, and elsewhere.)

Lifting our hearts and minds to what your people can contribute and how your abilities grow, we share that it will represent two steps forward and one step back, into the future, or even worse if your course of sociopathic leadership in politics is not neutralized.

This is serious.

We wish to bring people to the knowing that they can create peace and harmony in their lives, in their families, in their workplaces, and in your cities and your world if all will think this way.

Like pebbles into the pond creating ripples of peace, these intentions will transmit to the dark places and illuminate what is there for all to see.

Let there be light—be the light—sweep away the darkness.

The Russian government claims that they now have an intercontinental nuclear strike weapon that can travel twenty-seven times the speed of sound. Is this one of those foreboding concerns of our time?

Where is proof and where does the inflated truth run over into the not so truth side of reality? Well now, we say this is a media frenzy and much ado about nothing. There is little truth and no proof and therefore no need to look further.

What science in this country can accomplish is strong and quite influential and impressive, but what this country sets out to do is conquer and vanquish and strong-arm others to the extent that they shoot themselves in the proverbial foot at times for entering into research and development with bad intentions. The Universe does not like this and support for their ongoing success is not there.

Do not wait for the other shoe to drop.

Speaking further on the goal of neutralizing "sociopathic leadership", I'll cut to the chase: which countries are in most urgent need of leadership-from-the-top reform, and why?

One word fits all: corruption. European and Asian countries, South American countries, Russia, China, and who is considered the one to manage and set a good example for all? The USA, which is in perhaps the weakest position of all given the explosive actions of your politicians, again. Allowing the actions to be taken that place all in fear—we question the need and there is no reason for this complacency.

It is a sad situation that portends more sadness to come before the sun rises over the lands and peace reigns. There will be upheavals and overthrows and election losses that make the minds of many hurt for trying to explain and understand the trajectory of current politics on your soil. It is a conundrum—these next many turns of your Earth planet, and when it is making sense once again, it will be well into your future.

We wish to say that your world is in turmoil and chaos now politically. There is to be repercussion and it will be felt as ripples on the water for some time—escalation occurs, and lives are lost.

It is sadness to the Universe, and we speak of ripples on the water—these ripples now extend beyond the galaxy and reinforce the view of your interstellar friends that your planet is set on a course of self-destruction, immolation.

That *is* very sad.

Here in the United States, we have much division between our political parties. Citizens are nearly divided down the middle and both sides have no interest in seeing the other's perspective; both believe that they are in the right. You could say it's a cold civil war.

It is our wish that your people spend more time accessing their own Higher Selves to rewire their ways of being. Too often there are sheep following where there should be rams leading. Those currently leading your world powers are doing not a good job of it. In your soon time will be upheaval and a not pleasant experience for many, but it will result in greater input by the people in the make-up and running of governments.

It is time now to know that the days and decades of sitting back and watching corruption unfold, without defiance from the people, is over. There must be choices made and actions taken to remove from world power those who are leading your people into disarray on the world stage.

The time is now to take your power back, all of you, and stand up for what is right. Reversal of fortunes for those in power and raking in the many big moneys for their own pocket lining—this is underway and must come to the forefront of your news as a happening thing and be stopped.

How do you walk through each day knowing corruption is and corruption spreads and you have no recourse? Of course you do: stand up and say you do, then follow your hearts and move into the next stage of cleanup.

It begins with you.

Sometimes governmental lies and industry corruption can feel overwhelming. You said that change comes as we continue to grow our powers and abilities. What powers will we develop that will turn the imbalance of power from the government and industry giants to the people?

There are now those who understand that change comes— change in the way of implementation of the new order. This means that those who sit back and take from your world will have slim pickings and those who step up and give will be the receivers. Is this as it should be? We think so.

Penelope, the time comes for whose role it is to improve the lives of those around them to be the recipients of improvements and those who diminished their world will be diminished in the eyes and hearts and minds of those who see truth.

Coming soon, *all peoples will see truth and work on instinct*—much more than in recent generations of your civilization. In past civilizations this was the case, but intuition and intuitive action has diminished to the point of extinction almost in the masses. For those with the gift, they know the truth is out there and it soon becomes close to all and visible.

Bringing forward the gifts of telepathic communication improves life and changes life to the degree that it is all but unrecognizable. Think on it: that you can understand the mind and wishes of someone who needs not speak the words. What can be hidden away? The truth *is* out there, out there in the ethers for all to access. That is the meaning, don't you know?

This will separate the wheat from the chaff, as they say.

Going forward in business and politics will be quite a different affair. Think on it: what can be hidden or buried or not discussed? What truth can be avoided and what untruths covered? It is to be the greatest change that your world has seen in a very long time.

Moving into this era will happen quite naturally as a shift continues in your earthlings who are open to their spirituality and their gifts and talents regarding communication: the unspoken variety.

Oh, my goodness, Pax: it's now becoming apparent as to why it is imperative for us to seek our spiritual development and our innate abilities—it's the way to truth, light, and peace.

It happens seamlessly until one day it is observed that lies and untruths are recognized for what they are, and the "wool" can no longer be easily pulled over the proverbial eyes of society. People just become aware that they know or understand things and live their lives more acutely. It is a beautiful thing to see develop.

Those who are slow coming to this place in their lives will understand that time will unfold as it should, and they too will come to a time and place where the ability materializes. There is no specified timeframe for this other than to say that those who are further along on their spiritual paths will recognize it in themselves sooner and be able to counsel others as to its imminent arrival for them.

Wow.
And, what does "doing business" look like in this new era?

Transparency is how it looks. As we have spoken, there is no hiding of thoughts and intentions. Think of this and smile—those who purport to be well-intentioned are seen through the microscope of intuition and transparency and must either change their ways or become a fringe player on the stage of life. Honesty and idealism prevail.

This is revolutionary.

Penelope, this is the time of all times for those who begin to experience this gift, and gift it is.

Clearly, this is the change responsible for much greater future changes in your world as infidelity and greed and fraudulent actions make way for transparency. Think of that.

Our way is to advise you of what is to come, to fortify you for the experience. Positive and more highly evolved behaviors result and the greater steps toward harmony on your planet to be taken—go now and contemplate this change for it is a significant one for your time.

Again, we say look to the past for your future. These civilizations of long ago who routinely communicated this way will show you the way and there are messengers here now, of course, watching and readying for the new age.

It is poised to begin.

We speak of transparency in all, and this comes within a few generations.

As the mindset of your people changes to good and acceptance and love and honesty, so does your means of communication leave the written and spoken word much of the time and become telepathic thought communication.

Allowing for the fact that nothing can be hidden when thoughts are read, clarity and honesty become the norm. Other thoughts that are dark-energy-sourced or nefarious are instantly known as your people have reached a level of intuitiveness meaning nothing is hidden.

It shifts behaviors immensely.

Volume 6

Do Unto Earth
Pax and the Yellow Brick
Message

*"The Earth will not continue to
offer its harvest, except with faithful
stewardship. We cannot say we love
the land and then take steps to destroy
it for use by future generations."*
Pope John Paul II
Head of the Catholic Church
from 1978 to 2005

Chapter Seventeen
Your Mission Should You Choose to Accept It

*L*et's continue on our quest by identifying the important purpose that each generation has at this time in our history, and the ways in which every person can become the power to change the world.

Now that elders have the time and disposable income, many of them, we ask that there be a movement afoot to enlist them in the correction of the Earth's troubles, as they were largely responsible for the creation of same.

Why is it you feel the children are responsible for fixing the problems created by the previous two generations? This is nonsense. We say the children *will* lead the way to repair, but it is those with the money in their jeans who are needed as well to be the team members and leaders in some instances.

What is the role of those in their middle age?

While there are elders and children teaching, too many in the middle are not only not teaching but also not *listening*. This is to be changed. We speak on the why and the how and we have passion for this.

We continue our journey to aid your world population and it is not made easy—not that easy is required but it is a curiosity that what seems obvious to so many is bypassed and ignored by so many more.

All around you are people willing and able to step in and make the difference. Allow them to do so: allow them their rightful place in the solution to the problems they helped to create.

How can we learn from our wise elders?

Listen and learn, it is said. Study who has gone before and the messages shared. It is parents and grandparents with lessons to share that each person can avail themselves of. Be aware of what is gone before and what presents now and match the ways of finding successful conclusion.

We speak of these studies as familial as well as global, and all in between are present and recognizable by seekers.

A global study of the ways of our wise elders—it's a brilliant suggestion.

You regularly mention "seekers" which is especially fitting as we discuss our mission and purpose by generation and as individuals.

Now we ask for you to see the big picture. In the not too distant future will be the epiphany felt by the majority.

What is "the epiphany felt by the majority"?

This revelation is the awareness that your world is collapsing, imploding, and it is human caused. With this epiphany comes the look around for who to fix it and how and it is then your people look to the youth for guidance. It has been in preparation, as have they, and when the two meet there is action and result and the changes needed will begin. With the noticeable improvements comes increased trust and the circle of those becoming part of the solution, grows. This begins, of course, at the top of industry and politics and the removal of those holding power for their own gain. It becomes a good time of shift in energy and action for the good of all.

You have told us about special enlightened souls among us—starseeded souls, though born to human parents—many of whom are still children at this time and their purpose is of planetary healing. How many of these individuals are currently engaged in this mission?

Millions of wise ones to show the way. Greater numbers than these are required to encircle your globe and touch the areas and leaders and people in need of enlightenment. It is ongoing from now forward as it has been from generations past to current day.

They come in with joy and verve and idealism and energy to make the changes they see are needed on your planet. They will not be deterred—they are the leaders for your planet's healing and movement forward into your future. They bring change in their own way, sometimes with more noise and great amounts of righteous indignation—this is an enabler, this feeling, and spurs them on to right action.

They are old souls returning via reincarnation to lead, inform, and educate where there is need in the world: to be the bringers of new thinking and acting and tolerating and reversal of roles between teachers and students, parents and children—an upheaval of the best outcomes. That is, best outcomes if you hear the messages and trust in them to bring change and growth and fundamental light of empowerment to your world. Without this light there is no change, and without change there becomes more darkness for Planet Earth—an intolerable situation—so we advise to listen and learn and be the change you need to see.

Will the adults and powers-that-be listen to the guidance of youth?

The children are idealistic and noisy, loud in a good way to have their voices heard in the energy that they have available. It is now, in your time in history, that youth are given a voice. The reason is that now is the time youth are taking their voices to the streets and any place they will be heard. It is youth taking back their power. It is youth knowing they have a message and equally knowing they deserve to be heard.

The snowball grows in size and power as it rolls down the hill, and this is the manifestation of this group increasing in size and speed and strength to the extent that those in the way step aside and watch the advancing formidable object approach.

Attention is being paid to the advancement of this move-ment—not a snowball, but a tidal wave of youthful voices and intention.

It is power.

When the children are clearly wiser than the parents, it is quite identifiable by parents and teachers and world leaders who often fear them.

We can all recognize this phenomenon and there are now many known leaders among our youth.

To say they live for their missions is correct—they are the conscience of your planet's peoples now and lead in all areas of doing better for your planet's future. They try to lead and do where they make themselves heard, and they teach and live their best lives according to their mission and purpose.

What's your message to all people—all ages, all nationalities and cultures, all spiritual and religious beliefs, all abilities and challenges? We all want fulfillment and joy—what is each individual's mission in this lifetime if they choose to seek and accept it?

We are of the mind that your thinking generations are the oldest and the youngest—with the in-betweens just coasting. Is this the case? If so, we have much work to do to enlighten the middle ground and cause them to enjoy coming up with solutions to the Earth's problems. Meanwhile, we have the message for your people:

Now and into the future will be the greatest change seen yet in the history of your world, at least since the invention of the wheel. With that came the jump forward in technology and thinking and increase in formal education about physics, well somewhat later, but the path was already widening for the many. Curiosity brings development. Curiosity brings ways to make the difference and find solutions. This is what we ask for now in your world—sufficient curiosity about the next stage so that people want to know what comes next, what they can contribute next to the evolution of the species, and how they can each make a difference in their world.

Then "seek and you shall find" would be a good mantra for us. Let's talk about purpose: If we don't quite know our

purpose, you're saying that we can come to it through our curiosities; that through seeking and asking questions we find our path and become our purpose and legacy.

I've spoken to many people who say that they don't know what their life purpose is, yet in the depths of their hearts they do indeed wish to have a defining and important purpose.

Legacies are not just for the few but can be left by many. We say that each parent leaves a legacy in their own way, as does each child and adolescent and then again as an adult. It may not be earth-shaking or memorable for the throngs, but it will have left its mark on the family and friends circle inhabited by that soul spirit person. This is what we speak of. Each of you has the talent and ability to leave a legacy. Perhaps it is for you to determine in what areas you can do this and make the effort.

Moving into larger circles, like the pebble dropped into the pond creating ever-increasing circles of ripple, each of you can enlarge in your circle of influence and your circle of ripple effect and move into greater and greater regions of accomplishment. Do not question this for it is the case.

Knowing the destination is not always possible for Earth people, but understanding and recognizing the *feelings* that pull them toward an unknown destination is of great assistance. There are many times when one does not fully identify their chosen path but just *knows* it is somewhere out there and they can *feel* themselves on the right direction and path toward it.

This is very useful: if we don't know our purpose, we can *feel* our way to it.

How else can we identify our purpose in this lifetime and know that we're on the path of our purpose?

When you work within your areas of passion you develop them to their highest form, and you create your legacy. Find your passion and follow your heart. This is the direction for each of you in your lifetime.

Do not look without for direction; look within. This is where you find your strength and your drive and your zeal and your intuition flaring into higher and higher levels of function.

In the event that you don't think you possess intuition and untapped strength, just think for a time on what it is that would make you happiest in this lifetime. If you could give up all that detracts you from following your true path, what would you identify as your true path? If you could leave all responsibility now and find your truth, what would it be?

It's a pivotal question for anyone: *what would make me the happiest in this lifetime?*

Pax, I understand that you're not suggesting that we leave our responsibilities, but rather to unencumber our *imagination* in order to know our passions and purpose. Please continue.

This is the time to be free and open with yourself and identify your inner fire. And when you've done so, please ensure that you keep an open place for it in your life every day. Allow it the place for air to enter, to fan the flame and allow it to grow brighter and stronger. When this flame is hidden under a bush it is dark and airless and the flame dies. It is your responsibility, each of you, to open to that flame and allow it to blaze, shedding both light and power onto your path to awareness and allowing passion to rise. Only then is it that you experience true fulfillment and joy.

This is your mission in this lifetime: be true to yourself, honor yourself, and find your passion and joy. Not until you do is there peace. Your highest calling will be revealed to you and the rest of the journey is yours to chart. Trust us in that your life will be filled to the brim with peace and harmony and joy when this is your destiny found.

There are many people who are following their greatest passion, and yet it is not bringing them fulfillment. I'd love to help them crack this nut, so I'll give you a specific example and hopefully you can share some wisdom.

Here's the example: the "starving"—or at least struggling—artist.

I used to live in Music City U.S.A. (Nashville, Tennessee, of course) and I know many singers and songwriters who have given up just about everything to follow their dream, and now, after decades of pursuing their big dream, they are financially broke. You'd think that they are extraordinarily happy because they are following their dreams—in fact, they're "all in" on their journey—yet most that I know are not all that happy; they're deeply unsatisfied and still hoping against all odds that they will one day "make it" in their dreams. They want not to struggle anymore and to be able to make a decent living doing what they love, and why shouldn't they want that?

What advice can you give these individuals? And, are they somehow doing something that prevents them from manifesting this peace and joy and the accomplishment of their big dream?

Within each seeker is a level of intention to find their truth and reality and passion. In some it is extinguished regularly and replaced by hope, whereas in others it burns brightly and is impossible to extinguish despite roadblocks in their way.

Oh my—hope is not a dream-maker.

It is the *degree* of intention to succeed that propels a person toward their chosen end, not the intention alone. Many are interspersed with doubt and self-doubt and these eat away at the fabric of strength of conviction.

There will always be degrees of success achieved as well as what is strived for. Many believe they will be happy with C-circuit and others believe B-circuit suits their level of talent and that achievement will be acceptable. Yet others remain convinced that nothing but A-circuit will be their reward and refuse to accept less. It is controlled by the individual, this level of "success", and where is their finish line. Each may reach a level of success they hadn't previously experienced, and yet feel they deserve more while at the same time settling for where they are. This is a mixed message to self and Self.

To each there is an expectation and to each a doubt about their ability or level of talent—*these control the result.*

Doubt is indeed an insidious force.

The popularity of Law of Attraction material which states that like energy is attracted to like energy has many students of metaphysics somewhat worried that to have a doubt-filled day will cause them to repel their dreams and goals. Personally, I believe that energy vibrations are contagious through an osmotic effect and are not just operating on attraction.

Is it possible to simultaneously have great expectations and some doubt and still be successful?

Human nature is that these exist simultaneously.

Doubt not about the success of the plan but whether all components of the plan are *optimal.*

So, doubt is useful at times, for instance as a red flag that helps guide our path away from potholes and wrong turns

on our journey. Yet, I'm still curious if a little doubt is an unequivocal dream-killer or a natural part of the journey. Should we train ourselves to *never* let doubt enter our consciousness as it relates to our inspired purpose?

Doubt is not to be considered always as lack of trust, but often a thought that another way of doing the task may be better. This is not more than considering all aspects of a situation.

To have no doubts is to wear blinders and not consider other ways. If those in science did this, the explorations would cease, and progress stalled. It is good to remain open to options. Some would call this doubt of the original plan; it is not so—it is strength to remain positive and open to receiving alternatives.

Chapter Eighteen
Operation Envision

There is a popular law of attraction philosophy (I think it was introduced, in more recent times that is, by the Abraham-Hicks books which were also channeled Spirit writings) that offers this formula to manifesting your dreams: ask, believe, receive. While many have read these teachings, there are those that still cannot make this formula work.

May you please speak to the essential steps for manifesting goals and dreams?

Set *Intention* that it will be, whatever your *it* is. This is a direct line from wishing to wanting to making it reality. This is not rocket science—everyone can control their own destiny in this manner by using power of intention.

Empowerment is the word and the key to clearing the clouds in your life so that the future you desire becomes visible.

Trust (Believe) In Self is key, for without that there is nothing but hope. Trust in one's own ability brings it from hope to reality, that each person can manifest the good in life that they wish for:

it is a reality and each person can create their own reality. When one travels in faith in self and trust and follows ones' heart, one is on the correct path for themselves at that time and can expect great things to come.

Vision. When one *sees* a higher calling for themselves and trusts that they deserve that and can, if assisted, find their way to that place, they can allow peripheral things to drop away from their daily journey in order to follow their chosen path.

Action is the result of Empowerment and comes after Trust in Self and Vision for the goal. One can take Action and if they "fail"—one can become empowered to understand failure is a part of Action and to be accepted as it comes as a stepping-stone to what will come as success.

Then comes *Focus,* for without this there is no dedication of *Intention* to the task.

It comes full circle. This is excellent, thank you.

I'd like to expand on Trust/Believe. I suspect that our every unit of thought creates what we believe, and so perhaps it is our thoughts that are the power in this step. If so, that makes it a lot easier for us to understand how to believe something that has yet to manifest, because even if we don't yet truly believe it, we can most definitely train ourselves to think the thoughts that support the dream.

What your people "get stuck" on is the Trust in Self portion. This is the derailing of most ideas and intentions—this lack of trust in self to complete the intention. Without this faith and trust in self, no amount of intention will rule.

We often experience a period of waiting in the process of dream creation: waiting for others to make decisions, waiting for the right timing, etc. As we discuss pursuing

our goals and manifesting our dreams, is patience a virtue? Is there a *lesson* in patience, whereby if we have patience, the outcome will be the one that we desire or perhaps even a greater reward? Or, is patience simply required in these instances and so we might as well have it?

Patience with self is the meaning.

There are those who find that if "it" doesn't happen for them immediately, they have failed. No so, all things happen as and when they are intended. To be aware of this and allow what is to become often takes a few turns of the world and it is to be noted that no amount of angst will cause your Earth to rotate faster than She wishes to rotate. Learn what can be changed and what you must change within yourself to accommodate what you cannot change—this becomes wisdom.

The "secret to success" is a catch phrase used by many self-help gurus and it's an elusive quest for many. May you please talk about the secret to success?

We are here to speak of poverty this time: poverty not of money but poverty as it pertains to fulfillment, happiness, peace and all that it takes to make a rewarding life, and how people mistake the important components of a happy life for those that are really superfluous—and, how to know the difference.

"How to know the difference" are indeed the operative words here.

How can someone know their true wealth and what would fulfill them?

That can be answered only by the individual, as the question of what their success looks like is theirs alone. Each has his description, each has their own needs to be met through their personal success, and rarely are two alike.

Within the heart of each person is the Happy Place where their heart sings when involved in their chosen activity, and where they know they are in alignment, completely, with body, soul, and spirit. This is the personal barometer of their level of secret success measures.

What can someone do if they don't love what they do day-in-and-day-out, wish for change, and yet feel hopeless to break out of the cycle?

Oh yes, this is the part where visions play a role and these persons are asked to *visualize* themselves exactly where they want to be, doing just what they want to be doing, and viewing their lives as they would want them to be.

Then it is for them to take steps to understand what they must do to change their situations, slowly and bit by bit, to effect these changes.

For them to understand it is doable is key.

Okay, let's look deeper at visualization. It's a powerful tool for our empowerment, happiness, and the manifestation of our dreams and goals.

We can call it "Operation Envision"—to create the life that we want.

Small steps, one at a time, will result in big changes down the road. It is best to progress in this manner and any target or goal can be reached and accomplished. Yes, it is the case.

At times I have envisioned something with diligence, I completed all of the steps and homework to earn it, and

then it didn't work out or become manifest. In this example, let's make an assumption that the dream was both envisioned and believed to become reality—what was missing or went wrong if the dream wasn't realized?

There is often a missing link which is *Trust*, trust in self and Self *that it is the right end-result.*

You did say that Trust in Self is where we get stuck. To leave it out might be like leaving out yeast in a recipe for bread; you'll make something, but it won't rise.

Although, what you are speaking to here is that sometimes a voice or knowing within us does not trust that a direction is indeed the correct or best course. So, trust in self is imperative to reaching our goals, however, if that trust just cannot be found or conjured, then we might want to revisit the goal. Is this what you're telling us?

Yes, it may also be that this is not to be, despite the emergency of beliefs that it should become reality. Is it the case that the Higher Self may sabotage the dream, as it is not the best possible outcome for the dreamer?

When the window opens to reveal that only another door is presented, it is time for reflection.

This is good advice.

And, is there such a thing as "everything is meant to be" or "it wasn't *meant* to be"—or do we make our own reality and that's that?

Indeed, it is in as much as one tries to make something become reality for them, and if it does not, there is the consideration that the Universe watches and provides what will be the optimal path to that person's future. This is a balance and to be looked upon as so.

While there are transparencies in the field of consciousness creation and personal reality being managed by the individual person, there is also the overarching love and care emanating from the Universe. How often do you exclaim that "the Universe provides" when something went opposite to your wishes yet proved to be the best outcome?

You are to manage the balance between viewing and aiming for your goals yet allowing for deviation when your chosen trajectory proves wrong. Not everything is to be dissected and completely understood.

As you are speaking, I'm realizing that *you* have a vision for us! What is it, dear Divine Wisdom Source?

Moving ahead in time we see that all peoples can learn to manage their lives this way: envision what it is that will serve them best, then take small steps toward that goal. It is not disruptive to themselves or those around them, but it targets the spot where happiness and fulfillment will be found, for all involved. It is the case and can be readily accomplished.

You will see that this spreads like the ripples on the water when the pebble is thrown in—it spreads quietly and envelopes all around it. It encircles those in the center and encircles that rock which finds itself suddenly in a strange place: the middle of the pond. When it was quietly lying beside the pond and someone picked it up and threw it, relocated it without warning, those peaceful ripples spread out and marked its spot—marked that it had arrived in its new place, all around it the welcoming ripples of peace. This is the way of your world, in future.

We ask for all people to visualize the world they want and act accordingly.

Expect the best and it will be.

Finding those who ask for peace but do not practice it, the ripples will be the reminder to practice serenity in their lives, daily. Allow the people their time to come to terms with how this is accomplished. Your world did not deteriorate to this stage overnight, and it will take some time to repair.

Put out the peaceful energies and spread the ripples of serenity throughout your worlds, touching all who are within your range. The ripples return to you in this way.

This is illustrative and lovely.
How do we become our Higher Self?

A journey to one's Higher Self indicates a spiritual journey to the inner strengths and wisdoms held in the soul as experienced and gathered throughout many previous lifetimes, accessible now to help aid and guide that person through this life's challenges.

Sharing that wisdom with those along the way is a value; teaching what is known and has been positively experienced in past lifetimes is a blessing.

Accessing this Higher Self wisdom comes through trust and patience and finding quiet and focus to receive the thoughts and images that come on request during meditation, for example.

Let's talk about meditation and its benefit to Higher Self connection.
Many years ago, one of my spiritual mentors told me that I should meditate every day in order to reach my spiritual goals and carry out my life's purposes. For our readers, what is meditation, why is it helpful, and what's the best way to do it?

To use another term of contemplation, or substitute walking in nature, there are variables to be considered. Meditation in its truest sense is a removal of all outside stimulation while focusing within, focusing on a problem needing solution, focusing on one's inner strength and bringing clarity to a question or a day or a need for cleansing of daily life and seeking purity and inner peace. There is much to be gained.

Many refer to their daily swim or walk in the forest or sitting by the ocean as meditation, and if it brings this level of peace and clarity to them, who is to say it is not. However one finds their peace and clarity, it is their beneficial time and place and can be their way of meditating—the end result may be the same.

If every person were to raise their consciousness to the level of Higher Self, would it be Heaven on Earth?

This is precisely what the consciousness movement on your planet is endeavoring to create. When masses of minds are raised in positive energy and intention, magic happens.

We are here for the purpose of adding to our discussions for your Earth people about their progress toward spirituality and how developing this within themselves enables them greater strength and focus and wealth of attributes.

Ours is to deal with the way of humankind to achieve this and support the way of acceptance and inner strength required to achieve. Our inspiration is based on the support of your Earth people in their rise to self-mastery and empowerment to be their best selves and know that achievement of goals comes from inner strengths.

Chapter Nineteen
The Holy Grail of Empowerment

I've noticed that you're very careful not to have a religion created around you. I appreciate that. And, I feel like you are trying to tell us something that we don't really "get" in most of our religions: you're trying to tell us while we have created deities, that in actuality *we* are the source and *we* are the creator. Is this correct?

Well now, isn't this an interesting philosophical consideration? Are you? Would we say you are not when this would slow your progress to finding your Higher Selves? We would not dash those hopes and desires and *destinies*: you are what you believe you are.

Some of you believe this and act accordingly, while others only follow guidance laid down by organized religions. To explore is good and to question is better, and to do both even more enlightening.

Follow your heart we say, for it will not lead you astray.

We wish to share the word that the path to spiritual wellness and personal power is not such a long or convoluted one, but it takes trust in one's self to undertake the journey. We will facilitate that journey and the carrot on the end of the stick will be the greening of Planet Earth. Most feel badly about the pollution and the poisoning of your planet, and most bypass the route to change because they don't know that they can be a conduit for change themselves.

Do highly evolved souls incarnate at times in order to help advance humanity's spiritual awakening?

Always there have been those advanced in thinking whose mission it is to lead their fellow citizens to better ways: the enlightened ones who wish to circumvent the status quo and make their lives and those of their fellow mankind, better.

This makes me think of Jesus: was Jesus sent to us at that time to help us reset our direction?

And did it work?

I think it worked, although I do wonder if religion is a construct that might not be in alignment with His original intentions.

At that time there was a leader who began as a wise child, teaching the adults the better and higher ways of thinking and being, and Jesus was his name.

Jesus *was* the "religion" he taught and created the following that exists today. He did not think of religion as a thing, it was how one lived, treated others, carried values and moved through life. Jesus had no intention to separate or divide or create a named religion that would do so. His was the gentle way of inclusion and love for all, and this teaching continues today that all are equal in the love of their deity, if it be rock or saint it is not relevant—it is the personal choice of each.

Ahead of his time and not afraid of conflict, he was a leader in the field of giving all for his cause. He left a legacy—the great ones do.

This sounds like it could be an excellent new academic field of study: what is "the field of giving all"?

Do understand that giving all means to make it a life's passion, commitment, and priority, and place nothing in higher importance.

Has Jesus ever reincarnated on Earth before or since the time that we know of Him from some two-thousand-plus-years ago?

This is indeed a good question and yes, Jesus comes back regularly to continue teaching and in many different colors and creeds. His wisdom is designed to enlighten those in need, and is there for the enlightened, also.

The Jesus soul, as it is currently in your world, will continue the task of leading by example—it was and is a simple way of living to show the peaceful way. Those who take note will be touched and this is the way. The purity of existence is shown toward all. Living in this manner is unchanged as the lesson by example.

There are many major and minor religions in the world, and each has a unique figurehead or variant to Christ in the form of a divine messenger or prophet.

Whether he be called by the known name of a religious leader or a political leader or a kingdom ruler, the continual appearance in aid of bringing peace and harmony to your world is the purpose. He or she, as the time dictates, is showing the way to higher power for your people, the purpose does not vary just the container, the body, the appearance of the one sharing the way. It is to continue, as your people have not yet got it right.

We have much work to do as a people, however, what specifically do we still need to get right?

You ask what your Earth people need to "get right". We suggest your racist and divisive ways of living, acting toward one another, warring, greed, polluting your Earth, and destroying nature for profit to name a few are areas needing change. Narcissism is another.

Practice spirituality rather than separation: there is a world of difference between what is and what could be, if only there was such recognition.

That was direct and to the point.
I noticed that you don't use a capital letter when you say "he" in reference to Jesus. Why is this?

Jesus was a carpenter and one gifted with infinite gentleness of nature and wisdom. His was not the intention to become elevated on a pedestal of any making. His wish was to teach the little children, to teach the teachers also, and to sit in temple and speak to those who would hear—this is where he was happy. He went nowhere and met nobody without speaking his truth—it was his way to be and his wish was for those who heard his message to follow in his footsteps, in other words, adopt his gentle way of being.

No such elevated thought of practicalities such as naming a religion after him were entertained: it was not his way, or his goal, or intention, or even within his comfort to have this applied to himself. Not so. He was a messenger and one who walked in purity of intention and action.

He accepted all for themselves and preached and taught his messages as though all were one, which in his heart they were. That there was Jew and Gentile as well as the many other faiths and deities brought across his path in his travels was of interest but not used to determine who was and who was not worthy. It was not the case that he determined those who would go on to peace in the higher realms and those who would not; his was the way of acceptance not division.

It was the wish of Jesus at the time that his disciples would follow him in his teachings and go their way spreading the word. Some did and some did not. Those closest to Jesus were most inspired and kept the faith.

The true intention of Jesus was that people live their best lives in wellness and holiness. It was the way people achieved this that differed. In the time of Jesus was poverty and inability to move beyond it for the many. To share the higher wisdoms and belief in a heavenly place as a reward for those who believed in his word, Jesus brought hope to those whose daily lives were toil and trouble. It was this faith in his teachings among the people that gave them a belief in reward in the heavenly place of rest coming to them for lives well-lived.

(Postscript: I will continue to capitalize pronouns when speaking of Jesus. The quest for self-empowerment, while critical to enlightenment, can peacefully co-exist with each person's religious beliefs and traditions.)

Is Jesus one of many messengers and have there been others at His same level of enlightenment?

Many, of course, have come and gone over your history—some more famous or well-known than others. They have been leaders in art and culture and astronomy and architecture and philosophy and literature and religion, too. All had messages for your world, and all left their mark somewhere.

Is Jesus-the-son-of-God a child of God in a higher way than each one of us is a child of God?

Chosen to show the way and do so without fear, to be a teacher and live the message—a much-heightened position in the hierarchy we say.

Will Jesus come again?

It is the case that when the-end-of-your-world-as-it-is-now comes to your planet's wellness, that entity will appear once again as a leader and educator.

Time moves and shifts and need grows throughout the galaxy. Do not think yours is the only source of turmoil in existence; help is needed in other worlds as well.

Will Jesus be coming again *to judge* all souls? I'm specifically asking about this word "judge".

Not so, we say, as there is no such narrow version of the messages shared by Jesus, as one example. It was never the intention of Jesus, as he was in biblical times, to judge, and as he continues today to return to your world as teacher—there is no intent to judge who was naughty and who was nice. As a spiritual teacher, judgment is not a part of the program. *Inclusion and love are the program* and understanding and willingness to understand are the higher path taken.

To do one's best and live a life in *love* and *compassion, giving* and *sharing*, is to be the message one wishes to share. Tolerance and love for all is and was the message and will continue to be.

Love is the key and acceptance of all people.

If Jesus Himself were to speak now and re-teach His message to the world, what would He say is His message?

Live your best, love all, and follow your heart; do kindness and practice respect for all.

Believe and trust in yourself to be your highest and best. Blind faith is not for all.

Forgiveness is key: forgiveness of self for not rising to one's heights, forgiveness of others for their transgressions toward self or the world at large. It is the way to finding peace within the heart, for holding on to malice and blame and vindictiveness creates darkness in the soul. Without forgiveness there can be no path forward. There will always be one foot stuck in the mire of blame and disregard and even hate, and this clouds judgment and action, and all thought not only on this topic but on life in general. It is like harboring a germ and knowing it will grow into a disease—makes no sense—it is for all to know that removing the germ and sending it away in love is the way. For love, when applied to another, creates an unknown and unexpected, very often, response that involves dissipation of the dark cloud and return to wellness in all involved.

Trust in this and apply it where needed. You will see.

Love, acceptance of all, non-judgment, respect for all, forgiveness, belief and trust in yourself—this feels right.

Pax, you frequently tell us that to trust in ourselves is the key to empowerment, and that our empowerment is the key to having the courage to live a life on-purpose and

to making a difference in our world. May you please speak again about the great significance of our empowerment?

While we have the best in mind for all, there are times that we are not able to provide, and each person must use their inner strengths to envision what and how they want their lives to be and then allow it to happen. No pushing of the envelope is needed. The best will be for each person when they "let go and let God" as we say. Follow the path laid down by many moccasins walking it previously.

More than anything, we need to believe that we have the power to change our own lives and the world. Yet, it's a hard thing for most of us to believe that we have the power within ourselves: it's like assuring a High Schooler that they will ace a PhD dissertation someday, even though that moment is so far in their reality's future. And yet, you know that it will be.

Set the Intention, Believe in self and Trust in the outcome. This is it, the Holy Grail of empowerment.

The Holy Grail of empowerment—I like that. This formula for empowerment closely mirrors the keys to manifestation that you gave us earlier and so I will deduce that empowerment is the forerunner of manifesting our highest dreams. I'm following the yellow brick road.

The inner strength that people are developing in your time and the virtue and the trust in self all relate to empowerment and self-awareness and the ability to take responsibility for their own reality.

This is the growth of the human psyche and we expand on the thought that while each of you does create your world as you wish it to be, each one of you must understand that the greatest attribute is trust: *Trust In Self* and trust in your spirituality. This is the next step to walking your true path.

Understand your gifts and talents and what you have learned in the past lifetimes. Understand your challenges and limitations, some also brought forward from those past times. Then, have a look at the big picture and know you will be able to grow and fulfill your role as it is laid out before you in the great blueprint of your life and lives. You have a plan, you do. You have the ability to walk the walk or go off the rails. Your choice.

The bubble you may have around your head will burst when the reality of your responsibility hits: the responsibility to yourself and your spiritual development so that you may give back to your world today and fulfill yourself along the way.

This is a necessary component to healthy and rewarding living and it is for you to understand this. Don't think you are just passing through and will not leave a footprint. You will—either a positive or a negative footprint. And the size and depth of this mark left on your world is determined by your courage.

The size of our mark in the world is determined by our courage?

Your life will expand, or not, depending upon your courage.

We wish to focus now on humankind's ability to lift oneself up by the bootstraps and move into the role of leader when confronted with the need. It is too often the case that people wish to follow as it is safer—it can always be someone else's idea and if not successful, someone else will take blame.

It is time now for those who have this habit to look into themselves for strength and the knowledge that sometime, somewhere in their past, they have been capable of decision making. Why is it they abdicate this responsibility now?

We say to go forward in the knowledge that everyone has a gift and talent in leadership no matter how small and taking one step at a time toward making judgments and taking action will feel so very good and rewarding—so do it.

Take the leap and go for the brass ring. It is your right and your gift from the Spiritual World to reach out and grab the opportunities to thrive and grow and excel and blossom.

People who deny their ability to make a difference in the world neglect to take sufficient responsibility for their inaction. The sadness is when their power is lost to them it is lost also to the world. To be impactful, one must believe and trust in oneself. With continued consciousness-raising in this area, the end result is a race of self-assured, highly evolved people seeking peace, tranquility, purity of mind, and purity of the environment. This is the future for your planet—the crystal dream. We ask you to move forward in this goal.

Change is as change does, and you are the catalyst; each of you.

Take the leap of faith. You will be blessed in the result. Never doubt this. It is your birthright. The guides who share your growth and journey are there with you, ensuring that you have a resource when in doubt. This is your journey and you are on track if you feel it in your heart.

Then we say, follow your heart and go in peace and love.

Chapter Twenty
Heart, Peace, and Love

*Y*ou have three themes that repeat in your teachings: "Follow your heart", "go in peace", and "love". Each of these is an important wisdom for us, and I'd love for you to speak to each and to underline your message for us.

Yes, we begin with the discussion of human nature in times of struggle and we combine with the lessons of finding empowerment in the face of confusion.

It is our belief that your people have strength of conviction and intention to do and go and create, all of these are obvious to them at a time of wanting, but when times of pressure come there is hesitation to take the incentive and follow their own thinking. Rather it is the case that too many will be like the sheep and await the dog to come with the shepherd and round them up and direct them on a chosen path.

We wish to speak of how it is for people who want to choose their own path but lack the strength to believe in it being the right choice for themselves.

Then let's start there, please.

Beginning in early life for many people is the need to follow direction from parents, teachers, bosses; all have the effect of deciding what is to be for a person—this is to be tempered with selection, by that individual, of their own choice and own path. How to trust that it is the right choice is the complication.

When a person understands their physical and emotional selves, they recognize signs, and the physical body will always send signs and signals to indicate if the choice made is the best, or not.

What does it feel like to follow your heart? How would we recognize if we were following our heart, or not?

Warm and glowing and smiling happy is how this feels.

You must consider doing a test of self where you ask for your own opinion on a planned direction. Yes, that is asking your self if the considered direction will be right for you. Be still and await the feeling in your heart—not your mind—await the feeling of warm and peace and calm and joy, or find the feeling of cold and constricted and tight and trepidation. Which one do you think will be that to be followed?

This is a visceral reaction to a question and your Higher Self knows the way. If you will listen to this message and follow what you feel in your heart, you will be following your heart, which will always show the direction and passage best for you.

Following our heart is a decision-making tool?

When we speak of the feeling in your heart, or ask you to follow your heart, we mean that there is a visceral feeling in that place which, if felt and understood, will confirm what is right and what is not right for that person.

We speak of the feelings of cold and fear versus the feelings of warmth and glowing—is it obvious which one is a signal for what response? If a person is faced with a decision, a choice between actions, trust in self that the physical body will signal the correct direction. When the thought is held to go with choice one, how do you feel in your body, your heart area? Do you give it time to consider and await the physical response? Is that response one of warm and glowing and pleasant and maybe tingling? Or is that feeling one of dread and cold and revulsion and upset? This is the Higher Self describing the outcome and showing the way to the correct choice. To trust in this will always lead to the best possible outcome.

And, this way of decision-making can be counted on?

At no time will your Higher Self lead you wrong.

There is much history of past lifetimes and current related experiences to draw upon when showing the way and the Soul knows—this is the Higher Self, the Soul and all is understood and available to point the way to the right choice.

Trust in this and follow your heart, we say, for it is your inner compass.

To elaborate on the idea that our Self also speaks to us through sensations of the body—I know someone who gets a rash, only on her left arm, when something is a hard *no* for her. I have another friend who feels she will vomit when presented with something she's not keen on. And, another friend who has an instant bowel reaction when she hears bad news or feels insecure about something or someone in that moment.

Does everyone have their own unique body reactions as signs from our higher consciousness?

To each his own, yes.

These visceral reactions are to be listened to and followed as signs to go or to not go in the considered direction. These are *cell-memories* tuning in to the frequency of what is presented and quickly advising the body and mind of the best possible direction for success.

Are some Higher-Self-communication physical sensations universal and therefore experienced by most?

It is for each person to know their own personal reaction to danger or pleasure and their fight or flight reactions.

Based on each individual's past experiences, these reactions appear instantaneously and when least expected in many instances. It is for each of you to feel and consider what is presented and even if not fully understood, it is advisable to follow in the direction indicated.

And, what about goosebumps? Getting goosebumps when something "feels right" is an experience that I've had and it's common to the point of having been accepted as part of our vernacular—people say, "Oh, I just got goosebumps!" when something is very good and deeply resonates with them. Many people say that goosebumps are Spirit talking to them; some say that it's the presence of a spirit or a deceased loved one saying "hello". What is the cause of goosebumps (in this context)?

Validation of the idea presented, positive validation for the person presenting as witnessed by the person hearing the idea.

It is a confirmation of right and correct action to be taken.

It is an interesting psychosomatic reaction and common to those who known themselves and their Higher Selves and understand to go within for answers is the way. Those who do not may consider the goosebumps as a cold chill and think no further—such a shame this valuable tool is not more greatly utilized by your people.

Again, we advise that going within for your guidance is the way. Your Higher Self knows the way.

To what other inner tools would you like to alert us?

Consider lessons for a form of meditation to reach one's inner core of strength, needed in your time of confusion.

Wonderful. May you please give us a lesson on this?

We begin by asking that all who choose this do so with open mind and heart and trust that their inner core is strong and pliable, and the guidance will serve them well.

As we ask for you to go into your inner self and find your soul power, we ask you to focus on your core, your solar plexus and combine this with your heart strength. To coordinate the two brings the power intensely and to have the two synchronized completes the power. Merging the power centers brings the ability to consider the soul's messaging and what is best for your feeling and knowledge combined and how these transmit into the way forward in life.

It is for you to stay in this space of core power and present your feeling and question to your soul power for clarity.

As the inner humming begins, so comes the knowledge you seek and so comes the growth of strength of conviction.

The way forward in personal power.

I can imagine that this will be instruction for future meditations, and people will follow and teach this. Thank you.

Do you have the energy required to trust in self and Self when those around are paralyzed by fear and distrust and begin human behaviors that are counter-productive?

I hope so; please go on.

Through the practice of meditation and taking small actions based on self-direction comes empowerment. It is the thinking that one can make one's own choice followed by that action—this is the formula for beginning a revitalization of one's own way of being.

To look outside for a situation but to look inside (one's self) for affirmation, this is the way. It involves trust—always it involves trust and more and more is developed as success is found.

The inner signs and signals allow for choices made in confidence and actions the same. Speaking one's truth is key and walking the talk also.

To believe in self and know that others look to you for direction brings a sense of rightness to an action. When one leads and others follow it is a signal, and that signal brings confidence and repeat action of standing in one's own light so you may illuminate the path for others. This is your choice and your destiny.

We wish you to understand that in this time on your planet these lessons in self-empowerment are needed. This will remain so going forward as your world is in turmoil and will remain so in different ways that involve your environmental protection.

Next, let's look at your instruction to "go in peace". As a message it appears straightforward, however in practice it

can be less so. (Regardless of whether it's applied to inter-personal relationships or international relations.)

To go in peace indicates going through life and your world in peace—a way of life and being, not just a thought. It is the solution to all.

We are here to continue with the growth and development of your people into higher functioning individuals and your Earth population, as a whole, into a more cohesive group of humans on the globe. We wish to speak more of working together for solutions.

Too much of fighting and vindictiveness enters into conflicts and no thought of peaceful resolution is considered. We wish to speak again of the value of being the peaceful warrior.

We're listening. What more can you share with us of the value of the peaceful warrior?

Of what value is love and tolerance on a global scale, and teaching the way of peace and inclusion?

Well, yes—what value? They're your words, not mine, my dear Divine Wisdom Source. Please continue.

Holding together the framework of your lives and infra-structure of your world organization is the value. Showing the way and walking the talk. Growing of each self into a being of love and forgiveness, acceptance and trust sounds like weakness to many; trust us when we say it is strength of the highest order.

Do you not understand this is the way of the highest order of beings who accelerate their wellness and continue their jour-neys to the Ultimate Warrior status? What is this? Well, it is the peaceful-Self interacting with those in need of great awareness of all that the Universe has to offer. There is no way to fathom it all without higher learning and open heart; open mind is surpassed by open heart, and it is this that differentiates those who will elevate from those who cannot as they are held back by an intellectual need to grasp it all.

This is a *heart-based* exercise, this higher understanding, and minds do get in the way of acceptance. Be prepared to come to this understanding, as it is the way to continued living, as you know it.

You have been warning us about our dangerous pollution practices and the rampant corruption in our governments and corporations, yet these largely continue. It must be frustrating for you to watch what we're doing to ourselves and to our planetary host. You've told us that you are benevolence, non-judgment, and love, and for anyone who reads your words, these are felt. Yet, I wonder: are you also sometimes angry with humankind, or perhaps disappointed or frustrated?

These are emotions you must feel for yourselves.

We have no judgment, but observation is clear. The forward motion that is not forwarding, as it should on your planet, in terms of growth of awareness and caring for your Earth is bringing us sadness. This is ours to exclaim.

I hear that you have a personality; it comes through in the writing. However, do you have emotions or feelings?

We have explained our range of thoughts that bring feeling, though non-judgmental. We offer the reality of sadness for what we witness. Aside from that we have enjoyment of this communication. It is the lightness of feeling in this communication that brings us joy. Ours is to continue our dialog in order to pass along helpful guidance as needed and it is our blessing to contribute.

Dear Pax, what else should we consider in our world as we seek to unsoil our governments and corporations, and heal our planet?

The great movement toward world peace that is mentioned by many, but not seriously pursued. The *elevation of pure intention* coupled with personal power, brings transformation to your Earth people and a raising of the vibration globally. It becomes the magnet that changes your world. This is our wish for our contribution to world peace.

From the elevation of pure intention coupled with heightened personal power, comes transformation to your Earth people and raising of their vibration globally. This is the sequence. One begets the other. Without heightened awareness of the nature of Pure Intention as it applies to the individual, there is no sequence of events toward world peace.

There needs to be personal peace and understanding that no boundaries exist to success in bringing a higher vibration to world actions and people. There must be a desire and plan for world peace, not simply a wish. Without intention a wish is powerless. The primary message is bringing power to the people to make the needed changes.

May you please expand on "elevation of pure intention"?

The nature of pure intention is not achieved without a vision and a goal.

What is the intention and by what method will it be achieved? Pure intention, of course, is the purity of heart and mind. This is written and this is strived for in certain segments of your population. It is to become the way of your people before a critical mass is reached which enables great change.

Much time will pass and much more is written about the need—right now your world is in turmoil to the extent this notion cannot be heard or seriously considered while people are being persecuted and genocides are in the minds of some.

Change, it is said, begins at the top and some world countries demand change and there will be change in order for a light to be seen by your people as a possible and potential end to strife.

For those who monetize what should be benefits to humanity, a fall will come which enables positivity to be regained.

Regained positivity in our world today would be providential.

Penelope, our willingness to put forth these ideas and dialog at this time is that it is a requirement for the continuation of the flourishing of your Earth population to *function as a cohesive unit* rather than a fragmented and protective/possessive population. This idea comes from the top down and so we shall also speak to those leaders who present divisiveness as their way. There is no future in this, much disputed by those who practice this way, but we will show it for what it is—folly.

Please do speak further about those leaders who present divisiveness. This is your soapbox and the stage is yours to speak *directly* to the leaders of our world.

It is the time in the history of your Planet Earth when a pivot is required, and that is to the need for inclusion.

For some, that you continue to sow the seeds of hatred and fear is to your own detriment. How you have come to the place of power is questionable and how you remain there, even greater. It is your lesson in this lifetime that your actions are contrary to what your people will benefit from on their own journeys to wellness and prosperity, self-esteem, and flourishing families. Your need to elevate your selves at the expense of your followers says much about your lack of inner worth.

To all, it is past time to take a lesson from peaceful warriors of past and begin to sow love and forgiveness, tolerance and lessons of wisdom, and inclusion—it is yours to share.

Love needs to enter your way of life as it pertains to all, in order for your people's survival.

Lastly, please speak to your steady mention of love, to be love, and to go in love.

Love has been shown to be the strongest of emotions and mislabeled as weakness by many. Not so, as it is the most difficult of tacks to take in considering resolution.

We wish to speak more of love being the way to all ends, the way to live and the way to think of all as it pertains to methods and means of resolving differences. This we wish to teach and will provide examples of this on a personal as well as international level.

Oh, please do.

Love in the heart translates to love shared, and on a personal as well as global scale, it is the great equalizer. Love brings tolerance and understanding, heart-filled acceptance and unconditional support. For this to become reality there must be love of self. Is this understood? For love to be given there must be love of self and trust in self and belief in self—these are lessons to be learned and practiced.

It is the way of those who devote lifetimes to scattering seeds of acceptance: there is no difference in color, race, religion or any outward sign of attachment to group or nation. There is only an interest in what resides inside a person's heart—this is the key— again, not the mind but the heart. Learn the difference. One can say and one can feel. It is the *feeling* part that rules, or should.

As we talk about love, I want you to know that I love you. You're very lovable, you know? In fact, you have said that you *are* love. I infer from this that you are the noun and the state of love—Love with a capital "L". Do you also love, as in the verb; the action of love? Do you love *us*, Pax?

Love is as Love does, it is said, and it is our way to be this and show this and offer this and spread this as the way of being for all.

Love is the answer; Love is the way to a future of peace and harmony among your people. When decisions are made based upon what is best for all, this is showing Love. When actions are taken that bring peace instead of warring, this is a decision based on Love.

Do we Love? Indeed, it is our way of being that we teach Love and harmony and walk the talk. Love energy extends to all who are in need, also to those who seem less in need. Our Love is Universal.

Love is the answer. Love is the way. You've been telling this to us for many, many thousands of years, haven't you?

Yes.

To fully develop your heart and mind and walk in the heart love, which you share with all, this brings you to a place of rising above the negativity and bewilderment troubling much of humanity in your spacetime. Hate is a limiting and debilitating emotion, which rules many and is to be eradicated from your civilization.

It takes teachers to undertake this project and make the difference in your world. To bring love and order to those around you, to spread love and intention for peace and healing throughout your civilizations, and to act on the need to heal your people and your world, sharing peace and harmony from your heart to the ethers and back, this is the love and the light that is the universal human.

Chapter Twenty-One
Superpowers You Didn't Know You Had

*H*ow does it work between the Spirit World and us when we need your help? Should we "phone in" for help by calling on Spirit for guidance and assistance?

There is respect that help is given when help is requested. All people have the ability to communicate with their own Spirit Guides if they trust in this as a resource and a possibility.

Does the Spirit World hear our prayers? Does prayer work?

It is our surprise that this question has been asked. However, it is a question the many of your Earth people consider and we wish to state that as personal intention works, so does prayer. It is a belief in the resolving of a problem that drives those who do believe to seek validation from their sources. If it be a religious or a spiritual source is of no matter: it is the individual belief in cause and effect—if they ask, they will receive, and this the case in prayer.

To trust in the process is key: to state the concern and the request for relief and ask for guidance or support in a decision— this is the way. To bring trust to the outcome and belief in self and Self, this enables the moving forward in knowing the personal decision was the right one.

When a person prays, they are including the request for input from their Higher Selves, their souls which contain the wisdom of their ages, their all, their many lifetimes, and this is a source of right action in all ways.

To each their belief and to each their way, but prayer as called by many names, works.

Let's take this opportunity to share with our readers a number of tools that they can use—superpowers (if they choose to use and develop them) that will aid them in their effort to place their trust in themselves, to build confidence in their instincts, to live a life of purpose, and to *be* their Higher Selves.

We understand there is a movement to seeking the Self and it has begun everywhere. We applaud those who are self-seekers. Always trust in self. Seek your higher power for answers. Do your muscle testing to determine what is good for you, swing those pendulums, and otherwise use the tools of your intuition for guidance.

May you please explain both muscle testing and pendulum swinging? Of what benefit are these and how are these practiced?

The use of a pendulum to define right from wrong for an individual has been practiced for thousands of years.

While the method is basic, may you please tell us how to swing a pendulum and apply it to decision-making—what motion signals a "yes" or a "no"?

One does not swing a pendulum, however, one holds the string still—it is the pendulum that swings in response to questioning. What motion signals yes or no depends on the individual and the pendulum and is determined prior to beginning questioning. This is done by testing to have the pendulum show its yes and no responses. In the case of Carole Serene and her pendulum use, her pendulum shows "yes" as a forward to back motion and "no" answer as side-to-side motion. Further, if the answer isn't clear, the pendulum will either rotate in a small circle or remain motionless, pointing straight down while trembling with the string slightly vibrating.

What is the metaphysics of the pendulum?

In any energy work there is the trust and respect and relationship between the object—pendulum in this case—and the energy and Higher Self of the operator. It is energy that allows for the connection between these and the result is Spirit involvement in showing the way forward.

The pendulum is a tool, an object of focus to show the energetic response to a situation.

Basically, why does it work and who or what makes the pendulum move?

You ask why does it work? Trust and belief and pure intention to communicate through Spirit are the way.

The beauty of the pendulum is that it knows what it knows because it is a collection of wisdoms coming through you to bring the responses. These wisdoms are a combination of the Universal Wisdom, your Higher Self, the guides with you, and the great and overall view from above which sees all.

And now, please expound on muscle testing—what is that?

The use of one's internal regulator to determine what is best for that individual body/mind/spirit entails asking within for the answer and allowing the body reaction to determine response. You may extend an arm, for example, parallel to the ground, and have someone attempt to push it down while you hold the thought of what is being considered for yourself. If the strength of the body holds that arm rigidly in place, it is a positive, whereas if that arm is easily pushed out of position and down, it is a negative.

There are other tests, but this is effective.

I will begin practicing these techniques. They sound easy and, well, fun!

I'd like to ask you about circles. Earlier you said: "We should like to point to the wise ones of past times who circled their people and taught lessons of conscience and caring and working together to keep all people healthy and fed and educated."

Actually, you've mentioned circles a few times in our writings and now is a good time to explore the significance as a philosophy and a tool. Please tell us more about circles and encircling the people.

Wisdom shared in circle is a significant part of life for many cultures.

The strength of a circle is unbroken; the circle brings together those in equality. There is no first or last or front or back or head-table or backbench, there is only equality. It is the power of all to contribute equally and be considered equal.

In this configuration people know they are not one above another. There is clarity of who brings what inspiration and feeling to the group, who sees others as equal contributors to the cause or healers to the need presented. This is wisdom, this knowledge of gathering in circle—it is knowledge of human behavior responding to circle gathering: love and tolerance and understanding of the needs of others in circle results in wisdom sharing and gathering and successful outcome for the purpose.

That's profound.
I wonder if simply changing the shapes of our dining and conference tables from rectangular, square, and oval to circular could help in creating a change of consciousness in our societies.

Yes, and why not?

There are countless examples of circles being used by our ancient ancestors, such as the circles of Stonehenge, and there are modern examples of famous circles as well, like the five Olympic Rings. Gosh, even planets are circles—well globes, technically.
Does the circle *itself* hold power?

There is power in the circle as it radiates energy back to those forming the circle—it is an incubator of ideas that are tending more toward peace and solution than to confrontation and isolation. It is ancient and powerful and effective. It brings equality to all in the formation going in and is a great equalizer of power. When entering negotiation with the knowing that each has equal power there is a shift in energy and *this is the secret.*

We have many tools at our disposal, even a power-full shape.

Let's talk about the superpowers that we have within. How do we become multi-sensory beyond our currently known abilities?

Ah yes, this is a fine beginning to a subject which each of your Earth people should address and if learned, will make a great difference in how all communication is achieved and interpersonal relations improve.

As it is, most of your Earth people have and rely on five senses, if they are fortunate to have them all, and that is sight, hearing, smell, taste, and feel. Most go through life relying on those to prove what they choose to believe. What is lacking is the sixth sense, the intuiting of what they do not know and want to—intuition is valuable and key to a well-rounded individual.

What is not understood by your many people is that this is a powerful sense that was, at one time in history, integral to survival. It came to be known, over time, as a piece of witchcraft and therefore fell out of favor and people stopped relying on their inner sense to determine their next step. It is such a valuable tool to determine another person's intention as true or not, a story as viable or not, and a direction taken for themselves wise or not. It is the time now to begin the resurrection of this powerful inner strength. Having the ability to just know if something is right for you is amazing to many but to those who believe and practice this skill, it is invaluable. Trust in this and know that your Higher Self has the means to show you the way. Believe in your own inner feelings, that little voice inside of you, that knot in stomach or other bodily reaction to tell you the direction is right or not—it is in you to find and use.

Trust in your Higher Self, your Soul, to take into account all around you and determine for yourself what will serve your highest and best good. You have the ability to place yourself in a leadership role, using your higher powers, your intuitive self, your multi-sensory self to show the way for others. To talk the talk and walk the walk, it is said, is to be authentic and to live this way, taking in all your power and teaching this to those in need, this is the higher calling.

You have nicely opened several topics here.
Is my "intuition" the same as my "Sixth Sense" and the same as a "gut-instinct"—and the same as my "Higher Self" for that matter?

They (your intuition, Sixth Sense, and gut-instinct) are the sum total and one, while Higher Self awareness is of greater depth and reach. Do you know that these are your sum total of past lifetimes knowledge base that can be accessed at any time?

I do now.

It is there, and if you feel it, act on it. We are aware of the fact that many do not allow these thoughts and feelings in, do not listen or accept them as a benefit and do not follow the message, believing instead in the guidance of others for their life decisions: such shame here.

Your inner wisdom is always your guide if you will allow.

How is a Guardian Angel different from a Spirit Guide?

Do we know that it is? Who is to say, but how each person refers to their personal angel is their own way.

Ooh, okay—good to know. So, a Guardian Angel and a Spirit Guide are our names for the same thing. That's helpful.

Do we also have loved ones who "watch over" us—those who have passed over into the Spirit World?

For some who believe a deceased loved one has come back to protect them, this can be reality in that the spirit chooses to not leave what they consider their new role of protection. Often a person feels that energy and recognizes it and applies the name they know.

For the many there is their inner wisdom at work and on that they rely for guidance. As we have stated, how it is termed varies, as does the degree to which people respond. Just know the inner guidance is key.

We also share that in many instances, the guardian angel held responsible for avoiding disaster is really the person's inner wisdom, their Higher Self if you will, advancing warnings that are heard and acted upon. This is often the way and how it is termed is not of matter: it is a gift then that a person in that situation avoided harm by hearing and following that guidance, that intuition, that guardian angel, that inner voice.

Wow, Pax, this is a new thought.

You said, "in many instances", and this infers "not always". So, my first question is: who are the Guardian Angels that save us on the occasions when it is *not* our own Higher Self providing the advanced warning?

To each his own: how do we identify who is with whom? Is it your deceased loved one or friend or another taking the role? It is not definable in this way. Sufficient to say it is a *love energy* walking with you.

What or who exactly are "angels"? I mean this in the sense of a bona fide angel with wings and all.

An angel with wings is a historically inaccurate portrayal of this energy field, but if your people wish to see this protective energy as winged, it would serve well your commercial purposes. Love energy is angelic, wings or not.

It's kind of funny when you think about it because, of course, a being-of-Spirit would not need wings to "fly" or move around. This is a logical and humorous revelation.

Pax, there are readers who will wish to ask their own questions and get feedback from the Spirit World. I've come to understand that we all have the ability to access the great wisdom known to our Higher Selves, and that with practice and right intention, many can and should seek to communicate with Spirit. May you please give your thoughts on this?

We know that opening to channeling and the ability to use one's sixth sense is becoming more and more prevalent and also considerably more accepted than recent generations past. We say this is part of reclaiming personal power. The ability to utilize all senses is what has been missing—flying on one wing, as it were.

To begin to see the benefits of following gut feelings, following urges and hunches as they apply to everyday life, will be empowering to those who see the results of doing so. There is no grey area here, people. When you act on a hunch or feeling or what some would recognize as intuition, and it brings you through a situation safely or avoids potential danger or improves business or personal life situations, this is clear and the self-fulfilling aspect of it not to be denied.

This is how to go from skeptical to practice openly, and how people will begin to speak more openly of the cause and effect and what happened when they listened to their Higher Selves (intuition) and what happened when they didn't and should have.

It's abundantly clear and it is the beginning of the movement that will create the groundswell of action and trust and openness about this practice until it becomes mainstream and common-place and widely accepted as fact.

Next to the heart, the power of the mind is the greatest power you have, and it is too often overlooked in favor of physical power; mistake.

Well then, because our thoughts hold the power to manifest, should we get in the habit of regularly scanning our thoughts, checking to monitor the negative and focus on the positive in the same way a computer might be constantly running a background scan?

For people to understand that the body hears everything the mind says is to know that the scanning required is not simply the mind, but the heart. The feelings within self are telling, and a body knows what is. A feeling of darkness and trepidation signifies negativity for most, while a feeling of hope and light signifies positive, slight variables of course. It is for each to examine their feelings as well as thoughts when determining what to keep in order to act upon, and what to leave behind.

A good reminder.
On a different yet similar query: how do some people move objects without touching them or bend spoons with their mind? (You mentioned "bend the spoons" when we talked about "collective consciousness".) And, how do some people levitate an object? Are these tricks of magic, or laws of energy and physics? Or, is this the power of the mind, as you say?

Physics and energy and frequencies and mind-power combined.

If we wished to, how could we go about exercising this and other powers of our mind?

The first step is to trust one's self: always empowerment is the goal.

Without trust and belief in self, nothing happens that is memorable or extraordinary. To understand that harnessing personal power is the source of your abilities is the beginning. We have spoken much on this and will again, but for now it is to be understood that each person has great personal power if they will acknowledge it and go within to experience it.

Teachings of parents and others in younger years either support or deny this, and if one grows up not believing in oneself, it is not too late to begin the growth into a high functioning human. It takes belief and trust and a certain amount of excitement to meet the new and stronger inner self.

Always go within for these conversations with self. The body hears everything the mind says.

I think it's time that we understand much more about those signs and signals given by our body, and our physical sensations and the feelings within our body.

Let's touch on the seven chakras of the body and their purpose and meaning. We have plenty of good books available on the chakras or energy centers, yet I'd love to hear your take on chakras.

We say they are energy depositories in the body and each holds differing forms of energy and frequencies. These centers may become blocked and result in poor or no energy transmission throughout the body, bringing dis-ease in many forms.

Mind-power use can result in clearing of blocked energy in these areas, also energy healing and clearing techniques. If these chakras remain blocked the result is a body/mind/spirit out of balance.

From where does our "gut instinct" come: is it the body, mind, or spirit?

We are pleased to say that it is *soul-connection* that gives warnings.

Perhaps we can offer a mini tutorial for the reader in how to practice, exercise, and develop their own intuitive abilities. If you were leading this class (which you are), what would be the first lesson?

In our way of leading we would encourage all to know themselves, feel what they accept and what they reject in themselves, go within and learn their strengths and follow it with knowledge of why they would develop psychic abilities: do they believe in this or is it a game? How will they utilize heightened psychic abilities, to what end, and to what *benefit*? Do they understand that trust in themselves is key? Do they believe that they can contribute to humanity and to their own personal and soul growth through an added dimension to themselves?

There is thinking to do and an understanding of the bigger picture. First one must know one's Self and understand that respect for all dimensions must exist.

Pax, I'm eager to learn more about increasing our personal power and unlocking all of our innate (yet unused) abilities. I suppose that to unlock something is also to open something. May we start there, with becoming open?

We are here to speak on opening to channeling and opening to awareness from all places in the psyche. We say that all peoples have this ability if they choose to access it. For the most part it is kept under wraps, and if people do have inklings or hunches or thoughts about things, precognition etc., they either dismiss it or considerate it coincidence. We know there is no such thing. Serendipity yes, but of coincidence we say it is drawn to be in that place at that time for a purpose.

To speak of living on purpose is to include getting to know one's self in all ways, including one's gifts and talents as they pertain to higher powers. Why is it you think of developing talents like piano playing and tennis while ignoring one's own higher powers such as telepathy, intuition, and the ability to communicate well without spoken words?

It is now time for people to understand this is the way of the future and to stop being concerned about what others will think. We shall speak more on that later.

Each person has the potential for sharpening all of their senses and those unafraid will find much pleasure in touching on each one and finding ways to increase their personal powers.

It is only a matter of time until it becomes commonplace for people to seek out teachers and coaches to help them in this regard. Do not think it won't be helpful in business as well as personal life. Do you not consider that knowing who to trust is a benefit in business? In developing intuition and inner knowing, one can move through life in the avoidance of negativity and that which will not serve their highest and best needs. It is simply an awareness of a depth that comes only through this, and a self-trust that allows for decision based on the reality of the situation as intuited and known without question. When people communicate telepathically, in time, all will know the thoughts that cannot be hidden from each other, and hiding truths will be a thing of the past.

In the near time comes the resurgence of personal power building without thought to individual limitations. You are to know that your personal powers are *limitless* if you believe it is so.

All people should share the goal of helping all others with their spiritual development: the development of each individual's ability to access their inner superpowers and contagious light energy.

Each is owed their potential and to fulfill it is an obligation and a trust. To use that wisdom and knowledge and ensuing skillset to the best and highest degree and aim the use of that learning toward the well-being of mankind is the objective: say this and know this and plan for it.

It is your destiny.

Pax, I've come to know Carole Serene Borgens as a partner in these projects and I enjoy hearing about how you connected with her. It will also interest our readers because many will wish to know how this level of communication is accomplished. However, there was a time that Carole did not practice this communication and when she didn't know how to do so, but she was a seeker of metaphysics and spirituality and she sought wisdom and learned and practiced. May you please speak to this?

Carole Serene was chosen as our channel for her purity of spirit and willingness to commit to our message and the sharing of it. This is an agreement of souls for the higher purpose. There must be mutual respect and reverence for the process, and it is not to be taken lightly. This is a gift not given to any who have not made the commitment to be the vessel of communication in purity and love. Carole Serene had spent many years studying metaphysics and learning the level of respect she held prior to our connection.

And, what is not advisable when it comes to communication methods to attempt with Spirit?

There are ways of communication that people have chosen, such as Ouija boards and séances, and these will bring through spirits wishing to communicate on any level. They are to be considered somewhat troublesome in the hands of thrill-seekers and those playing the game for not well thought out reasons.

There is a level on which a person could connect with Spirit through a medium, or as a medium, and care must be taken to protect self against negative spirit(s) communication.

Please explain how the process of communicating with Spirit can successfully work for the highest good and for each and every person who desires this form of communication with pure intention.

Each person has the ability to communicate with their own Higher Self to access wisdom and guidance. First look within to know yourself. Go within to your Higher Self, as described, and begin to access Universal Wisdom from there.

Always speak the protection of asking for only the information that will serve the highest and best good for all, to come through yourself.

Spiritual wellness is held by all and choices are made for future roles in the growing into a spiritual being. There are choices and levels and we suggest each has its place in the chain. Whether to teach or to welcome or to facilitate or plan to return through soul in a further incarnation—all have their time and place and peace is.

When you say, "speak the protection", is this to be done out loud, and could you give us some words to use that could help as a guideline or suggestion?

Whether spoken in words or thoughts is immaterial: it is the intention that brings the power. You may ask for only the information that will serve the highest and best good of all to come through you.

You may ask for the presence of your Spirit guides in general or by name and open a question and answer dialog. And when your session is complete you may give thanks for it and formally state closure of the session then. This process becomes a joy when the way is found to begin knowing this other aspect of yourself and it is enlightening and comforting.

What are the "future roles in the growing into a spiritual being"? (I feel like this is an important line.)

This is a topic of interest to many who consider spiritual wellness a need in their lives. To what degree is the question often considered, however, and only the individual can know their own level of commitment.

To become a follower or a leader, to teach or to learn, all are probable in different periods of a lifetime.

There are no limitations when one feels liberated and able to follow their heart, their dream, and find a path to begin their journey, even though the destination is unknown the need to travel the path is sufficient to carry them along and through what comes, finally identifying the end goal is the bonus. From there it is the soul's journey toward that person's destiny.

Being transported along the path with the assistance and guidance of one's Higher Self is always a probability if one is open to this as possibility. Reality is such that each may dictate and direct one's own path to the future and in so doing will be further empowered to live their dream along the way: the knowledge that each person controls their own destiny—the ability to trust in one's ability to chart their own life course and create the reality they desire, wish for, and place their intention toward, that they will not be stopped but supported by the Universe in their dedication to making their life the reality they choose. This also is a mind-set: if it is believed, it will be, but if doubted, well, the steps toward culmination and fulfillment become steep and difficult. No matter the challenges ahead, the destination can be reached through trust in self and Higher Self to get you there.

There is the realization that personal power was the source of all accomplishments. This is an amazing realization and empowers one to continue striving for and reaching all personal goals. Each has this ability to grow within themselves and make a difference in your world. This is our wish for your people that they individually and collectively understand they have the power and they are the power, and this power of one, collectively, when combined with good intention, can move mountains.

Can we really *move mountains* with our collective good intentions or is this a metaphor?

It is both. Consider the mountain as an insurmountable challenge in life or a need to change on a broad scale. With the collective energy of those focusing on the desired outcome, miracles happen. We do not wish to place Mt. Fuji in another country but be aware that the exercise is to not dissolve the *particles* making up the mountain and relocate, but to dissolve the *energy of a situation* and replace it with positivity where required.

Much like dissolving clouds we say: focus and believe, and magic happens.

Volume 7
Do Unto Earth
Pax and the Next Evolutionary Leap

"I thought that thirty years of good science could address these problems—I was wrong. The top environmental problems are selfishness, greed, and apathy, and to deal with these we need a cultural and spiritual transformation. And we scientists don't know how to do that."

Gus Speth

Top U.S. advisor on climate change, former Dean of the Yale School of Forestry and Environmental Studies, and winner of the National Wildlife Federation's Resources Defense Award

Chapter Twenty-Two
What's Next in Clean Fuels

*W*e have traversed a lot of ground so to speak, and now let's turn our attention to future fuels. On this front, will you please help us to be the change we wish to see?

Yes.

Thank you.
Pax, we can no longer wait for scientists to make the progressive discoveries because in many cases (though not all) the scientists are funded by massive for-profit companies— often owned and operated by traditional fossil fuel interests.

Ground oil is neither sustainable nor clean and will indeed be replaced when greed and corruption within the fossil fuel industry is replaced with saner heads. Until that time there is behind-the-scenes exploration of alternatives, and technology is there but it is hidden from view in fear of replacement of the massive monies being lost by corporations in control.

Yes, and it's not fair to the masses.

May you please tell us which technologies to pursue that will replace the fuels and tech that we currently use and that is so damaging in terms of emissions and pollutants?

In past times and future times, parallel universes and off-planet technologies evolved to the point of thought power.

There is no need for fueled vehicles as teleportation is the thing; there is no need for burning fuel for heat as cracking together ions in technology produces what is needed.

The replacement for crude oil, in terms of propulsion and heating/cooling and more, is not a product but *a method* of alternative fueling. Some methods are in existence and in use, such as solar, wind, and other liquid-type fuels, gasses, propane, and more. They are and it is available and in use in some areas but not enough.

There is a large gap between where you are today and these methods, so an evolution takes place bringing electric power into use more and eventually giving over to a replacement with solar and wind and hydrogen and then to ion-specific power. Clean energy replaces all for the betterment of Planet Earth.

Moving ahead in time, your world will self-destruct at the current pace of pollution. It is for you to consider now that beginning change in transportation is crucial to the survival of your air quality. There is no way around this.

As you have created a population whose need for instant gratification extends to all things, you have also created the monster of gasoline engines overcoming your air to the extent it is brown in major areas. Think of this—brown—and you allow it to continue. What is wrong in this picture?

It is time to slow down and think of the alternatives.

You say there is a large gap between where we are and future clean energy sources. Let's look at it: Are we under-utilizing solar power? Will we develop a completely different way to think of and use solar energy?

Solar power is almost a thing of the past while it tried to become the future. Technology moves rapidly for you now and this passive source remains a reality, a resource: it along with wind-power, in certain regions, can be a source of reversing current overuse of hydropower. There is more to come in energy sources and as your world turns, so do the options available. They will be revealed in time.

Rather than collecting solar energy in a passive way as we do now with the use of solar panels, is there a way to use the sun more like an interstellar charging station?

Within current technology there is experimentation and change comes. To harness the sun-power is seemingly now an old technology, but there is much new to be understood and it will as time goes on, yes. Filtering the heat and separating it from the burning rays is a portion of this development, and using the ultra-violet aspect for other purposes exists. What can be accomplished here is huge and more will be known in your soon time.

Gosh, this is when I wish that I was a physicist or engineer as I'd love to dive into this sentence that you give us regarding the future of how we actively use solar power: *"Filtering the heat and separating it from the burning rays is a portion of this development, and using the ultra-violet aspect for other purposes exists."*

Let's hope the baton of wisdom is passed to those who can work on development.

And now to the subject of fossil fuels and ethanol, and the move away from their use—this we say is the way.

To reduce or eliminate fossil fuels from your reality is a campaign for many now, and it is beyond time to manage this into reality.

There is no further need for dirty fuels. What the need is now extends to fuel to run the electricity used for non-combustion engine vehicles. Clean fuels from nature are useful in reducing to fuel sources.

Farmers will retool and change crops from those not serving them well to something of a future use on a grand scale.

Is hemp the crop that will serve them better, or something else also?

It is one, yes, and when fully utilized as replacements for your world's great uses now, the farmers will want to adapt to this as commercial uses will be great for products, not food specifically. Textiles, containers, food source and so much more can be achieved through using all components of this product. And it is rapidly growing and sustainable.

Is there a fuel source that we're testing that is a waste of our time?

To use soy for heating and propulsion has not been fully considered: that it will not sell on a world market must be thought of and to retain these crops for development at home is the way. More is to be discussed but again, looking to the past to find the future is the way.

To clarify, are you saying *not* to pursue soy for heating and engine propulsion? Some of the arguments against using soybeans as biomass is that it would heavily soot unless shelled and the oil extracted, and also that the high oil content would cause heavy black smoke. And yet, soy is being considered as a heating bio-fuel.

It is the case that it cannot and should not be utilized for this purpose. There are clean fuel technologies: look ahead to these rather than attempting to retool and clean up after a source not well suited.

What about soy as a fuel for engine propulsion?

Not a source of propulsion to be spending time on developing when others are highly advanced, clean, and next-generation fuel sources of non-fuel propulsion.

These are known in your labs and are to be trusted to be revealed when the time is right and when the engines for use are ready. This applies to intergalactic travel specifically, and while your current jet fuels are efficient, there are alternatives coming that are cleaner and less destructive to the biosphere.

We wish to consider the new uses for current crops and say the farmers need not fear, but they do need to remain open to change. Technology as it develops now will affect their decisions and serve to guide them to a place of energy renewal and Earth stability.

The farmer, once again, becomes the producer and savior of the people, just like in past times.

It sounds like something exciting is coming soon.
Is there another heating and cooling power source worthy of some discussion that we haven't yet covered?

A form of gas that is non-toxic and clean and is filtered from outside air. We point to the availability of sustainable energy found within the Earth air and which can be extracted.

A gas in our regular air can be a heating and cooling power source? Let me think about this.

Hmmm, let's look at the components of air: 21% oxygen, 78% nitrogen, and the remaining 1% is a mix of argon, carbon dioxide, and methane. Well, wait a minute—our air also includes atmospheric humidity, otherwise known as water vapor. A water molecule has three atoms: two hydrogen atoms and one oxygen atom. So, therefore, hydrogen can be added to our list of gases available in plain air. Is hydrogen the gas in our air of which you speak? Is that the gas that you refer to for heating and more?

It is a component of what may be when extraction is accomplished, yes.

After some digging, I found something that seems to fit. Is the following method the one to which you refer in using hydrogen from the water vapor in our air? "Photocatalytic water splitting into hydrogen and oxygen using semiconductor catalysts is an effective method for converting solar energy or sunlight into clean and renewable hydrogen fuel. This process is the most promising and renewable choice for the generation of hydrogen."

It sounds good, yes? And it is and will be when focus is placed on development.

Okay, we now have an interesting method to look at for heating and cooling in particular. I want to be sure that I'm

not missing anything else: There are also scientists working on hydrovoltaics, the molecular generation of electricity from water. They discovered a bacteria protein (Geobacter microbe) in air that links together and with the help of atmospheric moisture, the protein chain can generate an electrical current by way of a patented generator device called Air-gen. However, the power generation output is low at this stage of development.

Is this technology worthy of attention, or is the extraction of hydrogen gas from atmospheric moisture the direction of which you speak?

You have not yet progressed to the understanding of combining techniques and ingredients to simplify the process. When all is said and done, it will be noted that at this time in history the operational method of power creation and the components required were with you but not seen by you.

You've said this twice now and I'm paying close attention.

Water vapor extracted from atmosphere is doable and may be the pathway *for now*. It has applications in some areas, and that would be helpful.

Non-fuel methods exist, such as magnetic, and are in development that will take them far above your water vapors and gasses, these will go the way of the dodo birds also and become a blip in history.

Chapter Twenty-Three
Future Travel

*W*hat is our next small step to look at with regard to our vehicle fuels?

Your Earth science is on it. The technology is there, development in process, and clean energy—when it is permitted to surface without challenge by old industry—will sweep the present into the future. There must not be interference for the sake of money—from "those"; they know who they are—and there needs to be inclusion of their modified industry into the future fuels movement.

It (your next small step) comes in the way of extraction of a useful substance from the current source, useful as an additive and support fuel for future transport. It is known now to science; it needs to be known to the people, also.

Do you know there is a correlation between hemp and ethanol found in gasoline fuels?

No, I don't know about that. I know that ethanol comes from corn. I know that decades ago Henry Ford created the Model T automobile to run on gasoline as well as hemp

fuel, and that some researchers are again looking at and testing the efficacy of using hemp oil as an environmentally friendly bio-fuel to replace non-renewable fossil fuels.

We've been drilling and fracking for one hundred and fifty years and it is high time we fully replace crude oil. So, I'm going to straight-up ask you to impart us with future fuel ideas and tech. Please do tell: what's the scoop on the correlation between hemp and ethanol (which is basically just alcohol) that is found in gasoline fuels as an additive?

Yes, it is the case that hemp can be a component and an efficient one.

Let me state the downside of ethanol.

Currently, it is ethanol that is used as an additive in gasoline. It's made from corn in the United States, sugar in South America, palm oil in Southeast and East Asia, and rapeseed in Europe. For a minute, let's talk about corn. By far, the lion's share of the world's corn supply is being burned up in gasoline as the additive, ethanol. (The United States is the largest producer of ethanol in the world.) The ethanol industry burns up sixteen billion gallons of ethanol per year as a gasoline additive, and this increases every year. It takes twenty-six pounds of corn to make a gallon of ethanol. Holy corn! One acre of land makes about 328 gallons of ethanol per growing season.

Due to this insane market for ethanol and the incentive to profit from making ethanol, indigenous prairie lands have been converted into corn crops. This only serves to increase the greenhouse gas footprint as carbon that was formerly stored in the grass is released into the atmosphere (where it joins other pollutants like nitrogen and combusted gasoline used to process the corn crops). Not to mention, the vast expanses of corn fields are tilled at the expense of the local wildlife's habitat. All of this still says nothing of the argument that corn is a food grain and would be better used to feed the world and end famine.

Please jump-in.

Hemp is a replacement component for others in short supply, or the land on which to grow them on short supply or poisoned by pesticides and unclean air and water. There are rainforest and other location crops not previously used while some are gathering wealth in keeping their products in high demand.

It is not only about size of growing area but rather about efficiency of use as a component.

Ah ha! So, hemp in place of ethanol in our gasoline is actually more effective.

A change is afoot to revise thinking of how to use resources and to amend what was with what will be. We are saddened by the loss of clean air and water and soil in which to provide what is needed for your continuation.

Sure, it's sad. It's also asinine, what we do to our environment.

As the environment becomes a bigger topic and a topic of debate, some environmentally conscious individuals are grappling with the idea of no longer travelling by airplane. However, life today is such that taking weeks to cross the ocean by sailboat is not realistic for most. Should we stop our air travel?

Should you throw out the baby with the bath water? To stop airplane flight would not be possible in your society. Commerce would grind to a halt as a result and what do you foresee as replacement for airplane flight we ask?

It is for your science to create fuel sources that either do not pollute or do so to such a minimal degree it is known to be the very best you can do.

Until your people learn teleportation, transportation will be on wings and wheels with ships to fulfill water-crossing needs. Fossil fuels are not needed for propulsion of any of these—we speak of alternatives so take heed and work toward these ends.

Hemp has turned out to be a superstar plant as a plastic replacement and an additive to gasoline to replace ethanol. I wonder what else it's good for. Could hemp be developed as a fuel for propulsion of our airplanes as the alternative to fossil fuel?

This is but one of the potential replacements now being considered by your science, and it is one that will *not* be top choice in the end.

What will?

There are derivatives of gasses that stand a chance of being useful when modified, as also there are atomic or nuclear derivatives that could prove useful when modified sufficiently. Much is currently in place as is experimentation on not just replacement fuels but internal combustion engine design change to the extent that acceptance of alternative fuel sources is viable.

To reduce fuel weight in aircraft is a benefit as well, enabling larger payloads and cleaner operation.

Liquid fuel is not necessarily the way in future, it seems, even if held to by those reluctant to change.

What do you think of electric cars? The upside is not burning fossil fuels, but the downside is that electricity comes from methods that are not all that clean—we don't often think of this when it comes to electric cars.

The production of electricity requires fuels that are not clean in the overall picture of this means of transportation.

At the level of automobile use in your civilization, there is no way to reduce emissions either in the travel or the production of the method of propulsion. Until your way of living is altered and your lifestyles change to include less travel on a daily basis, the need for travel vehicles continues and increases. First the lifestyle changes and then the lesser need for transport. Cycling and walking are the way, of course, but in your current world it is scoffed at by those whose fast lifestyles require fast transport.

Always look to the basics for answers.

What *method* of alternative fueling can replace crude oil use altogether?

They are many and varied and range from *magnetics,* to *fission and fusion,* and on to what you consider *batteries.*

However, the future battery will be miniscule in size and via *magnetic fusion* will propel *transportation* methods of your future.

(Note to reader: magnetic confinement fusion generates thermonuclear fusion power that uses magnetic fields to confine fusion fuel in the form of a plasma.)

There are those currently experimenting with propulsion techniques that leave fossil fuel in their dust.

That's very good news.

When the clouds part and the way becomes clear, a burst of development becomes evident that takes your people higher and farther than you might now expect.

It is the fate of all to be busy in one place while developments come in another.

That's an interesting statement.

In your future time comes the organization of science into different departments and new ones emerge for study.

From what sector does the future method of propulsion come?

It is the section of physics that focuses on particle acceleration, in small scales but *greater intensity*, to be the place to look for propulsion and fuels of all kinds. Soon enough there will be breakthroughs in physics that will be declared monumental and ceiling shattering.

Look to your current students to know the secret and find the way, to show the way.

The development of an ability *to split what was thought to be solid* and divide with fission becomes a daily reality that changes the way of doing things.

Looking to that a little further shows that this ability exists and is being used in *other ways*. Look to it for a spark of change in the ways of heating and cooling, moving through space or moving through villages. There are options and small *masses* produce *monumental* amounts of energy.

And it brings clean to the forefront of human life on Earth. It cannot be monetized as fossil fuels but when time passes and those in the forefront of sustainable living have their power restored, it will be the focus of the future.

We leave it to you now to explore.

Do not consider this to be unreachable for it is yours to take and know that those other-worldly friends watch and support this breakthrough. It is to your benefit to find this means of great change as it takes your civilization to a new level. All is to be well with it.

This reads like instructions and can be used as exploratory steps to follow.

Very specifically, what is the best next direction for our travel needs (prior to the advent of using thought for teleportation)?

Particle acceleration is the thing; it is a thing and in active practice in science. To apply it here and now, in your time, is being done within science. It has yet to move into the daily reality, but it *is,* and it exists and can be harnessed by those capable.

May you please expand on this?

Particle acceleration is a scientific process that produces energy—this is a simplistic explanation. Like splitting the atom, it brings new and powerful sources of energy, specifically jet propulsion; an integral part of your Earth life, is aided.

What is the best use of this particle acceleration technology?

Should you desire to travel to the moon or the stars or other planets, fuel is needed. Until such time as teleportation is mastered, these processes will continue to develop.

An ion thruster is the current form of spacecraft propulsion, however, at present it doesn't get us to other planets at light-speed or nearly fast enough to make other-planet travel reachable. What can you say about the mention of "ion-specific power" in terms of how it is different from the ion thruster?

We spoke of acceleration and particle acceleration and transportation. Use of these technologies extends well beyond "fuel".

If the particle acceleration that you speak of is "*like splitting the atom*", then perhaps it's *not* the atom that you are suggesting accelerating. You also spoke of "cracking together ions" for "ion-specific power". Is the future-fuel mentioned for use for on-planet travel and for heat and fuel needs the very same as the propulsion energy mentioned for use in interstellar travel, or are these two different technologies?

The ability to utilize existing fuels for heat and land-based transport remains constant. The use of liquid fuels for off-planet travel will cease as an alternate method of propulsion beyond lightspeed is further developed. It exists in theory and is becoming reality in testing by your scientific community.

When you speak of particle acceleration, is this the same as what scientists are researching at CERN, the European Organization for Nuclear Research?

We spoke of the evolution of fuel sources that rapidly now become propulsion sources utilizing no fuel. It is beyond this current discussion.

Okay, not CERN.

"Propulsion sources utilizing no fuel" is intriguing and I'd love to explore this. Will we get to the crux of it if I ask the right questions?

> Your questions are quite acceptable. It is the outcome of exploration that shall take further time and we do report on what proves best for your uses at a *later date.*

While the reader will flow from your last comment to this one, today is a later date. To be fair, it's only days after our last words on this topic, but I do have another question to flesh out.

Last night, at a dinner party, someone mentioned that the big answer to future interstellar travel will be "*plasma* propulsion", and so I wanted to ask you about it.

I found this description on Wikipedia for two types of propulsion modalities, each with their pros and cons of efficacy: "A plasma propulsion engine is a type of electric propulsion that generates thrust from a quasi-neutral plasma. This is in contrast to ion thruster engines which generate thrust through extracting an ion current from a plasma source, which is then accelerated to high velocities using grids/anodes."

Both sound like they could be a lead on the no-fuel propulsion systems and/or "ion-specific" power source that you hinted at. I don't know if I should bother you again on this topic at this time, and yet when someone at a dinner party brings up interstellar travel out of the blue, I wonder if this is a fluke or how the Universe whispers to me. I'd love for this work that we're doing to help our scientists so that they might then focus on the tech that's best for the purpose, and so my question is: is one of these more on track than the other in terms of the future fuel or future travel that you had referenced?

It is the case that ion-thruster is the work of the present toward the path to the future.

As it becomes easier to influence the ways of science to invest in this mode, it will grow further into commonality. Science trials repeat and grow and change and return ideas and theories and postulations, but the "meat" of it is in the doing, and we say those currently practicing with this method—testing and experimenting with it—are close to stating this will do the job.

Moving through space and time will become a need and currently is a want, so those involved are feeling pressured to develop a working model. We say they exist and are being tested in reduced size and power.

For these future travel technologies to not be hoarded by big industry or hidden away from public access, it would be helpful to know what exactly we are talking about so that the people can be part of the process. I'm enjoying putting this together, yet I want to make sure that I'm following the breadcrumbs down the right path.

This is the time to know that future technologies are presently in scientific laboratories and in testing stages. There is knowledge in select segments of science, not general knowledge, not ready for publication outside of science, but working knowledge and a believable piece of, perhaps not-so-distant, propulsion to move people and cargo through space. This hasn't a name at this time nor a pathway to existence that we are ready to examine, but suffice it to say, it will be. The end result is that planetary travel will be managed with the ease and fluidity as that of your intergalactic visitors.

Who are our intergalactic visitors of more recent times?

Friends from other galaxies. As we have said, they continue to "buzz" by to see how Earth peoples are faring but see nothing they want so continue on their way. As they believe Earth's peoples have decimated the planetary resources, they are saddened and don't wish to remain there.

Are there other peoples on other planets in the Universe that need this much babysitting from the Spirit World and buzz-by monitoring from intergalactic supporters?

There are and have been, yes, and they come and go as lessons are learned.

Many people have wondered about our technological leap forward in a relatively short period of time. For instance, our computer age seemed to arrive all at once, and it was a rapid quantum leap. Did our computer and Internet technology come from Spirit, from interstellar visitors, or from our very ancient starseeded ancestors?

Largely responsible for this quantum leap were those starseeds who brought their personal ingenuity and advanced capabilities to the technology: these young leaders in the science propelled development and still do.

***Young* leaders?**

Young leaders in the science—this means these leaders are *young in the science.* The science is also young.

As there is nothing new under the sun, your technology comes from the past to fuel your future. Your inventors who have come from past lifetimes in advanced civilizations are the disseminators of information that now moves you ahead in the practice of technology shifting. It is a time of greater movement in this sector and brings excitement to the fore as it pertains to inter-stellar travel development.

Will I be alive when interstellar travel is commonplace?

We suggest that interstellar travel is reality now, in your time, and will extend to widely practiced means of people movement within your generation. It is not now considered a regular means of travel for public use but will be. As the need on Planet Earth escalates and as the movement of off-planet exploration swells, the need will be met.

Your hydrogen and other powered transports are being finessed into another form that can journey light-years away in a speed previously unheard of. It is on the cusp of discovery now and will enable the thought to become action. This will determine the when, further science the where. In our speak we say the far time which, for an undertaking of this magnitude, is soon.

Can you tell us something—a clue—about what we need to look at to make this discovery?

This is a present theory for interstellar transport using no fuel, as you know it. Currently it is being made known to your scientific community and has far to go in development, but we say it will become reality and change the way of off-planet transportation. It provides for light-speed which enables otherworldly visitations routinely.

It is "being made known" …hmmm, interesting choice of words. Are our scientists creating no-fuel propulsion technologies from their own minds and through trial and error? Or, are they being *given* the information, such that

the technology is not their own and is instead from other-worldly beings or even from Spirit-inspired thoughts? And, furthermore, are such discoveries given only at a time when we can "handle it" and use it for good?

Oh yes, we say that when the student is ready the teacher appears, yes?

The no-fuel fuel, meaning no liquid fuel. Was it a channeled inspiration? Quite possibly. Where do brilliant ideas originate—from within or not? What is from within and do experiments take their course when one step leads to the next and a brilliant mind has an "aha" moment? Some of both, we say, that brilliance comes through experimentation, knowledge and divine inspiration also. It's a process and remaining open to all thoughts and ideas is key.

For the currently unknown no-fuel power source, is the following correct: *hydrogen finessed into another form created by smashing together ions is the "fuel" to be used for interstellar transportation.* Am I on the right trail here? You have said that it still has "far to go in development." What is my next breadcrumb on this? Or, if I've incorrectly put this together, please correct me and show me where I'm off.

The no-fuel solution to interstellar travel is in development now and will bring an exponential leap forward in space travel.

(I might be getting a parental pat on the head here.)
While I'm straining for an answer or a formula, I'm starting to get the idea that you're holding back for a reason—likely a good reason. And, it could also be that I'm not putting the pieces of the puzzle together very well at all.

It is known and will become a race to develop. With North American science and European science collaboration, the best will come in the way of discovery. Funding, of course, is always a deterrent when sufficient isn't available. As this project is of the highest priority, for some, it will soon become widely known and funding will be directed to it. Earth is not ready for this, but it will be.

Space travel to this extent will be fought over by private enterprise and become a scramble for superiority. Again, your people show their dark side. Nevertheless, science moves forward and those in the know now prepare for ways to utilize this discovery for their own advancement. It is a sad place your people have come to. We wish to scold those who know better and can use their influence to ensure idealistic values are retained and practiced in your civilization.

Carefully walking on thin-ice and with great respect and gratitude, I will go at this again. Speaking of the no-fuel power source that could power vehicles in space and on-planet—plus replace electricity, oil, coal, nuclear and all polluting and/or non-renewable energy sources—if this future power source is only in the hands of the few at the top and is therefore patented and monetized, the rich and influential are the ones who benefit and they become richer and more powerful, which further engenders disempowerment and poverty for the many.

That being said, I feel the responsibility to advocate for our people. At this time, what more, if anything, can you say about the no-fuel power solution?

Ah yes, this solution is in your labs now with the scientific community developing further test methods.

The particle acceleration aspect of this clean fuel brings your world closer to the edge of space on a regular basis. There are *more uses*, of course, which are revealed in your soon time.

For now, we say that the discoveries of today prove to be the basis for tomorrow's transportation methods and the advancement brings rapid change to your manufacturers—a quantum leap forward for all.

Like teleportation in a sense, it mimics the think and move through time and space way of going. The no-fuel aspect of this is to remain just that, for now, as there is no fuel needed and *soon all is revealed*.

You are very patient with me and I appreciate that. I am (finally) getting the message loud and clear, and that is that you are holding off—at this time—on giving us all of the answers to future fuels for interstellar travel, likely because you believe that the information could get into the wrong hands. Is this correct?

It is our pleasure to speak more on this topic when the time is right. For now, there are lessons to be learned by your Earth people to satisfy the need for cleaner living and cleaner energy and cleaner intention before the Universe provides and releases the knowledge to your science that enables such travel.

The planets with life-giving environments are there but inaccessible to you at this time. Undisturbed and clean they support life and civilization and await visitors. The sadness here is that the minute in time your Earth people do arrive they begin polluting and disturbing and leaving litter and signs of themselves—in similar ways they have decimated Planet Earth. Your "space junk" and debris left behind on your moon is an example. What is left behind is done, but going forward there must be concern for another environment's wellness, not just how to get there and claim it. This will not do. Until this practice stops there will be no forward motion in this ability to deposit yourself on the soil of another planet.

This is the one thing to be aware of: The Universe provides in many ways and protection against flag-planting and claiming of territory and ability to have no boundaries will not be tolerated. Only when your people become kind and aware of their responsibility in this matter will the ability to find alternatives become reality.

To the extent that your people consciously determine they will function with zero waste debris, zero plastics, and heightened respect for another planetary home, success in finding the optimum alternate location will be yours. Until then, there is much attitude adjustment to be undertaken.

To learn propulsion for space travel is one thing, but until your daily damaging of the environment is ceased, no amount of balance exists. Your obvious choices for the use of non-recyclable products to support life is a sadness to us and the obvious alternatives exist and are not recognized by industry as sufficiently profitable therefore are not given the research and development budgets needed to become mainstream.

Again, we speak of corruption and greed among your politics and your industry and commercial ways of manufacture. Too much is known to be abandoned as reality. This is detrimental to your future in all ways. We are displeased by this bold defiance of what can be healing for your planet.

We ask that the people of Mother Earth clean up their own planet and learn new ways of daily life. We are here to say that the future as you foresee it will be and the ways of travel and accessing a new planetary home will become known. Until then, the focus is to be elsewhere: on the corruption and greed to your government and your industrial giants and your corporate executive need for control and wealth and none of this qualifies your civilization to deserve a clean and pristine new home.

As the Universe watches over your actions and condemns them, the Universe also blocks vital technology from being yours if it is designed to overtake and damage another planet.

Your people are shameful in their actions toward your Mother Earth and are not welcomed elsewhere in your Universe. Harsh as this sounds, it is designed to cause soul-searching and inner soul visiting for each person's ability and desire to clean up their personal act as well as move to clean up for the greater good.

Chapter Twenty-Four
The New Scientist and the Seeker

*P*ax, I wonder what's the trajectory of our evolution and what will quantum leap us into action for the greater good.

You once mentioned "the next age of your people". I didn't follow it up then, yet I'd like to do so now. What's the next age?

Moving ahead in time, we see generations of self-motivated people working for the cause. This is needed. The cause is the preservation of your environment and your world as you know it. There is *a new breed of scientist coming* which revolutionizes the way earthlings operate and this will become evident in the soon time.

Is the new breed of scientists to be the Viralenologists that I've envisioned through the work of the Viral Energy Institute (*after all, this is what brought us together for our writings*)— the new scientists whose work includes the use of out-of-the-box methodologies of spirituality and metaphysics?

Yes.

Talk about coming full circle!

In that case, I would like to enter into our record here this new term and occupation that I feel should be commonplace going forward. Here's the definition:

Viralenologist (noun)

1. One who studies viral energy in social interaction, interpersonal communication, and for the betterment of individual relationships and personal development
2. A scientist or intuitive who studies Viralenology in environments and as the causation of large planetary pockets or masses of enlightened or heavy/dense energy
3. One who studies Viralenology for new and renewable energy sources, future modes of travel, new technology, and communication
4. An intuitive who accesses higher-stream-consciousness (a.k.a. Universal Intelligence) by way of the viral and osmotic nature of energy in order to learn from and share the wisdom-of-the-ages

Your goal, Penelope, can be to inform and educate now so your people change their thinking and acting and do not, in future generations, continue to do damage in other worlds. What you teach now will be taught down the line; future generations benefit, and your legacy continues.

As you know, I'm a believer in spirit messengers, conduits of Universal wisdom, empaths and those who intuit energy fields, channelers of Spirit, and those who have tuned into Higher Self wisdom through practice and intention. I believe that we need to tap into their line to higher consciousness and have them teach us the ways in which we can develop our own higher abilities. I also believe that we need to elevate Spirit channelers to important roles in our scientific community. If scientists would pair up with good and reliable channelers of the Spirit World, we would more quickly evolve in our technology, consciousness, and forward movement in all ways. Do you agree?

Yes.

I see a future where intuitives are regularly consulted by our scientists of all kinds, from astrophysicists to the engineers of our future fuels, and from medical doctors to mental health professionals.

There is indeed infinite wisdom to be mined when there is a meeting of the minds, as it were, and the resource is there for the taking. The great distance between science and metaphysics is understandable, between traditional organized religion and metaphysics also. There is doubt of value from one and fear from the other. Neither will mellow in the soon time, but Penelope, your stating this need for connection will begin a shift.

These could include the metaphysical practitioners, energy healers and teachers, researchers of the contagious nature of energy, students of the osmotic properties of energy and energy sharing, intuitives, mediums, and light workers who utilize spiritual practices and sixth sense abilities within science and traditional studies of science to enlighten themselves and the world.

This is the way of it beginning now and going forward.

There is much to be shared with those who are not on this higher plane of exploration of sciences, and it will take time to unfold. This is as it should be as during this phase many more of your Earth people are learning and understanding that they can make a difference and will be a part of the solution, not a part of the problem. And this is a lesson they will teach daily as they go forward into the population around them.

They are the New Orions who bring light into the darkness—they are the stars shining light onto and into the darkness to illuminate what is there. Once identified, they may begin to remove and repair and rebuild your society.

Is there any connection between your reference of the "New Orions who bring light" and the star constellation Orion known for its stars of bright light that comprise Orion's Belt? The three brightest stars are called the Three Kings and are known to be beacons in our night sky.

It is a name only, the name of Orion which indicates the brightest of bright.

These are the people of your world today who have seen the light and begin to bring their light into the darkness of unawareness among the population. The light is directed toward clean Earth resources and pure intention among the masses. It is the way of bringing about a return to simpler ways and purity of intention, honesty in all matters and a knowing that Planet Earth needs coddling and care, protection and respect, and teaching how this is done.

These are adults who have found their way to this place of understanding and found their need to teach and inform and share. These are the New Orions—those whose light shines brightly into the darkness of your Earth's present.

Wonderful. So, the New Orions *are* the Viralenologists—metaphysical seekers using enlightened thinking and feeling to arrive at scientific discoveries and future technologies of all kinds.

Yes.

You mention that they are adults. Are they exclusively among the adults of today, or do they perhaps include some of the enlightened young people who will also develop into the New Orions/Viralenologists of the future when they grow up?

They are enlightened ones, yes, and not of a particular generation.

There are many historical references to Orion, and also semi-recent popular culture references hinting at deeper significance such as in the film *Men in Black* (1997) where the galaxy is found to be hidden in a charm on the collar of an ET's cat named Orion.
Is "Orion" a clue to something bigger for us to explore?

Yes.
These, the new breed, have in common the greater good and the big picture for your Earth planet *as well as your galaxy*.
Cohesive planning and action is called for by these individuals and groups—they have a higher calling in their adult years and have seen the way. Having a voice and using it for the well-being of Mother Earth is their intention. Together with those younger who are committed to the same cause, they take action and enable those who watch and listen to know they may also participate and create change where needed. They are

clarions for the cause. Your world is blessed now with the upris-
ing of minds and spirits and souls and bodies for world repair
and wellness.

**To recap, the New Orions are the new breed of scientists:
enlightened adult-souls within all generations who have a
role for the greater good and big picture of Planet Earth
and the Milky Way galaxy.**

Yes. They wish to bring their zeal and excitement for
change-making to the forefront and allow their inner beings
and inner-voices to bring their strengths to the project of saving the planet.

They lead and they learn, and they teach, and they are *inclusive of all who can contribute*. It is their joy to become one with the
movement to peace on Earth.

What else should we know about them?

These New Orions are to be recognized and trusted, not
shut down for unusual or creative ideas that fly in the face of
tradition. Nothing new comes but repeating old ways, certainly
in the repair of your planetary resources.

Now it is time to trust in their recommendations and be the
voice that agrees to adapt to the new ways.

Within the movement will be those who *follow* and work
to create change, as well as those who *lead* and work to create
change—both are needed.

Quietly going where none have gone before in the intention
to create wellness out of destruction: this is the mindset of those
who see themselves as Earth healers, and this is the role now for
many to consider adopting.

If the goals are to clean air and water and soil and the minds of those who pollute, all these are needing individuals who feel the call to make the change needed now by Planet Earth.

There will be political change within your view in Earth's soon time, and that will enable a more peaceful change to come. Those in power who monetize their positions will find themselves on the outside looking in, soon enough, and those with inherent honesty and pure intention will be held to their ideals and lead accordingly. Change comes and your Earth is the better for it.

Your people are to know that it is a long-term plan to bring about the repair and healing your planet requires, but with the purity of intention you will find in new leaders, this task becomes a joy and like ripples on the pond, this feeling of pure intention spreads throughout your globe and is felt and emulated by Earth people. It is a good thing.

I think we're changing. I feel a groundswell of pure intention for Planet Earth. Environmental concerns are all the talk, and some action, too. Individuals are becoming aware and making choices to reflect this intention for planetary wellness. It's true that our governments are still moving full steam ahead in the wrong direction for the environment, however, the people can (and perhaps will) be the change needed.

Pax, I'd like to think that we are empowered about the physical reality of our world; empowered to make happen the changes that we want to see. Are you making a connection between our empowerment and the ability of the average person to make the discoveries needed?

Yes.

It is a time of change and becoming one of enlightenment tempered with wisdom and humility for those who thought they had the answers—they did not. And for those who thought they showed the way, well they did that all right, but it was not necessarily the best way.

We speak of the forces of nature and that means what is meant to be in your world at this time, what is intended, and what will result in the trajectory change that is needed.

I'm unclear (and I think this is important): what are the forces of nature?

We suggest that a "force of nature" is a movement that cannot be stopped, like a hurricane cannot be stopped as it is both a force and of nature. Those who come your way now to be the change that is needed are the forces of nature.

This is compelling and exciting.

As we speak of the "peaceful ones who show the way", they are the starseeded ones with integrity and passion that *come from elsewhere* to you as a gift at this time. They are the Crystal and Indigo children, and also, they are the New Orions—we call them by many names and the names themselves are not of matter. It is their intention and their goals that are of import to you and your Planet Earth. These are the voices to be heard, the integrity to be felt, the intention to be followed and the harbingers of a new normal for your world as time plays out.

It is for your people to trust in this, watch and learn, and choose your channel for peace. Each has a role to play, each has a need to contribute, and this is the time to know that the need will match the giving and the givers. To that end there will be change shown in a time and in a way you would not have considered. It is your time and their time and when combined, only good will come.

Trust in this and trust in yourselves.

Chapter Twenty-Five
Communication Through Consciousness

*I*s the Universe one ginormous organism?

All is one and one is all and interconnected in this Universe. What is in one place affects what is in another. It is the way of it. It is the linking energy that holds the Universe together, as that Universal energy holds your humanity in its protective grasp.

Is humankind sort of a metaphorical body part or organ of the Universe? Do we have an impact on the scale of the infinite cosmos?

Interconnectedness relates here and one affects all as all affects one. As it is important to not have extinction in the animal world it is important to not have extinction of a planet's race of people. One feeds another and one cares for another and to have a missing link is not productive—there is a resulting weakness of the whole.

How would the Universe be weakened if humanity became extinct?

As with links in a chain, with one missing the strength is compromised or lost. As with the Universal energy, such is the case that all of the whole makes up the strength of the whole.

Gaps in space are there for a reason, a distancing, and intentional. For something present to become not present is a weakening. This applies to the food-chain and the brain-chain in scientific development, and it applies to all aspects of life as you know it. Think on it from a familial standpoint: a family is strongest with all members present; remove one and there is a void that is never filled. It creates a weakness of emotion and, depending on the familial activity, a weakness of productivity perhaps. Expand that to the Universe and it is clear.

According to some of our cosmologists and quantum physicists, the Universe is *physically* connected, and not just metaphorically, metaphysically, or spiritually. Research from these cosmologists has shown that all planets and all stuff (and non-stuff, for that matter) in a galaxy are connected and "held together" in balance. Furthermore, all galaxies are connected to each other, so they say. Also, super-clusters (groups of galaxies) are connected to each other as if in a web. So, the whole Universe is connected.

Here are some questions based on these discoveries—
What is the mysterious power that connects everything? Is it a gas, an energy, or a force?

Well, it is the gravitational pull that is responsible for suspension of orbs in space. It is a push-pull result of being held together in the desired pattern. There is magnetic management of the distancing also, and planets and stars hanging in space do so with the magical threads of compression in place. Push and pull results in holding in place and not falling through the space they inhabit into another place. You do note that regularly there are comets and other pieces of the puzzle that break free and go streaking through the maze of orbs on their way to burning out. What is not intended to remain in space doesn't.

All is managed and controlled and finitely tuned to hold what is and what will be. Into the galaxies go the magical threads of what results in the dangling of orbs in the night sky for your viewing pleasure.

That was a beautiful description. You are a poet, Pax.
Speaking now again of our friendly intergalactic supporters, you said, "We access their wisdom through our conversations." I'd like to visualize how your communication with interstellar supporters works whereby they may pass on their wisdom to you and then to us?

As we have a teleporting and telepathic communication model, it is our way to communicate and to be.

The visitors who have been and continue to support Earth people's development do so as that is their role. They give of their technology and they give of their knowledge generally and offer to show the way to higher learning and functioning. They do this throughout their travels in the galaxy and farther afield. Where they are accepted, they help to advance civilizations and society. Often there comes an end to that acceptance so they continue to watch and await a potential need for their future interventions.

Should you wish to access the wisdom of extra-terrestrials, there are methods which do not involve us. Consider the application of remote viewing and the Higher Self accessing—always there are times and methods useful or not (and the time is not now to consider a direct communication with extra-terrestrials): this refers to accessing our own Higher Self wisdom for the purpose of intuiting ET wisdom. Here are two separate, or three in reality, existences: theirs, yours, and ours—and all on different planes, alternate realities and methods of communication. Allow time for them to meld.

Tuning in to another place to see what and who is there and what are the current activities. This technique has been commonly used by government security of highest level in times of war and cold war, to infiltrate from afar the operations of those they need to know. Spying it can be called. Viewing through the training to do so and utilizing one's psychic abilities to see the scene and report the details. Drawing what is seen in the "mind's eye" is a way to transmit the sight to paper for record keeping.

It's kind of scary (and eye-opening) that our governments have been using this ability to spy. I wasn't expecting to hear that governments use (what I consider) spiritual practices to spy for their own gain. Shouldn't this be illegal?

You overreact here as this technique is mind power in use for good. To know what a national "enemy" is doing is practiced globally and not a new technique. You might consider this being practiced for the good of the country and its national security. This is a widely practiced technique that is not only not illegal but is fair play: all is fair in love and war it is said. The use of this practice is more acceptable to many than entering a battlefield and shooting to kill. In fact, this technique and the knowledge it brings can prevent such action.

This sounds reasonable.

Recreationally it is useful to view a target of travel or family or road conditions—it is open to possibility. The practice of this technique is that, *practice*, and identifying the place one wishes to see and focusing on it, allowing the Higher Self abilities and strengths to function to the extent that a mental picture forms. Some do this as recreation. Others have done and currently do for national security reasons. It is not rocket science, but it is for the trained mind to achieve and brings great value to security needs.

Okay, I'm satisfied with that. Thank you.

This next question is going to be "out there" (ha! pun intended), although everything that we talk about is rather out there, so here it is: I know that you've said that our friendly interstellar supporters (who used to be visitors) do not visit at this time because we are too hostile and our Earth people and political culture is currently too volatile. Sooo, my question is, can I visit them? A little off-planet rendezvous perhaps? Maybe they could pick me up for a day trip? I'm being funny, yes, but I'm also perfectly serious in that I would be up for the challenge and would invite a meeting of the minds if they're interested.

Until you are able to teleport, we expect this remains a day-dream. Alternatively, Penelope, you may consider communicating through meditation: asking their assistance in understanding what more you can do to meet your challenges at this time is a beginning. Your intentions are honorable, and it will be known this way.

That you are an Ambassador for Peace on Earth in all ways is also *known*, therefore you may find contact.

I'm honored and eager to communicate via meditation.

Pax, these ETs are very interesting to us Earthlings; we're endlessly fascinated by them, actually.

I recall that you've previously said that we will be grateful for your guidance in this colonizing journey (yes! we are) and that you, Pax, "together with others of high-mind and experience in the Spirit realm, will continue to advance our support and ideas".

Who are the others of high-minds in the Spirit realm?

Those who have gone before and continue to observe and guide and send positive energy for the best possible outcomes for your Earth people are your teachers.

Their influence is felt in consciousness by those tuned-in to their Higher Powers and listening and following their hearts. There, in heart and mind the messages are felt and heard, the direction known as the right direction, shared for guidance and the knowingness that these are the ways now for your Earth salvation and healing.

How do we communicate with those guides in the Spirit realm?

Listen and learn, it is said, as above. Take the questions to your Spirit Guides, go within for answers always: this is the source for you.

I understand that ETs are physical beings in form. However, the Spirit World is just that—spirit. Through our conversations, I feel as though I know you in a way. Truth be told, I think of you as a friend and I even miss you between our chats. Is there such an experience as a visitation with the Spirit realm? To "meet" those of high-mind in the Spirit

realm—is this possible? Can I *know* you in a way that is experiential?

Experiential indicates having an experience as a result, yes? So, your experience *is* in communicating with us and this is the way of it. We could, however, develop a fictional method where you might say, "Guess who's coming to dinner?" but this would not become reality at this time or in your future, as we believe you would ask.

Yes, I would have asked.

Be aware of this three-way conversation (Pax/Carole Serene/Penelope) being unusual by any of your standards and quite unlike the day-to-day experiences of most.

Volume 8
Do Unto Earth
Pax and the Journey to New Worlds

"Our only chance of long-term survival is not to remain inward-looking on Planet Earth, but to spread out into space."
Stephen Hawking
Theoretical physicist, cosmologist, winner of the Albert Einstein Award, director of research (until death) at the Centre for Theoretical Cosmology at the University of Cambridge

Chapter Twenty-Six
Other Planet Colonization

*P*ax, how do people find balance between Earth repair and our journey to explore elsewhere?

Oh yes this is the question—how to find balance now with continuing efforts to clean Earth's environment while also forging ahead with space exploration. It is a balance of thinking as well as acting. It is a placing of emphasis and importance on both, simultaneously. How do your people think now about the need to maintain clean Earth while following the need to branch out to space exploration; where is the emphasis, the priority?

In our view of your world and people it seems that not much thought has been given to this question. Of course, it would be that emphasis is placed on getting through one day at a time, family and career and health and wellness, all which demand attention and focus. Most of your Earth people do not give attention to the question of this priority, this inclusion of space travel into their daily thoughts and actions. How is it to be that a question of this magnitude could enter the daily thought process of those simply trying to put food on the table and keep a paying job? It is not a priority.

When we enter into colonization of another habitable planet, will it be people with money and power that go first, and will greed and the need for power be factors that work against peaceful co-existence?

Well, it is the case that there will be an effort to introduce the need for purity of heart and thought among those first explorers. There is a division between settlers and those enabling the journey and settling, and there is opportunity to create a haven for those of pure intentions—in this way it is "utopian" in description and intention.

The power of intention among those facilitating this journey and this settling will serve to bring a higher vibration to those involved and endeavor to raise the project to one of purity of intention.

We understand that you will be grateful for our guidance in this colonization journey and we, together with others of high-mind and experience in the Spirit realm, will continue to advance our support and ideas.

It's inspiring and very emotional to know that help is coming.

And this is how it is.

For those who will pursue other planet colonization, what planet is the best option?

When it is considered time to colonize another planet, that new home will show itself. At present there is no knowledge of where or how to journey there, and not enough time to undertake a journey for most.

It breaks my heart to think of abandoning Planet Earth; she is so beautiful and blue and green, and I couldn't imagine a better alternative for us than to heal Earth and commit to her.

Seeking peace on your planet should be top of mind, not just how to leave it. Is it your people's belief that leaving for another planet will be a solution; that only the good and peaceful people will be transported? Reality is not so. Reality is that energy, healing energy, must now be utilized to clear greed and avarice on your planet. These are the basis of all warring. If there were a method now for your peoples to move to another planet, they would be "running away" from the poor conditions they have created on Planet Earth. In "running to" an alternative home, those who created the unfavorable conditions on Earth will simply relocate and resume their habits elsewhere. How long do you think this idyllic new home will be idyllic? First, heal yourself.

While we work to clean up Earth, can we also plan for colonizing another planet or must we complete our clean up first?

At the current rate of your planet's demise, it is desirable to make a Plan B for future generations: to speak of colonizing other planets is to reflect that which we have spoken of. There will be no clean air, water, or soil within one and a half generations, so how does the Earth population plan to eat, breathe, and survive?

This is not an idle threat—it is reality. There is already too much damage done to save all of the planet and populating of others will occur in the next generation.

Ouch. Colonization of another planet will become a *need* for humans?

The end of civilization on Planet Earth is a potential, of course, and there seems already a way around that with plans to colonize other planets while repairing this one: this should successfully avoid cataclysm. As your time shows poisoning of earth soils and air and water, continuing to support population at current levels is a challenge.

For those intrepid souls who seek to forge ahead with development of civilization elsewhere, transportation and methods in current development support travel to another planet to colonize, farm, and grow in readiness for increased population arrival.

This is done to relieve pressure on Planet Earth while repair is underway. It is the need to rehabilitate your Earth, not abandon her, so those who wish to travel and be pioneers and homesteaders on another planet will gladly do so. They forge ahead in the making of new lives and civilization, while those wishing to remain to repair Earth, will do so.

Earth people do travel off-planet to begin new civilization(s) elsewhere.

We have said that the need to remove large portions of your population to alternate locations exists, but the transport means do not as of yet. While they are being created on your Earth plane, they exist in heightened sophistication in civilizations elsewhere, off-planet.

Do you consider the possibility of combining the need with the resource? Can your Earth population see themselves entering the unknown in this way? Explorers and pioneers and those with no fear of striking out on their own to begin again elsewhere—these people exist.

That there is not yet infrastructure at the destination is a present-day situation and will change in your soon time. You have a space-station structure, but this is not what will be the home-base: it is a solid and on-land structure. If eating and breathing and life-functions can now exist on a space-station, a dedicated-to-the-process solid structure, situated on solid ground, can be constructed to host the explorers.

There is much to consider and much to be divulged of your Earth science as it has progressed in this direction but not been divulged to the public. We know and we share and there will be non-believers as well as those asking where they can sign-up.

It's now time to focus on interstellar travel and the colonization of an alternative home for Earth people while refreshing Planet Earth.

Does the plural in "colonize other planets" and "new civilization(s)" mean that we will set up a number of colonies on more than one other planet?

Oh yes, you will look to go big and colonize more than one planet.

To find suitable hosts, however, will take time but meanwhile there is exploration and preparation to be done.

Your science prepares propulsion methods to get you there as well they prepare ideas for supporting life on arrival.

There is no known destination at this time that duplicates Earth and will be the most like your present home, but that will come. First is the transport means to get there as well as a sense of where it may be that your next home is located.

The pieces do come together as the many branches of science work to answer the questions around this great undertaking. As your time progresses there is renewed energy put into this study and greater commitment by people to join the science making it become reality.

One step at a time and one day at a time and it will be.

To live inside a space station on a grey and life-barren planet sounds bleak to me. Are there no other beautiful blue and green planets accessible to us now?

Space travel time and distance determine the where, and your science determines the when. While there may be these twin planets—their existence in your galaxy or elsewhere is not yet known (to your people) nor is the method to visit. There will be no awareness of soon-time travel to a duplicate of Planet Earth, no, as planetary locations relative to your Earth Sun make it unlikely. Farther removed, however, there will be, even though not accessible at this time. It is not to be a focus of your current Earth science.

You will find alternatives closer and as technology catches up with need, those afar may be explored. For now, it remains a journey into technology and alternatives and time will bring the ways needed to undertake this adventure.

I guess there are some people who are into the lifestyle of living on a space outpost firmly planted on a life-barren planet, but I don't see the appeal. I like landscapes with waterfalls to admire and mountains to hike. I like peacefully paddling down quiet rivers, and hearing the birds chirp in the morning and again at night. I like the changing seasons and the smell of fresh rain on summer-hot terra.

Will the settlers of such a planet-station live indoors their whole lives, perhaps creating faux-outdoor spaces but never again knowing the reality of a living and lush planet?

This is dependent upon the destination chosen. Those who are comfortable with isolation from nature will be accepting. As there are city people and country people, there are choices to be made.

We do not describe all future planetary homes at this time as they are yet to be identified and chosen. Choices exist, or they *will*.

Those who travel off-planet initially are less concerned about the destination, and more about the journey.

I see—they'll do it for the adventure, the newness, the intrigue, and the science of it. Yet, for those like me who are enamored with a lush and living planet home, I suspect that you'd say that we should clean up Earth and take care of her if we love her so much. Of course, I'm with you on that.

In your world today is deep unrest and upheaval. It will begin to heal, yes, but in order to effect repair there must be not only awareness but the bravery of speaking up and speaking out, in peace, to what will regain integrity and purity of the heart of your nations around the globe. Some are there and some are close while others have driven themselves over the cliff and require a complete rebuild in order to function in integrity.

The mist is lifting and now you could not be clearer as to why this book's various topics are to be understood together: like the ingredients in a recipe that must be mixed together to create the desired outcome. All topics here are related to environmental repair. The eight subjects of *Do Unto Earth* are not separate topics at all, are they Pax? Together this is a complete message that says: Do unto Earth as you would have Earth do unto you!

Yes.

We ask that your people trust in their own voices to speak their truth to power and ensure forward motion for your humanity and not only for survival but to flourish once again as peaceful societies in respect and love for all.

We wish also to speak of resettling and new beginnings and the old ways brought forward to form the basis for new society. There is the moving to explore another planet with a view to settling. Preliminary work now being done in this direction shows promise and we can build on this.

Adding in assistance from those intergalactic supporters of old will bring an interesting twist and allow for a progressive journey into what-ifs and what is possible. Our friends from afar show the way, if permitted, to refreshing your ways and re-establishing a healthy Earth society.

Will ETs make an in-person visit to help and guide us?

In this present incendiary society as a whole on your Earth plane, not a visitation for the purpose in sharing wisdom for your future is possible. To which unsettled country would they aim and into which warring culture would they insert themselves with an offer so out of the realm of expected and logical sounding messages? Your planetary cultures are fractured and worsening and to think a peaceful entry into your world is possible at this place in time is not reality. The fear this would bring to your peoples and the intent to capture for their own future gain would be forefront in behavior and will not be undertaken as a result. There will be no further intentions to bring friendly and helpful visitations until your warring and greed and wish to maintain supremacy changes into your people developing confidence and empowerment to the extent they cease to fear what may be offered to them in peace. It just will not be.

Can we access their wisdom through our conversations, yes, and we will fill our energies for a time preparing Earth peoples to listen, to purify their own thinking and acting, to be caring about your climate crisis, and commit to behavioral changes that result in a wave of energy toward the repair of your planetary resources.

(Well, this answers the Fermi paradox.)
Will our next planet be a place of unity, peace, and bliss?

Well it is ours to say that "Utopia" is a state of mind, is it not? It is not a place and perfection is in the view of the individual and the judgment of that individual. It is not—outside of a fairy-tale—practical to think your world will rise to this description, either on Planet Earth or your next destination home. Your people carry corruption and greed, and this will not be eradicated within the next generation or two. There is much work to be done by your people and perfection won't be reality until this is undertaken, if ever. The creation of a "utopian home place" is represented by the introduction of peace and prosperity for all—these are not present on your current Earth plane.

A new home of the old and proven ideas for peaceful co-existence in a future time and place is the way.

Is Earth the fairest planet in the Universe (to put it in Magic Mirror terms) or are there other beautiful and life-filled planets out there?

Such places exist, yes, and in the eternal darkness of space, unexplored mostly at your time and place in existence, there are host planets that may be considered in your future. Vast in nature and vital in make-up, they could support life as you know it.

The immensity of space brings challenges to travel of course and this will be surmounted by your science, in time, with help from *future* technology as previously discussed.

"Eternal darkness" ...hmmm, I'm a bit concerned by our people's history of easily getting the message screwed up or attaching fear to it. While I know the difference between light (such as perceived by the sense of sight and an energy byproduct) and Light (as in enlightenment and highly vibrating intention-energy), and dark (as in the dimness of the visual sense of light) and dark (such as polluted intention and action which clouds the Light of goodness), others might require your reference of "eternal darkness" to be made crystal clear in context before they go off in the wrong direction with the message.

Eternal darkness is deep space. Not gloom and doom and fear darkness, and is to be interpreted as such. It is deep space your people wish to access. You may refer to the locations of habitable planets as the great unknown or the unexplored, but we suggest it is as we have stated: the eternal darkness of deep space which shall be illuminated by your finding and visiting them.

Chapter Twenty-Seven
Interstellar Travel at Lightspeed

*Y*ou've said that "our friends from afar show the way" in our project of exploring another planet's colonization. I'd love to know who is on the team! Who are the ET friends who will show us the way?

As your science becomes able to replicate the technology which brought visitors to your Planet Earth in past, the speed at which the project flows increases. Your military and government are aware of the history, location of classified records, and details of the transport vehicles used and reverse-engineered following crashing to Earth.

These records exist and only those in power know why or if they will remain secret.

Are you speaking again of the spaceship still held and locked up in secrecy at Area 51—the craft that crashed at Roswell?

Oh yes, it is so.

Has this craft been fully utilized in our ability to reverse-engineer, or is there still more technology and wisdom that can be uncovered from this craft by re-opening the records and vaults?

All that is known and has been learned can benefit by additional looks as technology continues to grow and advance toward what is there. Recognition of what is there will grow as your technology does and is understood.

The value is in continual inspection and comparing with what is currently known and what is in development.

I would imagine that reverse-engineering the craft would provide information about the vehicle's engine and propulsion system, yet I'm not sure it would explain how to harness the no-fuel propulsion source. And, even if our government intelligence and military has unearthed (ha!) from this craft all that is needed to reproduce the technology and no-fuel energy source to run it, this information is not disclosed to the public; it's kept in secrecy. As businessman J.P. Morgan infamously expressed to Nicola Tesla—if they can't put a meter on it, they don't want it.

Pax, will fuel one day be free?

Yes.

You've told us that the no-fuel energy source is a method not a product: it's free energy and will change everything from pollution to carbon emissions, and it will upset the geo-economic system, open new industries, end secrecy and corruption, and eliminate the 1% (or perhaps the .001%)

from holding society's power. It will essentially end the monetization of energy as a meter-monitored paid utility. And, it will allow for interstellar travel at lightspeed.

It also would mean the end of oil, coal, nuclear, public utilities, and even solar and wind power (which, while largely clean, are still monetized utilities like all the rest).

In addition, the open source energy method would shift the power from the very few with special interest and re-seat power with the entire population of the world.

Pax, the no-fuel propulsion source, if known by some, is not going to be released by our governments because they are tied to the stakeholders of big oil and the like. The suppression of clear, free, and equitable energy will continue unless We The People get a divine intervention or some extraterrestrial help.

Of course, there will be no interstellar travel without the means to get there by light-speed and beyond, and so let's begin to talk about the propulsion systems used by our interstellar supporters.

Pax, what can you tell us?

The spark of energy needed to propel and maintain space flight and travel is the catalyst, and that is known and being developed by space researchers now. It will be shared with those developing the technology both in public and private enterprise.

The energy is harnessed from deep space and this will become more known as science progresses.

I believe you're talking about Dark Matter. Crikey, Pax.

Time allows for continual recognition and inspiration to identify and unravel mysteries.

Some of our famous physicists from history such as Nicola Tesla and Hendrik Casimir brought in the idea of Dark Energy being a zero-point energy field: pulling energy from the quantum vacuum. Is the zero-point energy field the secret behind interstellar travel propulsion systems?

Partially, and it is currently in laboratory trials—the ability to promote and deliver a method of propulsion for space travel that is independent of fossil fuel use on your Earth plane. There is no means for storing liquid fuel in sufficient quantity on board a space travel vehicle that will serve a purpose designed for lengthy travel and return.

Dark Matter is something (or no thing) that our cosmologists still know practically nothing about.

Here's what we do know: Dark Matter does not emit, absorb, or reflect light, and yet we know that it has a gravitational impact because it bends light as it passes nearby. It is something, it has an impact, it is a force or power. Beyond that, it's a mystery to us and I can't help but ask for some enlightenment on this from the Spirit World.

What precisely is Dark Matter?

It is a place, emptiness, and a non-place all at once. It is a nowhere and an everywhere, a void to be filled? What is and what is not are in this void and it will become useful in time.

"It will become useful in time"—well, well, how compelling. Let's start more broadly. Dark Energy/Dark Matter does not contain matter?

It is the great void of magnetic being that results in swirling masses of energy. We suggest that this is a *place*, this Dark Energy, and it is of interest to those in the scientific community for its potential to hold secrets.

When the time is right there will be exploration of these places that results in the demystifying of all things related to space. For now, it is the darkness of knowledge that remains.

It is deep space. It is the place in the time.

When Dark Energy is understood, *all* mysteries of space will be revealed/known?

All mysteries will never be completely revealed as time passing creates more mysteries within the Universe. We may say that as humankind is ready for the revealing, it will be. *As we have stated, when the time is right.*

Is Dark Energy the last frontier of exploration?

At this time when focus is on what lies within Dark Energy, it will seem as though it is a last frontier. As the Universe continues to move boundaries over time, there will always become another frontier for exploration. At this time there is no final frontier.

Does Dark Energy expand?

Expansion and contraction is, and as it is, the density varies. Like stretching taffy, it can be smaller and thicker or greater and thinner. Where lies the strength do you think?

This is a puzzle for our cosmologists and theoretical physicists.

Does Dark Matter/Dark Energy have *intelligence*? If so, *who* (or what) is the cosmic mind behind this intelligence of Dark Energy?

We are here to say this is not the application for these places in time.

Be aware of the placing of these areas and their intention as part of the Universe.

Separate time from place from intelligence and it will be clear.

(More breadcrumbs. *The placing. Their intention.* Maybe the locations of Dark Energy are connected to their purpose and function in the Universe.)

You have referred to Dark Matter as anti-gravity and that its usefulness to us would be revealed in time. May you please expand on Dark Matter's origins and purpose?

This is the *weightless* and almost *indefinable energy* found in corners of unexplored space and it will contribute to your wellness when understood and harnessed. It is the void and the place of worship for the many. How is this meant, you ask? Those cosmologists who try to understand and control indefinable areas of space do worship at the altar of higher learning and endeavor to communicate with who and what may be present there. It is for them to continue the focus and the in-depth search.

May you please speak to a zero-point quantum vacuum system and how we can utilize this zero-point energy source?

This is a necessary forward motion in the space travel industry and together with science brings forward an integrated fuel system. The ability of some to integrate systems and take from each what will blend and meld and contribute to the whole is underway and the end result shows itself in your soon time.

I've been doing my research so that I might ask the pertinent questions, and I've learned that our scientists have

produced models and theories to explain the way in which the zero-point field works, however there is still a missing piece of knowledge. Some scientists say that the problem is (and I'm paraphrasing and summarizing to the best of my understanding) that they can't yet figure out how to interrupt the quantum field in order to extract some of the energy. Basically, because the field is a balanced bubble there is no pressure differential, and without that the tremendous energy contained inside is just a moot point: it's not useable while held in the balanced field because no pressure means that the power within is powerless (to us anyway).

It seems that our scientists are trying to replicate the zero-point field and figure out how to properly interrupt the quantum vacuum and therefore utilize particles of energy to create the thrust needed to power propulsion systems/engines capable of interstellar travel at the speed of light, or faster.

How do we replicate the zero-point energy field—that tremendous power contained in Dark Energy—in order to use it as the no-fuel power source?

We say it is not for you to replicate but rather to *harness* this—no need to reinvent the wheel.

Then, this means that we harness it in space as opposed to creating it on Earth through man-made energy generation. (This is a giant clue.)

It's believed by some scientists that the zero-point energy field is effectively used for interstellar vehicle travel because (perhaps in addition to use as the no-fuel spark of propulsion) it basically creates a spacetime bubble around the vehicle.

What do you know about the concept of the vehicle creating its own anti-gravity environment which essentially renders it massless?

You might say so, yes, and if this is the technology to strive for then it is achievable. At speed this becomes reality and eases the way forward. It also provides protection somewhat against exterior injury. An energy field surrounding a capsule can deflect potential harm as it travels through space.

Aye aye, Captain.
Some scientists say that extraterrestrial interstellar vehicles are operated by trans-dimensional physics, meaning that they cross through other dimensions to get here (to Earth) or other places in the Universe. Is this true?

It is, indeed, as the trans-dimensional aspect of it does create forward motion in propulsion. This is an internal fission and fusion, and these together work in tandem for propulsion. This is to be discovered and tested further and will be the way of it.

Until that time, we share that the off-planet trajectory now is to deep space, and this is where the technology is required.

And so, the big question is: *how* can we harness Dark Matter in space?

Harnessing Dark Matter in space is to be a continual study as it is not yet your time to so do. There are steps forward not yet identified and so we suggest that as science further explores space it will become clear.

There is a time for everything in your development and even in your old days it was known that the cart was not placed in front of the horse if forward motion was the goal.

In summary, we use Dark Energy while in space and harness it in space. And so, this leaves the question as to how

we get into *deep* space in the first place where we can harness Dark Energy for propulsion whilst in space.

Oh, yes. It is the case that off-planet exploration will become every-day in Earth people's future. In order to get into deep space there are many details yet to be ironed out, and many explorations of technology to be completed. At this time, we point you toward fission and fusion. Your science understands this now as it is the means of current travel. It is our intention to show your people the way of the future, yours not ours, as off-planet people know this technology and use it to buzz by your planet regularly. It is the science of motion put into play and combined with the spark of non-fuel, completes the circuit.

It's an electrical circuit at work, that kind of spark, and together with thrust and propulsion equates to forward motion. It is the simple action of current passing through that creates the fusion which allows the fission and the rest is projected upward. We should like to say it is not rocket-science, but in fact it is. (*Cosmic wink.*)

Chapter Twenty-Eight
The Secret Lives of Extraterrestrials

*L*et's reveal or dispel some alien life and otherworldly enigmas.

In searching for a word to call the peoples of extraterrestrial civilizations, would we call them "people", "humanoids", "aliens", or "beings"?

Well, they answer to many names it seems, and "visitors" is one, "watchers" is another, "supporters" another, and OPA's another (off-planet ancestors). ETs cover the differences between them.

You've told us that our ancient ancestors do not visit us anymore and they don't buzz by to check on us. Rather, it's *other* extraterrestrial supporters who have taken up this role of monitoring our planet and peoples. In terms of the difference between them, would it make sense that the beings who Starseeded us are OPAs while ETs encompass *all* interstellar beings inclusive of our visitors, ancestors, and those others with whom we've had no contact or history at all?

Do I correctly understand this?

Semantics is the carrier of clarity and this description can be used, yes.

Do all extraterrestrial beings have the same basic physical appearance with two legs, two arms, a torso, and a head etc. (Even if some have larger heads and almond-shaped eyes, and others don't?) Or, are there some OPAs that look like a cross between an *animal* and a human? (Like a lizard-man or something else from our science fiction.)

Science-fiction indeed—no references to lizards exist at this time.

There are differences and there are similarities in their make-up based on their functional needs. A similar type body, although differing in size is correct. Heightened senses, of course, and less dependence on vocal cords for example also differentiate them. Think of the advancements and needs of their existence and the evolution of their bodies and senses complements it.

I guess they don't use their vocal cords if they telepathically communicate. That makes *sense*.

We share that they are not so different from your Earth people in their wishes for peaceful existence while being very different in their intolerance for the darkness of behaviors among your Earth masters, political and industrial.

I wonder if some of our moviemakers are divinely or interstellar-ly inspired?

Is there any basis of truth in our movies such as *E. T. the Extra-Terrestrial* (1982) directed by the sci-fi visionary Steven Spielberg, and/or *Avatar* (2009) directed and produced by the great James Cameron?

We say it is the case that these individuals have the gift of seeing and knowing what is to come through their own sense of radar and sonar and other advanced traits they are blessed with. The tuning in to higher frequencies is their gift and their willingness to mind-transport to download what they see as the bigger picture, is a gift. This they use for seeing what may be and what will be and weaving these perceptions into their stories. It is based on truth and as we know—the truth is out there.

Did they come to these pictures and stories accidentally or were they inspired as a result of Higher-Self-communication? Is it to be believed that their imaginations were unaided in these understandings? We say those who attain a higher level of spirituality see what others don't and receive what others don't by way of what is to come, and these are fine examples.

Indeed, they are.

I'd like to ask you about crop circles. This is one of our mysteries surrounded by significant conjecture. Though many crop circles have been manmade, many others are still unresolved conundrums.

Pax, were any of the crop circles made by aliens? If so, why?

Indeed they are and are done so to send messages as well as to announce their presence and ability to do so. Much is done in a playful manner by those who buzz by, just because they can, and if the humor is to be understood, it is to pique the curiosity of Earth people—mission accomplished!

Ha! Playful aliens: this is about the most amusing thing I can think of!

It is their intention to send a message that they are nearby. Humor is shared by most species and they are one.

Well, then, I believe the question should follow (because we've not been able to work it out): *how* **do they make those crop circles—with what equipment?**

Blowers, big blowers that thrust down blasts from their ships and flatten terrain is how.

Aimed in different directions it creates patterns and the view they have while making this art, and they consider it art, gives them the ability to manage small details.

There are elements of radiation and other-world gasses that contribute to the make-up of the thrusting tool.

It is a joy for them to paint their pictures in this way while not harming anyone or anything—like spending the night in an art class it is.

I'm in love with this! I can almost hear a symphony orchestrated to complement this scene. I just can't get enough of this image of jocular and artistic aliens making their crop circles. It's ironic and magical and elegant, and yes—funny!

I would guess that the blowers are not just for making art in wheat crops. What is the primary function of the blowers?

These are the thrusters that allow for propulsion and reverse thrusters also, stopping must be considered. There are variations on these in operation and they function in numerous ways.

When these craft move through time and space, they do so in different trajectories than your earthly airplanes, therefore their requirement for the ability to change pitch and speed and direction in nanoseconds makes them unique in your way of building.

And do they "blow" the regular air atmosphere from outside the craft, or do the blowers blow something that originates from *inside* the craft?

Outside air is rearranged to allow for progress, and systems from within the craft mix with this outside air to complete the picture. It is the fact that the mix of materials creates a composition of metallic nature that touches the Earth field to change the composition of the area. It can be traced that foreign intervention has taken place.

It is a signature like those found on an artist's canvas, but not visible.

"A composition of metallic nature that touches the Earth field." I'm repeating this for emphasis. (Calling all engineers!)

To explore more of the alien arts—do they have music?

Well yes, it is the case that there is music, which to them is not your music sounds nor would it necessarily be pleasing to you. It plays in each operating system for each being, and theirs is the pleasure *as they create it.*

Come again? I want to make sure I'm getting this. What is "each *operating system* for each being"? Is their operating system their brain or nervous system or their cell memory? Or, do they have a computer inside them, as the term "operating system" would indicate to us?

Ah yes, and that *some* are programmed for specific tasks indicates an operating system. And no, they are not robotic even with this variation to the theme of upright, two-legged intelligence.

You knew I would ask.

Yes.

As a hybrid they vary from both but accomplish similar tasks. There are those that are task-specific, purpose-built, and they contain the artificial intelligence referred to.

A hybrid type of ET with artificial intelligence built in— I'll have to think on this one for a while.

There are levels of intelligence, and there is artificial intelligence, also, which serves a purpose that is useful and decreases numbers of task-managers in a crew in travel. Isn't it interesting to think in this manner, where you can have a hierarchy with leaders and workers, and how does this deviate at all from your current military with officers and grunts as they were once called?

It is the case that these helpers are artificial intelligence to the extent they are task-specific and happy about it. There is no intention to become more and this makes them valuable in the team.

But, they're *not* robots?

Not being robotic is a part of the joy. They are part of the team in place and choose to remain in their place in the hierarchy.

That they experience joy is a nice thought.

There are levels of action and responsibility and "humanoid intelligence"—all are intended to do no harm to Earth populations.

Are aliens considered "humanoid intelligence"? I'm trying to understand this reference as we discuss ETs.

"Humanoid intelligence" is that which is *recognized* by humans and relating to their own. This is not identical nor is it close, but there are similarities sufficient to be recognizable. There are variations within intelligence that will or will not include such extras as compassion and humor and empathy and enthusiasm, so, when so it resembles humanoid in nature.

Oh, gotcha—"human-like".
We've been enlightened to ET crop circle art and now I'd like to ask about even stranger (and disturbing) events that have also been attributed to aliens: cow mutilations. Is this the doing of aliens, and if so why?

There have been such investigations as you mention, and this is the way of exploring what is in places visited. Curiosity of what is on your Earth plane only, and not considered with any emotion, simply a curious examination.

It is not to be repeated in the ways of past.

Well, I do consider it with emotion.
Why cows?

Useful and purpose-built is the cow and it interests as this animal provides a substance, milk, which is the basis for many items in a healthy diet, and many more to become useful. Can it be replicated on another planet perhaps? Milks of varying types exist and from various plant sources are available.

(I'd imagine that ETs would surely be curious about why we breed and eat so many cows. "How strange," they must think.)
There are people who say that they were abducted by aliens. Have aliens indeed abducted some human beings, taken them aboard their ships, tested on them for a time, and then returned them? If so, why? According to the individuals who claim this experience, it was terrifying for them. In my view, this is a violation of an individual's free will and, if it has truly happened, we need to understand it while simultaneously understanding aliens as friendly, which you have said they are.

The exploration of evolution of your Earth people is the curiosity leading to these incidences.

It is a fact there have been borrowings of Earth people for the purpose of inspection, close inspection in some cases, and this also was done out of curiosity and to document the human condition on your Earth at that time. It is the way of recording what is versus what has been and their record keeping extends to all things.

The buzzing by accomplishes some reconnaissance, but the close encounters are, or have been, utilized for deeper detail about humans on Earth.

Close encounters—I'd say!

Some of these alien abductees say that their DNA was taken for alien procreation, or that they were forced to have sex with aliens. Is any of this true?

The taking of DNA is simplistic but the sexual contact is less so. It would be against the norm and if investigation and examination of a deeper nature was required, perhaps it was so.

Procreation elsewhere by human standards is not a reality. The curiosity about methods for so doing attempts to be answered by close contact. It has been done and may be again, knowing it is research on the part of ETs for future consideration and species survival and flourishing.

Sometimes your answers require reading and re-reading. Like works of philosophy, they are for pondering.

Is this research for their own survival and flourishing, or is it related to the survival and flourishing of humans?

Oh yes, it is the ET future lifestyle survival. It is their interest in knowing all there is to know so they may apply as needed to their own culture. Procreation and ongoing life is a great concern and interest and curiosity drives their research. All is well in this and curiosity answered is curiosity resolved.

We say the reasons for human contact at any time are intended for long-term *good* as the divide between ETs and your human inhabitants of Earth narrows.

Remember that as your Earth people continue their intention and direction toward other planet colonization, there will be meeting and mixing: you will not be alone. You will be moving into another neighborhood and into another's territory where your rules do not always take priority and your perceived supremacy could be challenged, intellectually for certain. Think on this.

Oh, I'm thinking on it, Pax.
How do aliens procreate? Let's go there.

They do not replicate the habits of your Earth people. To arrive fully formed and informed is their way. Wisdom is inherent.

I'm trying to imagine how a species procreates in a way in which they arrive fully formed.

Creation comes in many ways and to build in response to a need is one.

Birthing of an idea rather than birthing of a baby as is known on your plane—this is the way of it.

Okay, that's a concept that I can follow: the birthing of an idea.

Some, while not all, are created with a form of artificial intelligence that is hard to distinguish from what you consider humanoid—these are made, not born.

These workers referenced are created for specific purposes with what you would recognize as artificial intelligence.

Yes, you mentioned them.

These workers are created, made, not born, arriving task ready.

We speak of aliens as we have described, some leaders and some task-specific followers, some are hybrids and some not—this division remains.

There are variations on your inter-stellar traveling visitors where some look like you and others not even close and some in-between. Know that the many and varied reasons for being have created many and varied types of beings who inhabit other places, other planets in other galaxies, and other times. To equate these beings with humans is not always possible. Variations exist and in ways beyond explanation here. Similarly, Earth people vary according to location, climate, and lifestyle and your system of becoming differs greatly.

Why would some alien civilizations have developed this integration with artificial intelligence, such as these hybrids that you mention?

This is not the way of all future civilizations but has become known as a way of forming civilizations ready for all, as focus is on building and growing and upward planning and thinking in an intellectual and scientific manner. This is a way of going for some but not all. Others find themselves beginning closer to your Earthly norm. Nothing out there can be expected to parallel your Earthly way—it just is not the way.

Those neighbors from afar have streamlined their way of living and to function in what they consider the primitive way of Earth has long ago been left behind. Not only is your Earth primitive in your warring and divisiveness and hate and abuse and lack of respect for planetary resources, but it is primitive in the way of creating babies which are not self-sufficient for many Earth-years, not productive they say, and not conducive to moving quickly forward in development of life while all attention need focus on babies and children.

It does take us many years to grow up, get educated, and become ready to be on our purposes. Yet, as you know,

we have no choice about this—it's just where we are in our evolution. *Or, do we have a choice?*

You don't, not at this point in your Earth time.

There are good things to be found in this way of grow-ing and living that suit your purposes. Your civilization, on the whole, is not ready for the advanced ways we discuss so leave that for another time and place.

What do advanced interstellar beings eat? Of what does their diet consist?

Pure nutrients created from the highest source of pure and clean origins. It is a diet of nutrients rather than flavors, as you know it.

Do ETs have religion?

Religion as an organized and named following of people is archaic to them: where a book is considered eternal truth although it was created by humans not deities; legends and stories that dic-tate obedience in daily behavior and belief in what comes before and after life—these things are not considered by them as useful.

What are typical subjects of education in extraterrestrial societies? Math, physics, telepathy...?

All is known by all and this is the way of it.

It is within the cells, this knowing, and extends to all aspects of the knowing of what is needed in their society.

To be arriving fully formed and initiated and educated, thus sparing the many years of growing in stature and knowledge—this is more efficient.

It is. And, it has me thinking of how much evolution we have yet to traverse. We'd better soon get past our pettiness and selfishness and greed and get on with the program!

I'd like to discuss the medical capabilities of ETs. Do they have advanced diagnostics or self-diagnostics? Is there disease in extraterrestrial communities? Are there hospitals on ET home bases?

Not in the usual form you are accustomed to in your space-time. Their clean atmosphere and living spaces maintain a level of wellness you would wish for. Their wellness is disturbed occasionally but they have the ability to scan their bodies for dis-ease, identify it, and make change and improvement. Their ability to identify what is amiss and make change enables a very low level of unwellness to exist in their lives.

Also, their bodies don't resemble Earth people bodies and the internal function and systems are quite different and more easily fixed, improved, parts replaced and otherwise returned to wellness. It is a combination of parts replacement and repair. There will be more to come.

Oh, that's right, you have spoken about cloning and part replacement.

Many of our diseases are created by stress or made worse by stress and anxiety such as heart disease and high blood pressure to name a couple. Do aliens have stress?

Is it possible that stress is self-inflicted in your society? We say it is and can be managed as well as alleviated. This is an anxiety that is perpetrated upon your people by society and is not a requirement for happy life—it's detrimental in fact.

Off-Earth visitors do not accept this stress as a part of their make-up and it is non-existent. It is a choice, don't you know?

I agree that stress is a choice, one that's hard for us to shirk, yet it's still a choice.

Do extraterrestrials reincarnate as we do?

These ETs you refer to have a make-up that allows for repair and replacement of bodily components and they do not die as your Earth people know end of life to be. It is a continuum of life that they enjoy and being dis-ease free allows for this. Your life cycles seems primitive to them.

This again goes back to when we talked about cell memory and the ability to create new organs and body parts as needed, just as a salamander can grow a new tail.

But let's take a minute to clarify this to be sure that we have an accurate and full understanding. You told us about the ETs who were shot down at Roswell, New Mexico in 1947: the crew died in the crash, although one alien lived for a period but then died due to the testing our people conducted on it.

That being said, although they don't die from disease or old age, do ETs die if they are in an accident?

As has been stated, parts replacement and repair is the way, so continuation of being exists. If a situation exists such as Roswell and there isn't the opportunity to be "fixed"—end of operation and function is experienced.

In this rare situation where they meet an end, do they reincarnate and return to physicality again?

It is a replacement of their beings that occurs. They are complete in their journey. Others will be created to take their place and this creation is a result of a need: if there is no need, then no further creation.

This is not to be confused with reincarnation, for this does not take place in that society.

You have said that ET beings do indeed have souls—everything does. Therefore, if they do meet an end of their physicality, what happens to their soul? Do they simply remain in spirit after that?

There is a division in types of ET beings with some being operational and others being ongoing components of their individual societies.

There are workers that come and go and have end of cycle experiences: there is a full-circle experience where end of life is end of purpose and end of cycle—all is closed with gratitude. There isn't the ongoing continuation of soul in that dimension as you now know it.

While others are designed to go on and remain as leaders and therefore will continue.

Now we ask for you to understand the great divide between your understanding of what is, and what actually is. There needs to be no further explanation at this time. As your world turns and change comes to attitudes and warring becomes history, forward motion comes to exposure to off-planet lifestyles and the ability to assimilate. It is in the far time for your people.

Do ETs have team sports?

Do you consider team sport as it appears in inter-stellar craft racing and play around other galaxies as their way, then yes. Enjoyment is taken from activities useful to the many—there are no egos to feed.

Pax, this is too good to be true. We have had aliens completely wrong! Many people think of aliens as heartless, even violent, robotic, or purely cerebral. But they're fun-loving, joy-filled, and peaceful in intention.

Now, let's look at the lingering rumor of alien presence on Earth. There are people who say that in the foothills of the Andes mountains in the area of La Noria, Chile, there is a race of tiny human-like beings that scientists have called The Atacama Humanoid. For many hundreds of years, up to and including our present time, it is claimed that The Atacama Humanoid, a race of small people just six-inches tall, inhabits the land. They are referred to by some Chilean natives as "The Gentiles". Apparently, a well-preserved body was found and studied by a number of scientists not long ago.

Are "The Gentiles" a race that was Starseeded to Earth a very long time ago, like all of our races? Or, are they a much newer addition of what we would call aliens or intergalactic visitors of more recent times? Or, something else?

This is an unknown dimension in *human* races as they have come to be. Much like other anomalies of nature, one in history does not a species make.

Local legend and lore as known throughout your world history is often just that and based not on fact. Certainly, what lives there now is legend—truth is not known.

Some of our well-known space theorists say that the planet Sirius B, the companion to Sirius (the brightest star in our night sky, also known as the "Dog Star", located in the Canis Major constellation), is an *inhabited* planet. Is this true?

Inhabited by what, we ask? Certainly, many planets are found to have micro-life and this theory can be proven by the presence of moisture that supports life. Not rivers or oceans or lakes, but moisture that can descend from what, cloud? Not in *that* place. So what is it? Left over from eons past and held in place by the pressure exerted on the surface by external forces. So much to learn with so little return. Your people will not travel there.

Are there, now, other intelligent beings currently inhabiting any other planet in our Milky Way galaxy?

Oh yes, Penelope, it is the case that they are out there, and this will become more evident in time on your planet.

As your science and technology advances, and as your governments allow for that knowledge to be shared with the people, a new level of understanding the big picture will emerge. When the people are considered partners by science and government, there can be forward motion in thinking and acceptance. While they are being kept blindfolded and in fear of this type of progress, there can be no acceptance or willingness to contribute to the cause. Being a part of the solution is preferred, not part of the problem.

Using our most powerful telescopes, would it be possible to detect another star/planet that is inhabited?

Astronomers do their best and technology continues to allow for building more powerful telescopes, but proof of habitation does not come this way. Visitation and travel will confirm. There is much to be seen and learned, and technology struggles to keep up with need.

We suggest the way to create more powerful viewing is through Remote Viewing. We have discussed this but not in the context of off-planet exploration—think on it.

That is a compelling suggestion.

It's a big galaxy. In what arm of the Milky Way galaxy is there a planet inhabited by intelligent beings?

In the time of ancients in your solar system there was much buzzing about in travel to explore other places. It was found that there are reasons to explore, as life exists in different forms elsewhere out there. These forms are advanced or not and vary widely from single cell to intellectual and scientific and advanced—all support one another and function independently of their off-planet cousins.

This circulation of energy throughout the star system was and is and continues to be. In another time on your Earth more will be known. What is to be is the veil of secrecy lifted and open travel and visitation, but as long as your Earth people consider space as something to be monetized and claimed, it cannot be without cataclysmic results. So, time must pass while saner heads prevail, and openness and inclusion of space travel and its consequences begins.

I can imagine that we could learn much about Higher Self attainment if we studied the lives and cultures of ETs. Do they regularly operate from their Higher Self as a common and natural way of functioning?

These beings *are* their Higher Selves as they function on a level of spirituality unknown to your people. Theirs is civilization advanced in all ways and we say it is to be emulated, and will be in time, your Earth time.

Meanwhile, growth and understanding of higher functioning is a goal. Your civilization has much to learn of peace and equality—begin there.

How can we emulate our friendly intergalactic supporters if we don't know them?

To become a spiritual being is the way. Your people shall begin to know themselves and what they may do to know their Higher Selves. The functioning at a higher level of spirituality is the beginning—it is the way to advance the cause and that cause is elevation of functioning of all people—to consider the big picture, remove hatred and become inclusive; do not consider personal needs above all else. Consider others and consider the needs of Mother Earth as a higher calling. You all are spiritual beings having a human experience. Some do it better than others.

While ETs *are* their Higher Selves, do they continue to evolve their Higher Selves?

They bring to their collective the walking of the talk and living in the light of purity. One monitors another and their civilization dwells in the light—it is expected and enjoyed and provides the cocoon of wellness created by them for them. Higher technology is a part of their world and this in no way interferes with the overall view they have of their purpose for being: to continue evolution and education.

So, they are their Higher Selves and their purpose is their continued evolution and education. This kind of purpose is one that can be understood by those on Earth who are dedicated to our spiritual evolution and the studies of metaphysics, Higher Self development, and other vocations of science, knowledge, and truth seeking. However, many other people on Earth today would not be able to relate to this course of enlightenment as their *entire* reason for being. Many do not dedicate their lives to the quest for knowledge or the honing of talents and skills in any field. Many believe that their lives are about simple pleasures, survival, success as demonstrated

through financial milestones, or how far up the corporate ladder they are able to climb. The latter (and ladder) group might find a lifelong quest for evolution and education to be dull or unsatisfactory.

May you please speak to how and why these other advanced and enlightened civilizations (ETs and OPAs) grew to rank their spirituality and dissemination of knowledge as their top priority and purpose for being?

Ah yes, it is age—that is, age of their *societies*. It is said that age brings wisdom, is it not? And it is the case that they long ago left behind the level of chaos your civilization currently experiences. This comes with generations of change and how you describe many among your people now as unwilling to devote their lives to a quest for evolution, so be it: they will be replaced through attrition by those who will and do—it is the way of it.

We say that the shift in thinking and acting is now beginning. Although nowhere near a tipping point in your society, the surge has begun. When it becomes a tsunami will be within two generations and your people may be considered wise.

At their advanced level, what are the practices of other galactic society's peoples in terms of Higher Self development and spiritual maintenance?

Living it is the way. Alternatives are not known. It is the joy of being in the bliss.

What is "the bliss"? Many people experience happiness, yet not "bliss". Perhaps those people who experience bliss do so during moments of meditation, or when their child is born, or when they first tasted chocolate as a child, or when their sports team wins, or when they reach a goal such as summiting a formidable mountain, or another feat of physical, spiritual, or mental exuberance—yet these are periodical and not a steady state of living.

It would be greatly appreciated if you will help us to understand what bliss is, *where* it is, and what it feels like.

Bliss is to be found within your heart and mind. It is the knowing feeling of love in all things, wellness in all things, and harmony in all things. Imagine that and work toward it in your own life: this is our suggestion for your people at this time. It's even better than chocolate. Trust in this and accept it with love as intended.

You're kind of cheeky sometimes. ("*Better than chocolate.*") To briefly sidetrack, is humor a thing in the *Spirit World*?

Have we not indicated in our words and manner of approaching some topics that we indeed have this in our make-up?

Yes, you have.

All is not serious, all is not reverence, all is an amalgam of ways and to enjoy the serendipity and humor displayed forms a part.

Dear Divine Wisdom Source, I'm thrilled to hear that you have a sense of humor. In guiding us, no doubt you need one.

On a more serious note—you know, the day will come that the people of Earth are made aware of the existence of ETs and the visitations by our friendly interstellar supporters. This event is called Alien Disclosure, and it refers to a time or moment when our governments formally acknowledge the presence of ETs—all is divulged.

How soon from now will Disclosure happen? And why? Does something happen whereby our governments are left with no option but to admit to what they have known for some time?

If you ask about *time* we are at a disadvantage, as we do not know your linear measure. What brings about a disclosure would be mass visitation, but this would not be undertaken as your military would be called to order and hostility ensues. Your people are unprepared in their knowledge and trust and have been kept in this way deliberately to ensure Government maintains control.

That's unfortunate.

Our governments (and many people) worry about being attacked by ET visitors. Are there extraterrestrial visitors—any at all, anywhere of any race of beings—that would intend to harm us, war with us, or take over our planet? (I have asked this before and am taking another go to be sure.)

These interstellar tourists *could have* done any amount of harm over the last thousands of years had they wished to. It is not their intention now or ever.

It is to be known that action brings reaction, and should they be met with assault rifles, what do you think may be the reaction? There is much education to be undertaken among your people and there is no showing of readiness at this time.

We suggest that when the tsunami comes and your people are more enlightened and accepting of the reality of global healing and interstellar travel, there will be those ready to accept and manage the next phase of welcoming and inclusion.

We currently do not have any protocol for a post-disclosure world—at least not one of which the people are aware. Rather than waiting for a plan of defense and offense to be presented to us by our world governments, many people would like to get a protocol that we can all start to think about. What should be our guidelines of diplomacy with ETs? Can you give us a set of parameters that should be followed in our interactions?

The people of Planet Earth are not prepared, at this time, for consideration of what you suggest. Rigidity and fear in mindset prevails and it is ludicrous to think that sending out lessons of peaceful interaction expected is going to calm the nature of those expecting the worst. There are world leaders already speaking of weaponizing space, claiming territory, and becoming masters of those new universes. It is not in their planning to share and be respectful of those with higher technology landing in peace. It will not happen in your generation or some to follow. There must be further understanding of the need for peace and respect for all and combining resources for the greater good.

You are really driving this point home and I'm sure we need the repetition on this matter to get the message. Please continue.

As there are multiple nationalities together in a space capsule at the International Space Station, and they work together for the growth and success of the space program, so should your countries work together to consider the ramifications of life on other planets and what they can learn that may assist in the healing of Planet Earth.

More is to be learned and shared while continuing to refer to those from other planets wishing to bring peace.

There will not be opportunity for interaction in person until your world has taken many turns and change has come to your attitude and intention for control. When there will be interaction, respect and peaceful intention must be presented.

Releasing fear in people only comes through knowledge, and there will not be a sufficient growth of knowledge while the visitors distance themselves. The beginning is within your Earth people's culture to change the way of thinking, send the communication of this by the telepathic means of communication that will be common, and begin to function in peace and love. Only then, will it be noticed that a shift has taken place and perhaps it is time, once again, to entertain the notion of landing on Earth. As stated, another generation or two will grow in their enlightenment before this event.

On this topic, please speak directly to our political world powers.

As your people speak of space exploration and begin to consider funding more of it, there is talk of claiming territory and planning to weaponize space. What is this thinking and how does it represent purity of intention and peaceful growth in knowledge? We are saddened by this that the first thought, it would seem, is to politicize the next frontier, space, and begin with the thought of claiming and staking territory and meeting inhabitants of other planets with weapons. How is this any different from the current attitude of Earth countries' politicians?

To war and to conquer is what got you into this difficulty. Do you think that to begin space exploration with this attitude is the way forward? Clearly you do and therefore will receive no assistance from those of higher civilizations that could pave the way for your success.

You will witness failures where there need not be and losses that were preventable. Your unwillingness to go in peace is your great weakness and your point of failure. You are to consider this mentality to be less, not more, in the overall measure of mankind, and you are shameful in this attitude.

Foresight is what is lacking now in your population involved in this sector, and foresight will be needed. As you look through a limited vision hole, much like closing one eye or turning your binocular backward, the goal seems distant and difficult to achieve. Much more introspection and clarity of thinking is required.

That was direct. Hopefully those who need to hear are listening.

What is our test to pass or benchmark of enlightenment that will signal to you and the Spirit World that we have tapped into our Higher Selves, that we can be trusted with future wisdoms and technologies, and that we are ready and have earned the opening of our next passage?

Purity of intention is the answer here.

This is in the minority now and will not tip the scales into the majority for a long while. There are those among you now fitting this description. There is a small segment of your population with the passion for this endeavor and they are to be enabled to continue this pursuit: It is an idea whose time has come. They are the learners and researchers and believers and quiet revolutionaries who plan for the interstellar travel mentioned. It is their purity of intention that singles them out for not only their work, but their successes along their path. As they work on propulsion for space travel, they quietly know the way and continue to process the steps required to bring it to fruition.

When it is determined by your science and politics that peaceful exploration of space is the way, without weapons and territorial attitudes, progress will be made toward safe and successful travel.

For your people to understand why they wish to visit off-planet or colonize off-planet—and how that will look in terms of spirituality, is needed. This is the foresight that comes from looking within and mining one's own internal wisdom. Each involved has higher powers and old souls that carry much wisdom—it is this that is to be mined.

Do not ask without, ask *within* for your guidance and fore-sight is found.

Chapter Twenty-Nine
A Place in Time

*M*y wish for this conversation is that we learn how to get from where we are to where we want to be in the journey of our consciousness awakening and spiritual evolution.

We see that there are those in fear of traveling without a map or a hand to guide them. There will be those who lead and those who follow, of course, but the road less traveled is the right one for many.

The road less traveled is a nice toss, as we say in television. Let's get on it. I'll let you go first. What shall we discuss?

It is indeed the case that there is a linear time thinking process among your people, and yet this is not the way.

Excellent, we'll talk about the subject of time. *It's a tickin'.*

It is all in a box and at the same time and can be accessed at will. The notion that one is gone and another not yet reached is incorrect. It is all one and you may move from one to the other readily.

One what is gone? Are you speaking of *moments in time*?

Moments, sections of time, spaces of time and place: all are simultaneous in their existence. Thinking your way from one into the other is the way. Much like teleporting it is the will that enables the transition. We share with you that it is the intention coupled with the idea that creates this reality.

This is a notion that is difficult for some to process, but it is, and it will be understood by many others. It brings excitement, does it not?

It sure does. Are you really saying that we can access all possibilities at will, and that nothing is in the past or future that we can't access now?

This is what we have said.

You are capable of visiting this idea and trying it out for yourself. It's like climbing a wall in that if you believe you can do so, you will, but if you stop believing part way up, you may lose your grip and fall. Inner trust is your power.

Do future peoples exist on Earth in some realm now?

The notion of "parallel universes" is one that can and has been experienced by the enlightened. It is a place and time where life exists and does so at a different pace and in a higher frequency than Planet Earth as you know it. As fascinating as this seems to many, it is reality. Future Earth civilizations will develop from both sources and as is the case now, some will move between these realms and bring back extraordinary knowledge and experience; they will be the leaders. This is the current situation, but those individuals are looked upon as intellectually superior and not spiritually advanced; both happen to be reality.

Oh, this is so interesting. Can I learn to move between these realms to bring back extraordinary knowledge? If so, how might I do this?

One step at a time, now, and the work you are doing is of value and needed in your place and time.

Is there a reason that you put "parallel universe" in quotes? Is there a *better* term that we could begin using? And, you say that parallel universes have been experienced by the enlightened: are these enlightened people from another time or from another place?

All of the above: from Earth, from another time and another place, and the term is parallel universe. It is somewhat widely known and experienced by those who pass between realities for higher purposes. It is a place, a thing, and has in our view, a proper name.

Do we affect those parallel universes? Do the current occurrences on Earth affect another, or many, versions of Earth in other times and places and space?

We say those parallel universes are what they are, in time, and function independently of Earth people and time now. To the extent that some pass back and forth between your present and those other times and places, there is a touching, therefore an effect, but it is a portal that opens for some and closes behind them. To pass between realms is done voluntarily or also involuntarily where the portal opens and access is given unexpectedly. It is a surprise at times but always a reason appears as valid for that person's lifetime experience, one or both. Teaching and learning continues and growth between these universes is the reason for such visitations. Working toward enlightenment, those who travel have contributions to make and lessons to learn along the way.

What's the purpose of parallel universes?

We do not identify a parallel universe as having a purpose but rather it is a place, a "like life" existence where the choices you have made in this life play out there differently, alternatively, as the choices you did not make here with those differing results becoming apparent.

It is an awareness of what might have been. It is an existence, another dimension in time that one can slip in and out of as through a portal.

Wow—just, wow!
If every choice and action has a life and path in another universe, then there must be millions—no, trillions—of universes.

I wonder if there must be *countless* other universes. Is that right?

Not every choice and action plays out in another universe. It is not so complicated. Countless other parallel universes are as those who choose to visit allow.

This is for the few, not the many.

Oooh.

In all other universes, is there a "me" as I know me; a me of which my soul is conscious?

No and this is not the way of it. Your choice would be for one.

For one what? One soul, or one awareness of one Universe?

Yes, both. Envision a room divided by a curtain. On one side you act in a play as one character and on the other you return to your daily self and lifestyle. You are one person living two separate lives and as you pass through the curtain portal your life awaits and you resume activity. You are one soul living parallel lifetimes, each drawing you in for different actions and activities and you may leave each for the other at will.

This analogy is very helpful.
By way of those vastly variant choices, do I have a different name, personality, appearance, and/or even a different soul history in other universes?

There can be a difference in most of these including place in time in history. There is a learning component to why a visit is undertaken. Learning of life preferences and choices for future, and which suits going forward.

Of all of the "MEs", could it be said that I am simply all persons and therefore every person is me and I am every person?

No.

While all of these many parallel universes are exactly as the name implies, are they also just one Life in that all is connected?

No. A different life or lifetime in each universe allows for information gathering and experiences and relationships to merge and determine which life to continue and on which universe time and place. It is an offering of what may be and what could have been. Slipping between and through portals allows for this and is for a reason and for the few.

Are parallel universes different places in terms of space-time coordinates or physical locations?

The notion of parallel universe is an alternative for those who access a place in their wishes and dreams and is not a given for all people. It is magical and mystical and allows for those who place themselves there to see both sides of a life and how it might have been if other choices were made. One may travel back and forth and learn from both. Ultimately, a choice will be made, and one lifetime may become the forever choice and staying with it and the associated people will be the end result.

I think I understand this better now.
Let's discuss time. Why does the Spirit World not operate within linear time?

We do not know that fixation on time; ours is a differing place and linear time is non-existent. It has to do with many facets of being non-solid in make-up. Ours is a way of being and not a moderated example of what science likes to manage. Ours is fluid and not captured in your astrophysical ways.

Did our relationship with linear time begin when we were Starseeded to Earth?

Linear time is yours and is based on planetary rotation. It is the way of your world.

You must understand that time travel, teleportation, and lightspeed travel also are not measured in a timeframe your people would comprehend. Think of time as a *place* not a measure of distance.

This will be mind-blowing for many people. But wait, you also said that Dark Energy is a place. (Any correlation, I wonder?) You said, *"Separate time from place from intelligence and it will be clear."* Let me probe further.

I'm trying to think of time as a place; can you further describe this to make the concept understandable for us?

If you were to put a box around a picture of where you are now—it is a place. If you repeat this process the next day, it is also a place shown in that picture. However, each is a place but in a different time—a different day—a same place in a different time. These are places in time. They show time in place.

I've just been out for a walk in the sun and I kept thinking of the boxes around the place, and how tomorrow it will be the same location—different time, of course—but now a different place in time. It can go on and on into infinity with that visualization.

Let's take our discussion of time up into space. Can space-time be folded like a sheet? If so, as it's folded, can two portals or pathways that were light years apart become folded into the same place? Does this make travel instantaneous between far off points in the Universe?

Oh yes, it is the way of it and the magic, also. When it is managed this way there can be teleportation in an instant. Think of that! Your world becomes a different place when this becomes known. Of course, at this time in your development you need a welcoming destination for earthlings and that will take some time to achieve. It comes.

When we colonize another planet, how will we count time or relate to time in that other place? After all, we use a twenty-four-hour system which is based on the Earth's revolutions around the sun. Therefore, what counting system will be used in other places with other suns and moons and so on?

You must know that all is relative to location and the structure of your twenty-four-hour method will not apply elsewhere. Your people who begin space travel in experiments will cling to this as a measure of progress, initially, and soon become aware of alternatives to this earthly way.

Evolution will take your people from Earth dwellers to off-planet explorers, and in that will evolve a need for new ways of tracking periods of travel and habitation. These are determined by locations and will serve your people well as they adjust to their growth as inhabitants of new worlds.

When in Rome, it is said, and in this new way of being the way will be found along with the place in time.

In past discussions, you have mentioned teleportation. I recall we talked about the disappearance of the Mayans and the transport of the stones of the Stonehenge circle and the Great Pyramids. Can you "tip us off" as to how we can make the jump in knowledge and technology to achieve the teleportation of products and people? What insight can you share regarding teleportation?

Teleportation is a thought process; an escalation of the mind over matter way. It is not a trick of physics but rather an intention.

Oh, so teleportation is not done like in Star Trek (with computers and instruments that deconstruct then reconstruct cellular patterns), and it's not done through the laws of physics by way of particles in quantum entanglement?

Deconstruct, reconstruct, think it with intention and visualization and it is. Also required is belief in this as possibility; infinite possibility.

You practice and function using the power of intention, and this is no different. To dissolve in one area and reappear in another; this is the speed at which one moves accounting for the illusion.

What's "the illusion"?

It is the illusion of being there one moment and then disappearing, or magically appearing in a place where you were not a moment ago. The illusion is that you weren't there the whole time.

That last sentence is one to ponder.
And what is astral travel?

This is simply the mind leaving the Earth body to travel to other places, perhaps other planets and galaxies, then returning to the body. It is often a sleep-originated practice where one visits elsewhere and returns with great or even profound experiences.

Can you teach us how to do it?

There are many books on this subject and learning the full aspect and ramifications to be considered are to be learned there. It is not a game and is to be considered fully prior to undertaking. Read and learn and decide—some who do this do not find their way back to the body in time for it to be still viable.

Yikes.

Others have brief sojourns resulting in increased knowledge— it is to be respected, this ability.

Do our friendly interstellar visitors return to learn from Earth herself?

In terms of their time of existence and past assimilation and learning, their purpose is to guide and teach. They do so from a distance while remaining obscure, usually.

It is your Earth people also who pass through the portals and return in a leading of a double life. Lessons to teach and learn, and if they alternate this is the way of it. Who is on the other side differs for each one's experience and is specific to their experiences and needs. Nothing is forever in these scenarios, and they serve their purpose and the portal closes.

It is a whimsical thing and contributes greatly to growth of Spirit.

What exactly are "the portals"? What does a portal look like and how does it appear?

A portal is a place not a thing and doesn't have a look. It is an opening in time only and not relegated to one place. Like a brief parting of a closed curtain, it allows passage between time and place. It is quite magical and is experienced by those who look for it as well as those unsuspecting who have a need and are given the gift of it.

That's right, you have told us that American pilot and adventuress Amelia Earhart traveled through a time-portal!

May you tell us more about time travel as a process of thinking?

Time travel is a *result*.

This is a big stretch for us. We don't yet believe that our thoughts are this powerful—powerful enough to result in travel through time. We know the concepts of our will, our intention, and our ideas, yet maybe you can help us out a little more because we're not practiced in using these tools in the capacity of time travel.

How can we take our willpower to that level?

We say your "willpower" is quite separate from this discussion. It is inner trust in self—belief in self to the exclusion of all else—that is to be further strengthened. It is intention combined with this trust in self and Self that powers you on your desired path. It is also purity of intention that completes the fueling of your journey.

I'd like to try this out, as you have suggested. I'd like to better understand this ability because I'm not sure that I do.

Let's run through a trial to find out if it is what I think it is and how it can work. First, I'll describe a moment in time that is in the future.

Here's the hypothetical example:

A replacement material to plastics-made-of-crude-oil has been discovered. As you told us, it is a composition of hemp cellulose together with other renewable and reusable plant-based ingredients. In fact, this moment is possible because our writings have been read by so many around the world and now people are aware of the possibility. The demand is creating the supply of this new material—let's say it's called "plantic". I choose to make purchases that support my vision for a clean Earth, and so, I go online to buy a set of plantic food storage containers, plantic food wrap, plantic straws and cups for an upcoming party that I'm hosting, and plantic baby bottles as a gift for a friend.

Okay, let's press pause on that moment. How can I actually buy those items when in the now they don't yet exist? And, if this is not the way to journey to this future place-in-time, or perhaps the future is *not* accessible in this tangible way, then please further explain this "result".

It is not the way of now to move those items from a future time to now in that you envision going to a future store to purchase them.

It is rather the way that these things do exist in *that* time period where you may find yourself and your experience of seeing and using those futuristic items would take place in that place in time.

If this is a parallel universe, so be it, but when you pass through the portal on return you will come back to what is *here* and in existence *now*, speaking of your Planet Earth. You will not move a futuristic washing machine through the portal because you wish to—but you may experience it on the other side and you may generate the idea for how it can be created on your Earth plane of existence in your present place in time.

You may live and learn, as it is said, and return with ideas and details and methods with which to replicate what you saw. This is the way of it.

It is being transported from place in time to place in time: a warp and a dissolution of solid, molecules disappearing and regrouping. We spoke of voice-commands morphing into thought commands—this is it but on a greater scale.

All right, time is a result and a place. When reading between the lines, I think that the meaning of "place in time" might be "place in place". So then, time does not exist, only places exist. Is this accurate?

If you listen to musical notes between the lines, between the notes, there will be a distortion of meaning. There are places in time and space, and all exist. To be in a place in time is to be in *motion*: life moves as time moves and places occupied pass between and through. It is fluid, this time, and so be it.

I imagine these snapshots of time in motion—like a motion picture; a reel; a film. I'm really getting this now!

In order for us to master teleportation, is the challenge purely one of mastering thought commands, or do we need to overcome time in some way?

Oh hah, to overcome time is not a requirement, rather to work with it and go with the flow, as it is said, contributes to this process. One must not be confrontational when one can be a contributor to the process and success of it.

Be one with the Universe.

Yes, yes! Go with the flow. Be one with the Universe. We didn't just make these lines up, huh? (A rhetorical question; we know the answer here.)

Is time teleportation and time travel the same thing?

Is this a philosophical question? To teleport from place A to place B moves the body, but did it really pass through time or arrive at a different time? Only if that place in time is located elsewhere.

Consider airplane travel on your world today. You may travel for hours but arrive yesterday. It's all relative. You will arrive at a different place in time, yes? Should you wish to travel to another century past—this is a different place in time where you may experience what was.

Time varies throughout the Universe, but time is and is a required link in the chain of Universal wellbeing. Many are those who state that time is not a link required to survive, but time is survival for without it there is no survival.

"Your time is up" is a long-standing expression meaning when you cease to exist. Think on this and understand the connection.

It's all beginning to resonate and I'm gaining a new perspective on time and place.

Imagine if you will, the technology race now compounded by the passage of time and advances in technology. It boggles the mind, it does.

Imagine also that the technology that you now find state of the art is obsolete. What do you envision will replace it? Do you have any idea in the changes of your methods of communication and traveling? It will look like a different place and civilization entirely.

We are here to say that the time comes when the next generation is approaching the age of majority, when what you now take for granted is wiped clean away from the operative methods currently known. Well, that is what is coming, and you should be prepared to accept the transition although some already understand and see the future.

What is the fifth dimension that I've read about in metaphysical teachings?

There are dimensions in existence that mimic waves like ripples of time.

In your current third dimension living you have the sights and the sounds and the thinking of what is.

In the fifth dimension of living you have all of that plus the intuitive and the enlightened gifts of life in your abilities.

While you are very happy and contented now without the knowledge of what is possible, you will be ecstatic in the experience of more.

"Ecstatic" is a powerful word. I want to vicariously feel that ecstasy through your words. May you please tell me a story of life in the fifth dimension? What is possible and what are our abilities in that dimension?

What can you imagine? What do you wish for? What brings happiness? For some it is prosperity and for others love, and yet others consider the elevation of their daily life over the present work and need to earn a living a form of life management. All are to be, of course, as the journey toward enlightenment will show.

Entering this place of your future will bring peace and harmony and is found through the evolution of your own way of thinking and being. Finding enlightenment of spirit is a journey and your civilization is not there yet; not even both feet on the path, as it were.

To be in this realm of all possibilities is meaning your purity of spirit brings purity of thought and action toward all things, people, and animals on your planet, and your intention is honorable toward all. A day in the life here is peace and purity and as though travelling with feet on clouds of goodness. All forward motion toward continued planetary wellness is agreed upon and managed quietly and with good intention toward all, as we have stated, and this overriding belief touches all aspects of life and living.

The fifth dimension sounds incredible. Although, I suppose we've skipped one: is there a fourth dimension and, if so, what is it and how do we bridge our path from the third to the fourth?

Ah yes, development of your people and the journey toward enlightenment brings this about. For your people to have realization that their "this" is not all they have or should strive for is a beginning.

We wish to show that all have the opportunity to grow in their spirituality and grow in their gifts and talents for spiritual journeys. To use their gifts for the betterment of others puts them on track for their higher evolution and to know they strive for increased awareness and ability to practice their talents also places them ahead of their present sedentary existence.

Growing in knowledge and purity of spirit is this next step and understanding their role as student and then teacher, completes the stages. To be blessed with the ability to learn and grow and then gift this to others is the journey for many, and as a journey, it feels like a gift.

The true gift is in practicing the new ways of higher living and higher learning and placing respect for all and purity of intention above all else.

This is our gift to you.

Going forward from here I wonder how our intentions and actions will shape our future. Let's go on a time travel journey of sorts.

Will we have the Internet in fifty years, or will it be something else? If so, what?

Oh my, this will look very different as will be the devices used to access. All will be connected through an energy field you can tap into, or not, and access all information and desired communication.

What will social media be like in fifty years?

Not a separate entity or entities as now, but a component of the central reality of communication through the Ethernet: all is one and one is all—it becomes an integral part of the whole which is the communication channels developed to carry all wisdom.

I guess the folks at Facebook and Twitter will want to diversify.

In fifty years, will moviemaking and movie-watching still be as popular as it is today?

It will but in a very different format. People will not sit in theatres when they can access all media as they move about and download all to their internal chip and view it as if they are in a hologram. It is a departure from your current ways.

That sounds very cool—we'll be *in* the movie.

If we changed nothing of our ways, attitudes, govern-ments, and industry practices, and continued on our current

trajectory, what would life on Planet Earth be like in just *ten* years?

Very dark in all respects: the beginning of the death of the planet which has already begun, but effectively crippling the means of growing clean crops as clean air, water, and soil are non-existent.

How about in fifty years?

Government would look very differently as corruption would have melded current major countries into others who rule by fear and manage as dictatorships.

Earth is polluted to the extent that food sources are no longer viable.

Off-planet travel is common, territories were claimed there, and war begins for dominance in space.

Very unpleasant.

On the flip side, if we implemented all of your suggestions and wisdom, and began now to follow our hearts, trust in our selves, stand up to government and industry corruption, and be the change we wish to see—what would life on Planet Earth be like in ten years?

There would be a resurgence of the need to leave fossil fuel production, limit waste into air and water and manage the Earth resources as did the aboriginal and First Nations before you.

Peace begins to be felt among world powers and it is felt that the world's people wish to support each other in finding the best place for each in their development.

And, then again, in fifty years?

Your planet will be more quiet: there is not the warring that has been in history and the feeling of peace prevails in all things.

There are bumps in the road still but the driving force in industry and government is to take the direction of clean and quiet and good for all.

Love prevails.

Imagine.

Trust in this and go in Peace and Love.

—Pax.

About the Author and Channeler

Penelope Jean Hayes with Carole Serene Borgens

Penelope Jean Hayes is a new consciousness author, television personality, and speaker. She has appeared on-camera hundreds of times as an expert guest on programs including *Dr. Phil*, *ABC News*, as well as international news specials and telecasts. She is the foremost leader in the field of contagious and osmotic energy known as Viralenology, founder of the Viral Energy Institute, and author of the book *The Magic of Viral Energy: An Ancient Key to Happiness, Empowerment, and Purpose*.

Carole Serene channels Pax, the Divine Wisdom Source. Carole is a former nurse and longtime student of metaphysics. She has been channeling Spirit since the early 1990s when she was chosen by Pax and given the title "Spirit Messenger". Carole continues to write and provide in-person and remote sessions for clients around the globe, and she refers to her gift of channeling as "the greatest blessing in my life."

Of this trio, Pax says, "A good team we three," and together they have written a number of books of great importance to humanity, our planet, and future.

www.PaxWisdom.com
www.PenelopeJeanHayes.com   www.CaroleSereneBorgens.com

About the Artwork

Designed by British book illustrator Andrew Green, the art of *Do Unto Earth* is more than just supporting illustrations—it depicts the interconnected lessons of this crucial message and gift to humanity, and illuminates the wisdom that enlightenment is available to us all when the clouds are cleared.

Like ancient cave drawings, the cover design is a storyboard in symbolism:

The iconic megaliths of Stonehenge aligned to the sunrise of the summer solstice above the stones, an Aboriginal playing a long didgeridoo handmade from eucalyptus, Atlas holding up the celestial heavens and Earth, a spacecraft hovering above Egyptian pyramids —these are all symbols of our Starseeded Origin and the ancient relationship we share with our first relatives.

Animal wisdom is represented by a peaceful elephant, Blackie the race-horse, and a mariner-guiding dolphin. A pair of salamanders tell the tale of medical advancements to come.

Australia's Uluru / Ayers Rock and the Redwoods of the American West remind us that Mother Earth speaks through nature, and the intuitive third eye and lips represent our senses awakening to new dimensions.

The friendly off-planet ancestor (OPA) reminds us that we are not alone, and progress comes when we live in peace, unity, and love.

Of this cover design, artist Andrew Green says, "Taking it to its root intention, it represents love and the way in which art is a guide-post, storyteller, and truth-teller throughout time."

www.AndrewGreenArt.co.uk

Index

Made in the USA
Columbia, SC
21 September 2020